Saints, Sinners, and

Saints, Sinners, and Sovereign Citizens

The Endless War over the West's Public Lands

John L. Smith

UNIVERSITY OF NEVADA PRESS *Reno & Las Vegas*

University of Nevada Press, Reno, Nevada 89557 USA
Copyright © 2021 by University of Nevada Press

LIBRARY OF CONGRESS CATALOGING-IN-PUBLICATION DATA
Name: Smith, John L., 1960– author.
Title: Saints, sinners, and sovereign citizens : the endless war over the West's
    public lands / John L. Smith.
Description: Reno ; Las Vegas : University of Nevada Press, [2021] |
Includes bibliographical references and index. | Summary: "Saints, Sinners, and
    Sovereign Citizens explores the history of grazing rights on the West's lucrative
    public lands and the battles between the Bureau of Land Management and
    ranchers for their use. The April 2014 armed standoff between Bunkerville
    rancher Cliven Bundy and armed militia allies against federal officers serves
    as the backdrop to the story of a conservative political movement and the
    resurgence of the radical right in the American West"—Provided by publisher.
Identifiers: LCCN 2020017792 (print) | LCCN 2020017793 (ebook) |
    ISBN 9781948908900 (hardcover) | ISBN 9781948908917 (ebook)
Subjects: LCSH: Bundy, Cliven, 1946– | United States. Bureau of Land Management.
    Southern Nevada District Office. | Pasture, Right of—Nevada. | Public lands—
    Nevada—Management. | Pasture, Right of—West (U.S.) | Public lands—West
    (U.S.) | Range management—Law and legislation—West (U.S.) | Land use—
    West (U.S.) | Right-wing extremists—West (U.S.) | Conservatism—United
    States.
Classification: LCC HD243.N3 S55 2021 (print) | LCC HD243.N3 (ebook) |
    DDC 333.1/6—dc23
LC record available at https://lccn.loc.gov/2020017792
LC ebook record available at https://lccn.loc.gov/2020017793/2020017793

First Printing
Manufactured in the United States of America

25 24 23 22 21   5 4 3 2 1

For Sally Denton,
So proud to share life's trail with you

Contents

Back Road to Gold Butte

With the ceaseless stampede of traffic on Interstate 15 overwhelming a bucolic morning on the desert, I pulled my battered Subaru off the trash-strewn highway seventy-five miles northeast of Las Vegas. It was April 5, 2014, and the United States Bureau of Land Management (BLM), with the help of private contractors, had begun rounding up Bunkerville, Nevada, rancher Cliven Bundy's wayward cattle. Bundy had been at odds with the federal government for the better part of a quarter century over the question of jurisdiction of the public lands on which his tough crossbred Brahmans grazed. His refusal to pay nominal grazing fees had backfired in court and on his home range, where with assessments and fines he owed the government approximately $1 million—more than all other western ranchers combined. Bundy's expanding herd had roamed many miles off his 160-acre family ranch and original federal allotment and onto ruggedly beautiful Gold Butte territory near the Lake Mead National Recreation Area. Uncle Sam had finally lost his patience.

It was a country I was acquainted with. As a boy, I accompanied my father and brother on dove- and quail-hunting trips in a 1944 Willy's Jeep around Gold Butte's rugged hills. After a long day, we slept under a quilt of stars that dazzled my young imagination.

My dad, Smitty, was born in the desert and knew every guzzler and seep spring for miles around. Where there was water, there was wildlife—and usually some rancher trying to eke out a living with the help of vast acres of federal land leased for pennies per cow. To outsiders, the land was barren, but to us desert rats it was a kind of paradise, albeit one that could easily bust a tire and leave you stranded.

On BLM land outside Caliente, we dove-hunted near a line of sunflowers that marked a trickling irrigation ditch on a farm belonging to a Mormon, as members of the Church of Jesus Christ of Latter-day Saints (LDS) were known. Crows heralded the start of the day, and in the chill of the early autumn light, so clear in my memory, a red-tailed hawk circled in the blue. A coyote, as still as a stone, watched us at a distance, then vanished into the sage.

The end of October signaled the beginning of deer season, and the hunting ritual moved five hundred miles north to distant Elko County near the Idaho border. With aspen, mountain mahogany, and scrub oak turning in yellows and reds, the big hills beckoned us to walk far while the light was good. I'd spend all day at my father's heel as he read the groves, gullies, and grassy springs. As part of the sprawling Humboldt-Toiyabe National Forest, this too was public land where cattle grazed under federal lease. We were visitors, and we respected the responsibility. We may have carved our initials on the bark of an aspen, but we kept a good, clean camp.

From cutting Christmas trees and cords of pine, years spent watching my father and grandfather pick away at so-so tungsten, fluorspar, and silver mining claims, we drew from the public land. Although we never tried to run cattle in the desert, we met many of the stubborn stockmen who did.

Some would have called us Teddy Roosevelt conservationists, but we didn't know it. We were just there to enjoy the public land, the West's great American Common.

Nevada was a special place in more controversial ways. Its silver-plated statehood during the Civil War had been a thing of suspicion almost from the start. With so much space and so few people, it became a speculator's paradise, a place that was hard to settle whether you were disciplined Mormon pioneers or the U.S. Army. With 84 percent of its land under federal control, and more than 60 percent of that managed directly by the BLM, federal influence over public land has been a reality in Nevada since the state's inception. Although some reporters, made breathless by the cowboy imagery and Old-West feel of Cliven Bundy's predicament, covered his travails under the mistaken belief that the rancher's disagreement with the federal government was a new phenomenon, such showdowns had gone on for many years under various names, most famously the "Sagebrush Rebellion." In Nevada, ranchers named Dann, Hage, Carver, and Colvin still generated heated discussions in the state's enormous outback. The influential environmental writer Christopher Ketcham was right when he echoed the West's great literary iconoclast Edward Abbey in observing, "One could write a post-war history of the West as a chronology of ranchers' resistance to federal regulation, and the center of resistance has always been Nevada."

But the debate over the use of public lands far transcended the issue of states' rights. As former U.S Department of Interior solicitor John Leshy, a foremost legal authority on federal public lands, has observed, "The nation wasn't formed until the founding generation decided the national government was going to take ownership of a lot of land. There was no intention, from the very beginning, that as new states were formed they would automatically become entitled to all the US public lands inside their borders."

The region was long-coveted but little understood. It had been home to the indigenous Goshute, Mojave, Paiute, Shoshone, and Washoe people, but that didn't prevent conquistadors from claiming it in the name of the Spanish Empire until the early 1800s. When Mexico won its independence from Spain in 1821, it staked the vast aridness as its own. That changed following the two-year Mexican-American War with the 1848 signing of the Treaty of Guadalupe Hidalgo, which ceded to the victor 55 percent of Mexico's territory, some 525,000 square miles, including modern-day Nevada. The stakes climbed higher with the discovery of gold in California, and suddenly the future Silver State was trampled by thousands of fortune-seekers, emigrants, members of the Church of Latter-Day Saints, and the endless herds of cattle and sheep it took to keep them fed.

Nevada's silver-lined statehood in 1864 gave it an official standing that its undersized population didn't rate, but the Property Clause

of the US Constitution gave Congress authority over federal property without limitation. The argument that all new states should be
admitted on an "equal footing" with the original states was debated
and defeated during the Constitutional Convention in 1787, but it
gained popularity nearly two hundred years later during the Sagebrush Rebellion, despite a lack of legal standing. In the twenty-first
century, the vast majority of Nevada's land remained legally under
federal control. That fact did nothing to end the fight for control.

It was Teddy Roosevelt, the twenty-sixth president of the United
States and the big-game hunting, progressive father of American
environmentalism, who said, "Conservation is a great moral issue
for it involves the patriotic duty of insuring the safety and continu-
ance of the nation. We have fallen heirs to the most glorious heritage a people ever received, and each one must do his part if we wish
to show that the nation is worthy of its good fortune."

A lot had changed since Roosevelt boldly embraced the dueling
concepts of conservation and development in a "new nationalism"
of resource conservation. Although rancher and governor John
Sparks had been a dominant political force around the turn of the
twentieth century, the modern Sagebrush Rebellion emerged from
Nevada in the 1970s as a protest platform for cattle ranchers who
complained of federal government overreach. The Sagebrush Rebellion provided a political whip hand for a new era of conservatives
who found the hats-and-boots imagery irresistible. Presidential
candidate and gentleman rancher Ronald Reagan proclaimed
himself a "rebel" in a 1980 battle cry and co-opted the stockmen's
laments about the BLM. The former California governor led the
charge, blasting federal ownership of land within the western states'
boundaries as unconstitutional. He rode the antigovernment wave
all the way to the White House, carrying every state west of the Mississippi River. His choice for Secretary of the Interior, James Watt,
paid lip service to the concept.

While the Sagebrush Rebellion grew organically before being
politicized, the so-called wise-use movement was spawned in a
political Petri dish in the late 1980s. Those at the forefront were representatives of mining and timber interests determined to counter

growing environmental activism in the West. Among the movement's earliest chief funders was conservative Colorado beer tycoon Joseph Coors. By the time Bundy entered the public spotlight, his views were little different from position papers found on the Koch Industries–backed American Legislative Exchange Council (ALEC) and American Lands Council websites.

Truth be told, there was little new under the blistering Nevada sun. The powerful and their proxies had long vied in court, Congress, and on the open range for control of the arid land's immense open spaces and lucrative natural resources. When it came to political clout, the state's cattle barons were as influential as their Comstock counterparts. In the late 1800s, John Sparks used hired guns to force his will on the land. After the turn of the century, Nevada Senator Francis Newlands's Reclamation Act of 1902 began a system of dams and irrigation ditches that moved water for agriculture, ranching, and eventually development. The fact that he was an avowed white supremacist didn't hamstring Newlands in Washington. The "Sagebrush Caesar" and U.S. Senate powerhouse Pat McCarran, born to the saddle, rode hard for ranching interests in an effort that sometimes produced unintended consequences. A stroke would stop McCarran before his vicious red-baiting and onerous anti-Semitism did. By hook or crook, many had sought for generations to wrest control of Nevada land from the federal government. The trouble was, to a man no one ever wanted to pay for it.

In the latter half of the twentieth century, Southern Nevada had become one of the fastest growing areas in the nation. Outside the halls of the state legislature, the frustrations of Nevada's ranchers grew with the rise of the modern environmental movement. They saw their once-unchallenged political clout shift toward high-rolling casino gambling executives and developers who dreamed of a glittery desert metropolis in Las Vegas—and were ruthless enough to go after precious water resources. In the modern era, U.S. Senate Majority Leader Harry Reid was the undisputed king of public-lands issues as he moved—at times controversially—between warring environmentalist and developer camps whose differences were as great as those Bundy had with the detested BLM.

But the court-ordered impound against Bundy included more than one corral. While a large pen had been set up in a bleak alluvial fan called Toquop Wash as a staging area for the transportation of Bundy's wandering cattle, the government also created a temporary corral out of orange plastic fencing in anticipation of a possible protest by the Bundys' social media–intoxicated supporters. A sign wired to the fencing read First Amendment Area.

As a native Nevadan and veteran columnist with the *Las Vegas Review-Journal*, the state's largest newspaper, I'd followed the recalcitrant rancher's battle with the federal bureaucracy for many years. For much of that time, he'd often been portrayed in the press as a local character, a one-note singer. With a printed copy of the U.S. Constitution in his shirt pocket and the legally flawed argument that the federal public land on which he grazed his cattle was actually owned by the state and under county control, the patriarch of a family of fourteen was a familiar figure around the Mormon pioneer village of Bunkerville. Not only did he refuse to recognize the federal government's jurisdiction, but he also claimed a "preemptive" ancestral right to the land because his Mormon relatives had worked it since 1877, just thirteen years after Nevada received its statehood.

In the months to come, I would cover the Bundy saga for Reuters, the *Nevada Independent*, and National Public Radio station KNPR and watch it spread from the backroads of Gold Butte and a Las Vegas courtroom to the Malheur National Wildlife Refuge in eastern Oregon and beyond, as journalists attempted to report it and political provocateurs sought to exploit it.

Bundy had lost in every federal court he set foot in, but by 2014 his message and increasing pleas for help had gained traction in recesses of the right-wing media often larded with conspiracy theories and "deep state" chatter.

His cause was divinely inspired, Bundy claimed, as part of his LDS faith. The document that guides his spiritual righteousness is the same one that guides his interpretation of the U.S. Constitution in its protection of "states' rights"—the Book of Mormon. Mark Twain once famously derided the sacred LDS text written by church founder Joseph Smith in 1830 as "chloroform in print." Perhaps to some, but the Mormon belief that the U.S. Constitution is of divine origin is written in the faith's Doctrine and Covenants, in which God is quoted as saying, "And for this purpose I have established the Constitution of this land, by the hands of wise men whom I raised up unto this very purpose, and redeemed the land by the shedding of blood."

Bundy's politics echoed fundamentalist Mormonism's obsession with local institutions and its paranoia about the threat from outsiders, whether they came from the federal government or the conservation movement. If the government had lost its patience, Bundy would use its growing militarized presence on his ranch to conjure up images of overreach and outright abuse by the BLM, the U.S. Forest Service, and the FBI. Viewers of sharply edited internet videos couldn't help but ask themselves, "All this for a cattle roundup?" For those who remembered the tragic debacles of Waco and Ruby Ridge, there was an increasingly uneasy sense that the government's livestock gather wouldn't go well.

What was never included in the Bundy family's prayerful propaganda was the fact that the ranching patriarch had long enjoyed the advantages of the federal government's grazing system. Beginning in the 1970s, he'd been able to secure a grazing lease for 150,000 acres of BLM land at a cost of approximately $1.30 per cow per month. Since a majority of the fees collected were plowed right back into federal programs to improve those same public lands, the West's legendary libertarian ranchers had long been the recipients of a form of free-range welfare.

But the Bundy case was no simple ranching saga. In an age of social-media celebrity, YouTube stardom, and citizen journalism, it would go viral in real time.

For years, in an effort to claim land he neither owned nor legally held permits for, Bundy had been improving springs and developing water rights on it. When he began grazing his cattle in the nearby Gold Butte Preserve—a stunning landscape of 300,000 acres of natural and cultural beauty that included wildlife, Native American rock art, and sandstone towers—the federal government had another reason to respond. Home to bighorn sheep and mountain lions, Gold

Butte was slated to be designated as a national monument by President Barack Obama, thanks to lobbying by Reid, Nevada's "Senator from Searchlight." Gold Butte's protected status became an irresistible straw-man issue for America's right-wing media.

No one had ever accused the Bundys of acting directly on behalf of the developers and extractive industry men who had long had their sights set on the region's gold, uranium, natural gas and oil reserves, scenic real estate, and precious water rights. But in time it would become obvious that the family's battle with the government was being exploited by many of those same interests. The BLM, with its clumsy cattle roundup, appeared to be playing into their hands. But on that early spring morning in 2014, there were no angry ranchers or curious tourists, and I was a head-scratching reporter standing outside the empty First Amendment Area. Even with no one around to see it, it was obvious that the cordoned-off area would only fuel the anxieties of those who believed the Mormon cowboy was getting a raw deal from government bullying.

Given that the free-speech pen was located several miles from Bundy's ranch and even farther from the government's corral of the "trespassing" cattle, the lack of attendance was understandable. I had driven to the area to see whether the BLM and National Park Service (NPS) could manage to round up a few hundred head of cattle without making it appear they were invading a small country. They couldn't.

Nearly every federal official I saw wore a semiautomatic pistol on his hip. Some cruised in unmarked SUVs with tinted windows. Given the lack of attention from even other members of Bundy's large extended family, the crush of security gave the quiet area a militarized feel.

The Bundy family's propaganda would draw hundreds of supporters to the Nevada desert in a ranch-style Woodstock. Led by Stewart Rhodes, members of the anti-immigration Oath Keepers left their "patrols" on the Arizona-Mexico border to stand with Cliven. The family made use of misleading videos to fan the flames of its "emergency" and called for supporters from throughout an America already fired up by right-wing media, such as Alex Jones's *InfoWars*, Steve Bannon's *Breitbart News,* and *Fox News* commentator Sean Hannity. Supporters, waving the yellow Gadsden banner created during the American Revolution and since appropriated by everyone from Libertarians and Tea Party followers to members of the American militia movement, gathered at the makeshift rallying point outside the Bundy Ranch they called Camp Liberty.

By the morning of April 12, 2014, the BLM had already decided to halt the cattle impoundment due to the incendiary situation. The government had intended to sell Bundy's cattle as payment against the fees he owed the government. Such a move on the part of the government would have been routine if not for Bundy's allusions to doing "whatever it takes" to keep his cattle amid the alarming presence of armed militia members, which prompted the FBI to raise its threat assessment. Federal agents anticipated the grave danger and thought a deadly shootout was likely. Bundy's Range War Emergency message, with his promises to do anything to stop the cattle impoundment, was being taken very seriously. Those who believe in the government's "black helicopter" mystique had their suspicions and paranoia reinforced by the display of federal firepower.

But on April 5, the prospects of a showdown still seemed distant. I drove three miles, left the pavement, then wound on a dirt road past worn signs touting "Ron Paul" and "Bundy Melons" and parked in the front yard at Bundy Ranch. Cliven and wife Carol were friendly. The constitutional lesson was the same one I'd heard from him and others before about state sovereignty, local jurisdiction, and the limited power the Founding Fathers had granted the federal government. When I reminded him that his views had been shellacked in federal court, where judges had consistently ruled against him, he returned to his constitutional argument. By now, I expected, Bundy's own cows could recite it.

With his broad-brimmed hat and potbelly, Bundy was easy to underestimate. His drawl at times made him seem unlettered. His focus on his own reading of the Constitution made him appear obsessed and could easily be interpreted as a country conman at work. Although he kept his conservative religious beliefs to himself that day, I had attended community meetings in which his praise for the Constitution's hallowed language sounded like nothing less than a sermon.

There in his tree-shaded front yard, his wife at his side, with the sound of grandchildren laughing somewhere in the distance and the occasional call of a rooster and magpie adding exclamation to the interview, the rancher gave his side of a story more than two decades in the making. He was, he said, the last man standing in a ranching tradition in the region well more than a century old. His sense of persecution was clear:

> When I see the forces they have against me.... You know all those vehicles, all the machinery, all those men, all those guns and all those badges, you know, they're only after one person. They're not after you. They're only after me. They're after Cliven Bundy. And they want to incarcerate me or put a bullet through me. That's the only reason they could be there. And that makes me ask the question: Why do they want me so bad?
>
> It's not because of my cattle. It's because of what I say. And what I say is they have no jurisdiction or authority here in Clark County. And they do not own the land. The land belongs to we the people of Nevada.

But that's not how the authorities see it.

He knew better than anyone that legal experts and ruling judges disagreed. The previous year, U.S. District Judge Lloyd D. George, a respected jurist and LDS Church elder who practices in a federal courthouse named in his honor, echoed previous rulings on the matter that "the public lands in Nevada are property of the United States because the United States has held title to those lands since 1848, when Mexico ceded the land to the United States." There was no trump card in the deck. The only question was whether Cliven was bluffing about doing "whatever it takes."

Meanwhile, Bundy continued to insist that his position was correct:

> You know, our fathers come from a foreign land, and they come to the United States, and they went through the Revolutionary War and all these battles. But they finally worked their way all across America to this valley. And it doesn't seem like the good Lord put me here to give it up. I don't know whether I'm put here to fight this battle or not, but that's where I'm at. My heritage has brought me to this point. And then of course my duty here would be to be a steward over this land. And of course I've been born and raised in the western culture here.

He waxed nostalgic and was eager to talk about his interpretation of the Constitution, a pocket version printed for years by the LDS right-wingers W. Cleon Skousen and Bert Smith peeking out of his shirt pocket. "What I want to do is grow something green and see a fat cow," Bundy said.

> And of course the other thing is my family, it's most important to me. I've had the opportunity to raise my family in a real nice environment, in the fresh air and greenness of the world out here. And of course that's worth fighting for. It's something I love. It's a passion. I'm a producer. It's probably what I would want to be known for more than anything. I produce something…my cows eat the forage and the water out there, which there's no other way to harvest that resource. And they take that resource and make an edible commodity for you, red meat to eat on your table. And that's what I do.

Was there room for compromise? None, according to Cliven, for in his mind to compromise would mean to compromise the U.S. Constitution:

> I have faith in the heavenly father. I see our liberties and freedoms being squashed…they're not only after my freedom, they're after your freedoms and liberties. They're after your public land. And they're after this rancher that produces food for you.… They have run or broke, however way you want

to put it, fifty-two of my fellow ranchers right here in Clark County. I'm the last man standing.

Cliven also claimed to be a steward for the wildlife, to protect it from fire, and to keep it available for the public. "You won't find a 'Don't Trespass' sign on my property...the public is welcome. I want you to understand I only own certain rights here. I don't own this property in whole. I only own certain rights here. The rest of the rights belong to we the people of Clark County."

He said more than thirty vehicles had gone into the backcountry that morning and a government staging area and command post had gone up quickly out near the highway.

In the entirety of the interview he failed even once to acknowledge that his failure to pay his grazing fees to the appropriate agency had precipitated the trouble he found himself in. Instead, he saw a greater tyranny at work. "It's unbelievable that this would happen in America," Bundy said, turning again to his love of the land and the hundreds of thousands of acres his five-hundred-head herd of cattle were wandering on as we spoke.

> I raise some of the best melons in the world right here. That's something to say. I've got some good kids, too. They're all products of this land. If I can raise good kids, good melons and good beef, I don't know how much more I can do. I've just got to fight the United States government to keep it.

The lengthy interview finished, I left the Bundy spread thinking the rancher wasn't so much a revolutionary as a heel-dragging Mormon cowman on the wrong side of changing times. It was a view I'd adjust considerably in the coming months. He'd gambled in every court he'd entered and consistently crapped out. He'd been warned for decades by the government and his own friends in the ranching community. And now the bill was coming due.

Then a strange thing happened as I pulled back onto the paved road. Three government SUVs immediately followed me. Up ahead, two white, unmarked SUVs were parked sideways and blocking most of the road. An armed federal officer dressed in green fatigues stood outside his vehicle.

Forced to come to a stop, I rolled down the window and heard him say, "You can go around." Rather than argue that it made no sense to block an otherwise deserted road, I quietly followed the instruction. I then realized that the government's attempt to force Bundy to follow federal grazing regulations was probably not going to end well.

Indeed, within hours, authorities had managed to take one of the rancher's sons into custody, but not before roughing him up and playing into the family's hype of victimhood against an oppressor. Davey Bundy had been taking pictures of the semisecret cattle confiscation and posting them on internet sites. A day later, more than a hundred people answered what they saw as a call in defense of "freedom" and drove to the Bundy Ranch to protest in support of the family. In the coming days, the voices of protest would increase considerably a few miles up the road, near the banks of the Virgin River at a place the family's allies called "Camp Liberty."

The modern-day western story playing out in Nevada, an arid land of saints, sinners, and sovereign citizens, had begun to circle the planet. Like true westerns of old, it was a dangerous tale with few white hats.

Saints, Sinners, and Sovereign Citizens

CHAPTER 1

We Join the Revolution Already in Progress

Notice is hereby given that a temporary closure to public access, use, and occupancy will be in effect for the dates and times specified in this Notice on public lands administered by the Bureau of Land Management, Southern Nevada District Office, Las Vegas Field Office, within the Gold Butte, Mormon Mesa, and Bunkerville Flats Areas in the northeastern portion of Clark County, Nevada. This temporary closure is necessary to limit public access, use, and occupancy during an impoundment of illegally grazing cattle to ensure the safety and welfare of the public, contractors, and government employees.

By the time the BLM's official notice of federal land closure for the purposes of impounding Cliven Bundy's cattle was made public, the rancher had already prepared and distributed official notices of his own. He was well practiced, having typed notices and proclamations for years in his long dispute with a federal government that, according to his view of the world and reading of the U.S. Constitution, essentially didn't much exist.

Formally notified on March 14, 2014, that the impoundment was imminent, within twenty-four hours he'd told a reporter he was "ready to do battle" with the BLM and promised to do "whatever it takes" to defend his interests. It was a veiled threat he'd repeat often in the ensuing weeks in an effort to navigate the fine line separating constitutionally protected free speech and a criminal threat of violence against federal officers and government contractors.

Bundy had known a storm was coming. One missive he typed was dated three days earlier than the government's notice. It declared a "RANGE WAR EMERGENCY" and made a "DEMAND FOR PROTECTION" from a long list of Nevada elected officials, headed not by the state's congressional delegation but by Clark County Sheriff Doug Gillespie. Bundy added in all caps that a "NOTICE OF CATTLE RUSTLING AND ILLEGAL SEIZURE BY CONTRACT COWBOYS, UNDER THE DIRECTION OF THE BLM, IS IN PROGRESS ON BUNDY'S RANCH, CLARK COUNTY, NEVADA." His demand was signed and notarized, calling for action from the county sheriff and state officials because, as he repeatedly claimed, the federal government held no jurisdiction over the land or his herd.

That same day, Bundy also asserted a lien against officials of the Cattoor Livestock Roundup, Inc., of Nephi, Utah—a family outfit often used by the BLM to gather stray cattle and wild horses and burros from federal public land and Indian reservations. The gatherings were usually controversial and occasionally litigated by animal-rights groups and members of Nevada's Paiute Tribe. The Cattoor company was among the most experienced in the business.

Other contractors were anxious to go to work, including Sun J Livestock, Sampson Livestock, 'R' Livestock, and Sky Hawk Helicopter Service, a company contracted to spot and direct cattle from the air. The BLM had budgeted approximately a million dollars for the cattle impoundment and had no shortage of willing contractors. That is, until the companies began receiving official notices of liens threatening them with "appropriate legal remedies" and even the "filing of criminal complaints with the proper jurisdictional authorities." The notifications ended with, "Cliven Bundy will do whatever it takes to protect his property and rights and liberty and freedoms and those of, We the People, of Clark County, Nevada."

Going after the government contractors, some of them fellow church members, was part of a multipronged approach the rancher used to foul the impoundment. It was no secret plan. He made his intentions clear with every missive. Legalistic letters were enough to make some potential contractors think twice. The tactic had worked repeatedly in 2012, the last time the government had scheduled an impoundment before postponing it, in part out of a concern for employee safety. That time, at least one livestock contractor said he felt "intimidated" by the family, understandable after Bundy said he'd defend his cattle with the help of armed ranchers from throughout the region.

Two years later, Bundy was back at the keyboard producing notices of lien and liability against a new group of cooperators with the federal enemy. After 'R' Livestock Connection LLC, a cattle-auction company based in Monroe, Utah, placed the sole bid for a $78,000 contract to sell off Bundy's cattle, it received a visit from Ryan Bundy, one of Cliven's fourteen sons, and others associated with the rancher's cause. Signs announcing Stolen Cattle Sold Here were posted. A government indictment would later describe Bundy's angry rhetoric as a threat of "force, violence and economic harm." Bundy's son, in fact, had accused the company's owner of selling "his soul to the devil for a few stolen cattle."

Threats aside, it wasn't as if locating and gathering Bundy's ornery stock was in itself a daunting task for the BLM, U.S. National Park Service (NPS), and private contractors. The personnel involved, their numbers kept secret as a safety precaution, were spread out across approximately 600,000 acres of federal public land, closing sections as needed for the roundup. By the end of the first week of April, 322,000 acres, most of them administered by the BLM or NPS, but some even belonging to the U.S. Bureau of Reclamation, were shut off from public access.

The government set up its incident command post just off Interstate 15 in Toquop Wash, about six miles from the Bundy Ranch. It was a heavily guarded but homely piece of drainage that crossed the busy highway beneath two concrete bridges. In a major flash-flood event during the late-summer monsoons or a downpour of biblical proportions, Toquop might send water all the way to the Virgin River. Command trailers and a corral were set up; a perimeter fence was guarded and monitored by surveillance cameras, with the cut of the wash and the two highway bridges placing the impound-ment site at a strategic disadvantage in the unlikely event of a con-frontation. But given the intimidating firepower on display—heavily armed federal law enforcement in military garb and flak jackets—such a thing seemed like long odds.

The odds shifted, though, when Bundy began to use the government's might against itself. He calmly gave press briefings that often turned into winding speeches about ranching and government overreach. Wherever the talks started, they always ended up with a lesson on the Constitution's divine provenance. By the time the last of the banners and bunting were draped and flags unfurled, Bundy was giving speeches from atop a makeshift stage flanked, for the first time, by armed security guards.

Often he would talk about his ties to the land itself, how relatives had been standing their ground in the area since 1877. Even at a young age, Bundy was proud of his extended family's agrarian tradition and ties to the area, but they weren't the region's first or most successful cattle ranchers. The Arizona Strip's earliest nonnative inhabitants began cattle ranching at Pipe Spring in the mid-1860s. By the 1880s, non-Mormon Preston Nutter operated an outfit with four thousand head out of northeastern Utah at Nine-Mile Canyon. Nutter expanded his range, controlling water holes and forcing his will on the land until 1936, when it took him back.

Family patriarch Abraham Bundy, taking advantage of the 1916 federal Homestead Act, determined to stake out and "prove up" a deceptively dry area in the Parashant country near Mount Trumbull with no available surface water and "next to none" below ground. Bundy family relatives had been part of the Mount Trumbull Wilderness and the Arizona Strip, an 8,000-square-mile outland known for maintaining a thriving polygamist community for decades after the Church had banned the practice of plural marriage. Although there was no evidence the Bundys had engaged in plural marriage, a family historian reported that Bundy relatives had been part of a polygamist colony in Mexico before moving to the Strip.

With Mount Trumball as its central geographic point, in many ways the vast Strip country was a place apart, a land not for the fainthearted even by the West's extremely rugged standards. It was there the Bundys, after the turn of the twentieth century, would struggle and worship and eke out an existence in one of the least-populated places on the continent. They established a dot on the map, more outpost than township, called Bundyville. They would run cows, farm in arid patches, cut timber, and never, ever give up. In his history of a branch of the Bundy family, Lyman Hafen reflected, "I have always thought of the Bundys as a tough-hearted and rugged family, the kind of people who could be cut to their knees by noon and back on their feet by evening. They were survivors."

Not all the desert ranchers could say the same. When Brigham Young called acolyte John Bennion to develop productive cattle and sheep-grazing land in the Vernon desert of western Utah, Bennion sent his son Israel to accomplish the difficult task. The son "learned quickly the trickster temperament of desert basin life" with hailstorms one moment and parched earth the next. "He became the apprentice of the prickly pear cactus, the grandfather silver sage, the severe western winds, and a handful of lingering Paiute Indians who taught him the tools of survival," descendant Janet Bennion wrote. "He was not able to make the desert bloom, as his calling demanded; on the contrary, he and other Mormon men sent out by Brigham succeeded in *overgrazing* the entire basin" and turning the grassland into a dustbowl.

The Bundys survived where the equally tough Southern Paiute, specifically the Shivwits, Kaibab, and Uinkarets, had hunted and gathered for centuries. By the turn of the twenty-first century, much of the region would be redesignated as the Parashant National Monument and encompass pieces of Utah, Arizona, and Nevada. It amounted to 20 percent of the five-million-acre Strip. By any name, it was a forbidding place, but as Hafen waxed, "Hope, in spite of heartache, springs eternal on the Arizona Strip."

To understand Bundy the man, it's helpful to consider young Cliven, who could trace his Mormon heritage to great-grandfather Nephi Johnson's birth into the faith in 1833. Cliven wasn't raised driving a big herd of cattle but rather growing prize-winning melons in the fertile soil of the Virgin River Valley. The oldest child and only son born to Bodel (Jensen) and David Bundy, Cliven was born on April 29, 1946, in Las Vegas. When his father moved the family to the 160-acre homestead ranch, one of approximately a thousand ranches in Nevada at that time, Cliven was raised more in the fields than on the range, and he excelled there. As a boy he would join the Virgin Valley Future Farmers of America (FFA) chapter, eventually winning a hundred-dollar National FFA Foundation Award. With his father away from home during the week as a heavy-equipment operator on construction sites, increased responsibility was placed on young Cliven's shoulders. He didn't shirk, embracing his responsibility to do work usually reserved for grown men.

By the time he was eighteen years old, he kept fifty acres in cultivation at home and grazed a hundred head of cattle on federal land the family leased for a nominal fee. The family would eventually advertise the quality of its melons in area newspapers. In an essay that was later quoted in a St. George newspaper article about his FFA award, Cliven explained that he had even bigger plans: hopes of expanding the melon field in production to one hundred acres, with the farm serving as a hub for the family's humble livestock program. Although the family could claim roots in the region back to the late 1870s, it didn't begin grazing cattle in the Gold Butte area near its homestead until 1952.

"With dad gone from the farm I had most of the responsibility of the farming, but when he is home weekends we ride the range and take care of the livestock," Cliven said. Although he had "six real nice sisters," the oldest of whom sometimes helped him hoe the field and work with the calves, "my life has been based upon farming ever since I was a little fellow; I love to farm," he added. "I thought I could do any of the farming since the age of five, and did just about everything from plowing to feeding the chickens and loved it all."

That included experimenting with fertilizers to increase crop production, planting new salt-tolerant grasses for livestock feed, and battling weeds. "I try to keep a close watch on my crops so that I will be able to catch any disease or insects that may need my attention," Cliven stated in his essay with an air of understatement uncommon for a teenager.

If Cliven's religious beliefs ever wavered when he was a youngster, they were surely strengthened on an early evening in late

February 1964, when he hit and killed three wild horses while driving his father's new car outside Bunkerville. One of the animals came through the windshield. The car was a total loss, but Cliven managed to escape with minor cuts.

Life around Bunkerville was isolated. Cliven was raised almost exclusively among white Mormons, a long way from any ethnic communities and the growing American civil rights movement. He would reflect many years later, after being accused of racism, "I didn't hardly see a black boy probably until I was a teenager. And I didn't understand their customs and cultures. And I didn't understand a lot of things."

By some measures, he'd come a long way since 1964. By April 2014, the name Bundy was best known in the region for Cliven's outspokenness on the encroachment of environmental socialism and his many legal disputes with the federal government. He had lost in every jurisdiction but the court of public opinion. There, he found allies among other frustrated ranchers, libertarian constitutionalists, antigovernment sovereign citizens, and angry conservatives. His goal of returning federal land to local control no doubt elated wealthy land speculators and developers—few of whom could have fully appreciated the long, unsuccessful track record he had racked up against the federal government.

Bundy's first federal grazing permit, signed in 1973, gave a clue about the challenges that lay ahead. A federal judge later defined the Bunkerville allotment area as an "ephemeral" range, that is, range that can't consistently produce enough forage for cattle "but periodically [can] provide annual vegetation suitable for livestock grazing." That meant his herd would need to be kept under control and would not be guaranteed a permanent home on the range.

Although already politically active and outspoken on the role of the federal government, by 1989 Bundy really had something to complain about when the desert tortoise was designated for protection under the Endangered Species Act. A key reason for the change was the destruction of fragile protected tortoise habitat by grazing cattle. Rapid development in booming communities such as Phoenix and Las Vegas was bulldozing tortoise territory at a record clip, and developers familiar with the political power structure carved out ways to collect the tortoises and transfer them to desert zones designated for their existence. The plan was expensive and met with mixed results, but it kept the bulldozers moving.

For those who knew Bundy's zeal, the new federal tortoise protections signaled nothing less than a sign of more trouble ahead. "Bundy appears to be the last of a dying breed as he fights the U.S. government's efforts to yank his grazing rights on the public land that surrounds him," Kenric Ward observed in his analysis of Mormon influence in Las Vegas, *Saints in Babylon*. "Bundy's crusade isn't just about the law or his livelihood. It's part and parcel of his faith." Allies in the press echoed the sentiment, calling Bundy's dubious legal strategy "a noble cause" battle against "the arrogant practitioners of an environmental religion."

Bundy considered the tortoise restrictions and pending wilderness designations existential threats, and he protested that protection and preservation of the environment would drive ranchers out of business. He told one like-minded group in June 1989, "Do we want to be run by a government bureaucracy, have our lands controlled, multiple use removed, and be locked out and dictated to? Isn't that what we call communism and socialism?"

When the U.S. Fish and Wildlife Service Biological Opinion used as part of the BLM's land and tortoise management strategy placed Bundy's grazing area in the heart of tortoise country, he requested and received a delay of its implementation. He complained that ranchers didn't have the same ability as developers to pay a tortoise mitigation fee to Clark County, but his lament went nowhere.

The tortoise restrictions and recurring drought conditions took a toll on Southern Nevada ranchers, dozens of whom sold off their grazing rights and stopped running cattle. The era of dryland ranching outside Las Vegas was coming to an end, but Bundy failed to get the message. Two days before the tortoise territory protection was implemented on February 28, 1993, he fired off a pair of terse "Administrative Notices of Intent," claiming that the BLM lacked jurisdiction over federal public lands, and that his "vested grazing rights" enabled him to continue to run his cattle without paying any fees at all. He stopped sending checks to the government and began receiving late notices. By July of that year, he received a "Trespass Notice and Order to Remove" his livestock. When Bundy asked for a time extension from the federal agency whose jurisdiction he claimed not to recognize as legitimate, he received one. But the wheels of bureaucracy were turning with or without his approval, and within months Nevada's BLM director received approval from the court to proceed with the cancellation of Bundy's grazing permit. When the paperwork was delivered to the ranch, Cliven accused the BLM representative of harassment, and one of his sons expressed the family's disapproval by tearing up the document.

The rancher was losing, but even his critics would call him clever. Two weeks after the BLM issued its final decision cancelling his ephemeral-range grazing permit, he wrote a check for $1,961.47—the amount the bureau had calculated the rancher owed for grazing eighty-five head of cattle for a year on the allotment. But instead of sending the check to the BLM, he sent it to Clark County in an attempt to advance his jurisdiction argument. The check was returned.

When the BLM sent bills and late notices, Bundy responded with "administrative notices" of his own, and late in the year when the BLM notified him that a stock contractor would be coming to the disputed allotment to gather some of the wild horses and burros there that were overgrazing the tenuous forage, the rancher served them with a trespass notice.

As the decade wore on, an increasingly frustrated BLM continued to attempt to resolve the dispute with Bundy without a physical confrontation. The delays seemed to strengthen his obstinacy. He declined to meet with BLM agents, and when he wound up in federal court in 1998, he represented himself as a *pro se* defendant. By then, Bundy owed more than $150,000 in back grazing fees and assessments. Not surprisingly, his argument failed to sway U.S. District Judge Johnnie Rawlinson, who ruled in favor of the government on November 3, 1998.

Although Bundy claimed in his court filings that the tortoise protection law, "if fully implemented, would lead to the end of ranching in Clark County," the judge wrote, "The decision from the BLM does not inform Bundy he can no longer graze livestock due to the protection of the Desert Tortoise, but instead reminds Bundy that his grazing permit" was ending and needed to be renewed. "For five years Bundy has been trespassing on public lands and his livestock have consumed forage," Rawlinson wrote. "The government has shown commendable restraint in allowing this trespass to continue for so long without impounding Bundy's livestock."

In another order dated November 3, 1998, the judge restated the obvious, that the federal court had jurisdiction and the US owned the allotment Bundy's cows had been grazing for free. She then ordered a $200-per-head per-day assessment for any Bundy livestock found on the allotment after November 30, 1998.

Bundy's appeal to the U.S. Ninth Circuit Court of Appeals was rejected. He lost another part of his argument when Clark County, acting on a new BLM Resource Management Plan for the booming Las Vegas Valley, purchased from the government the federal grazing permit for the Bunkerville Allotment for $375,000—officially in the name of protecting the desert tortoise. Many suspected that political calculations were behind the agreement—which was probably accurate. A 2002 BLM memo asserted that Bundy "has no right to occupy or graze livestock in the Bunkerville grazing allotment. Two court decisions, one in Federal District Court and another in the Circuit Court of Appeals, fully support our positions."

In the ensuing decade, Bundy continued to run his cattle. In fact, he expanded his herd's size and range. The BLM continued to attempt to persuade him to cease and desist, or at least return its calls. By April 2008, another BLM notice went out to the ranch, notifying Bundy of the cancellation of his range-improvement permit and cooperative agreement. This meant that his water troughs, tanks and pipes, and seep-spring development were no longer allowed on the land. Without them, the trespassing herd would have no water. In May, he sent the government a "Constructive Notice" that mentioned a refrain that would become his mantra for the next six years. He said he would do "whatever it takes" to protect his grazing rights and property. The government again appeared to back off.

Other ranchers, however, were watching. A 2011 notice by the BLM of its intention to round up his cattle was complicated by the fact that Bundy had let the tough-hided bovines wander widely and grow to an estimated one thousand in number. Just counting the animals was costly and time-consuming. When a 2012 roundup was mapped out and contracted, it had to be cancelled because Bundy threatened to have armed ranchers from throughout the region descend on Bunkerville to protect his herd. The BLM told a federal court that it took Bundy's threats seriously.

Once again, the U.S. Attorney was brought in to reaffirm rights and jurisdiction in the protracted legal battle of Bunkerville. Once again, the government found itself dancing to Bundy's tune of delay. On July 9, 2013, Judge Lloyd D. George reiterated the government's jurisdiction over the land in dispute, permanently enjoining the rancher from grazing cattle there. Once again, Bundy appealed, and once again, he lost. In October, the court ordered the removal of his cattle within forty-five days and reminded Bundy not to interfere with the impoundment. Once again, Cliven Bundy refused to recognize the judge's decision.

Although wrong on the law, Bundy was often right when it came to pointing out the obvious: the BLM and other federal agencies, such as the U.S. Forest Service, had a mixed record when it came to stewardship of the great American commons of the West. Plain politics and outright corruption often rigged the game and ruined the best efforts of the dedicated rangers and bureaucrats who most often caught the heat of ranchers' branding-iron rhetoric. When Bundy had exhausted his consistent but legally nonsensical claim that the federal government had no constitutional authority to lay claim to the land, he was living a legal fantasy.

So long at odds with federal land-management officials, Bundy family members weren't shy when it came to drawing lines in the desert sand on what they considered their land. For his part, Ryan Bundy often spoke of the escalating showdown with the federal government in biblical terms. In doing so, he echoed currents from the religious fundamentalist beginnings of the Mormon Church that dated back to the American faith's 1830 founding by Joseph Smith. This was one reason the government, in an attempt to calm tensions, sent a BLM special agent who was also an LDS bishop to seek common ground with Cliven's outspoken son. Like so many other attempts to resolve the two-decades-long dispute short of rounding up the rancher's cattle and hauling them away, this one also failed. Not only did Ryan repeat the family's refrain, but he swore he'd have several hundred supporters at his side to prevent the impoundment. But, interestingly, when the agent attempted to learn whether "whatever it takes" included violence, Ryan walked back from the line: "You interpret that the way you want."

During a time when other ranchers were focused on spring calving, Bundy was busy preparing for war with the government and implementing a propaganda campaign. He made little secret of his intentions, confiding to the *Daily Spectrum* newspaper of St. George, Utah: "First, I'm fighting this thing on paper. Then I'll go after the contract cowboys." That failing, he would "go after them with the media, with 'we the people' and whatever else it takes."

It was that last allusion that generated so much alarm in the offices of the BLM, NPS, and Federal Bureau of Investigation (FBI). Although criticized for their increasingly "militarized" presence, BLM rangers commonly worked alone in remote areas many miles from backup and often beyond cell phone coverage. In a rural West awash in weaponry and backcountry travelers who often carried firearms in their vehicles, whether for sport or self-defense, even simple citizen exchanges put rangers on alert. Although Bundy was widely known as a peaceful fellow who didn't carry a weapon, his disregard for well-established federal jurisdiction and his agitation and threatening language invited an increased-threat assessment. All the finger-pointing, paperwork, and tough talk intimidated some contractors, while others were less impressed. "They got themselves into trouble," a Utah livestock auction owner said, "and they can get themselves out of trouble."

Unlike other challengers to federal authority in the West, the Bundy family was generally forthright about its intentions. Family members produced videos of their confrontations with BLM employees and contractors attempting to satisfy the federal impoundment order. As March 2014 came to a close, Cliven and Ryan Bundy were captured in one scene leading a group effort to block a vehicle trailering horses and supplies for the roundup. Bundy himself gave away the plot line. "All those cowboys are going to be thieves who steal my cattle," the patriarch said. A video titled *Range War* would later surface on the internet.

Those who followed Bundy's career closely would recall the many times he'd stood before reporters to complain about the government's treatment, whether the subject was grazing allotments, the protection of the desert tortoise, or new environmental laws redefining wilderness boundaries and protections. His beliefs echoed earlier Sagebrush Rebellion rhetoric and ebbed and flowed with the work of reactionary Nevada ranchers like Wayne Hage and Dick Carver. What was different in 2014 was the gravity of the circumstances Bundy found himself in: after two decades of refusal to recognize government authority on federal land, he was headed for the last roundup.

Although some of Bundy's grown boys had families of their own and had moved away from Bunkerville to locations in Utah and Arizona, he called them back to the ranch. They would eventually be considered leaders of a conspiracy, with Ammon, another son, and Ryan topping the list. At first glance, they didn't sound, or look, like dangerous subversives.

Ammon was handsome, soft-spoken, and expressed a sense of spiritual patience that reflected his fundamentalist beliefs. The left side of Ryan's face had sagged with paralysis since childhood as a result of being backed over by a Ford LTD driven by his father. Three of the Bundy boys were filling the car's trunk with melons in the field when Ryan fell beneath a rear tire. Then just seven years old, he suffered a skull fracture and broken arm, but managed to keep his sense of humor intact. In a letter posted many years later on Facebook, he reflected that after receiving a cracked skull and being near death he understood that "Life was a bit rough at that moment."

He recalled how his father sent his brothers from the field to call for the sheriff and an ambulance. With Ryan bleeding profusely, his father "stopped to lay his hands upon my head and gave me a blessing of healing, by the power and authority of the Holy Priesthood, and closed his prayer 'in the name of Jesus Christ.' The bleeding stopped and we continued on to town." Despite the facial dissymmetry, Ryan was a capable and confident public speaker. He also expressed strong religious beliefs and had a history of challenging federal authority.

Cliven's sister, Margaret Houston, would also make news after she attempted to step in front of one of the trucks used in the government impoundment and was taken down hard to the ground by a BLM ranger. The incident was captured by the Bundy family's ubiquitous cell phone videographers and quickly exploited to advantage on social media. The video went viral and would later be credited as influencing the actions of some of Bundy's most loyal followers.

Although the threats of retaliation against Utah stock contractors continued, by early April it was clear that, however slowly, Bundy was losing his battle a few dozen head of recalcitrant cattle at a time. He called on his son Dave to return home from Utah. On April 5, 2014, Cliven made what by most measures sounded like a direct threat after seeing seventy-five head hauled to auction. "I've done quite a bit so far to keep my cattle, but I guess it's not been enough.... I have said I'd do what it takes to keep my cattle, so I guess it is going to have to be more physical."

Later that day, Dave Bundy was arrested and accused of failing to disperse when he tried to block BLM vehicles while photographing government personnel. Scuffed up in the process, he was later released from custody—but only after news of the arrest was widely circulated. The government was slowly winning the impoundment battle, but it was losing the propaganda war in what prosecutors would later lament were "false, deceitful and deceptive statements" by the family, which had also accused the BLM of excessive force and positioning "snipers against Bundy family members."

Seemingly mild-mannered Cliven Bundy seized the moment in the propaganda campaign. In furthering the call for assistance and action, he posted on Facebook, "They have my cattle and now they have one of my boys"—not acknowledging that his son had been dispatched for the precise purpose of disrupting the cattle transfer. "Range War begins tomorrow at Bundy ranch."

On April 7, Las Vegan Eric Farnsworth joined a swelling assembly of Bundy's neighbors, friends, and extended family outside the ranch in a rally that featured the American Stars and Stripes and the yellow Gadsden rattlesnake flag with the words Don't Tread on Me. The Gadsden flag was particularly popular with the modern American militia movement.

Farnsworth had come to support his longtime friend Ryan, who was already getting in the faces of government employees trying to carry out the court order. "Heaven forbid, we don't want to get anybody killed," Farnsworth said, warning Ryan to "keep your head on straight," despite the fact that the BLM had come with snipers, arrested one of Bundy's sons, and were "armed and ready to fight with fifty vehicles and how many manpower?"

In the days ahead, Clark County Commissioner Tom Collins would emerge as one of Bundy's few allies among Nevada elected officials. An electrician by trade, Collins had been a lifelong wrangler and rodeo cowboy who had kept livestock just a few miles from Bundy Ranch. A former Democratic county chairman and state legislator, Collins was known as a two-fisted drinker and a wily and personable politician who understood rural Clark County's mix of LDS Church members and secular libertarians. He chided elected officials from southern Utah who had encouraged participation in the standoff by warning them, "You'd better have funeral plans." He was also accused of calling a Utah county commissioner an "inbred bastard"—a remark he later downplayed.

For several years, Collins had attempted to broker a settlement between Bundy and the BLM, but he found recalcitrant parties on both sides. He believed Bundy deserved to hold some form of claim to the area his family had worked for so long. Trying to mediate, Collins said, "I'm trying to do everything I can to tell anybody who tells me they're coming here with loaded guns...to tell them not to come. The Bundys want peace. They don't want any violence going on, so all these gun-packing folks just need to go home." He may have been right about the rancher not wanting violence, but he was wrong that the Bundys were not inviting supporters with weapons to Clark County.

Among Bundy's vocal local supporters, the most distinctive was state legislator and future Las Vegas city councilwoman Michele

Fiore. With a political voice made louder by her own radio talk show, Fiore was a Second Amendment advocate known for flashing her weapons collection in a family photo calendar. As a councilwoman, she displayed a pink semiautomatic rifle on one wall of her office at City Hall. She was an unabashed backer of the rancher, mouthing his talking points and passing along social media and conservative web posts that sometimes had little relationship to the truth.

In a social media network just getting the "fake news" mantra in focus, misinformation abounded—much of it inuring to the Bundy family's advantage. It was also true that the government's insistence on a militarized approach fed into the family's narrative of victimization. The feds' decision to fence off a "First Amendment Area" was genuinely tone-deaf.

As negative press reports described the federal government's protest space, combined with mounting incidents surrounding the roundup, Bundy appeared to pick up an ally in Nevada's popular Republican Governor Brian Sandoval. "No cow justifies the atmosphere of intimidation which currently exists nor the limitation of constitutional rights that are sacred to all Nevadans," Sandoval chided the federal government. "The BLM needs to reconsider its approach to this matter and act accordingly."

One supporter, Blaine Cooper, learned about the Bundys from the social media messages that had begun ricocheting across the internet. Married and in his early thirties, Cooper lived in Humboldt, Arizona, and was previously unacquainted with Bundy and his legal predicament. He wasn't on the scene, hadn't read the First Amendment Area sign, and, as time would show, failed miserably at keeping his head on straight. He sometimes claimed to have been in the Marines, but multiple media outlets would report that there was no record of his military service. Cooper's personal views weren't hard to know—he literally broadcasted them. He was aligned philosophically with the "Resurrect the Republic 'Truth Radio' Broadcast" on the internet. One story was indicative of many on the far-right website: "Sovereignty—Your God Given Liberty & The Takeover Is In Its Endgame." On his Twitter account, Cooper declared himself a "huge advocate against government," stating there was "nothing more sickening than a corrupt government, and over oppressive government trying to take away freedom." With that outlook, it was little surprise that when Cooper first saw many of the Bundy family's edited videos on Facebook he responded with what he considered a call to arms. He took to the internet and wrote, "I say we go their [*sic*] armed together and help him fight if there was ever a time to make a stand against the feds now is the time...so let's go there 100 strong loaded to the teeth and shoot all of them that try to take this man's cows and land."

Cooper later admitted that he knew nothing about Cliven Bundy's decades-long losing battle against federal legal and juris-dictional authority. When he arrived at the edge of Bundy Ranch prepared for a siege, he was heavily armed and sporting U.S. Army camouflage fatigues.

Cooper wasn't alone. By Tuesday morning, April 8, Ryan Payne had arrived at Bundy Ranch from his home in Anaconda, Montana. Unlike others who traveled to Bunkerville who puffed about taking action in defense of the family, Payne had combat experience as a U.S. Army veteran. He'd seen the family's distress call on social media, had reached out by phone, and quickly gotten on the road south.

Payne, who would emerge as an important player in the Bundy saga, was disillusioned by his military service and the lack of a clear sense of mission in Iraq. He was looking for a fresh purpose and found one in defending the Bundys. Born and raised in the vast sub-urbia of Southern California, Payne's background was a long way philosophically from Bundy's backyard. He enlisted in the army at age seventeen, just months before the World Trade Center attacks of September 11, 2001, the greatest act of terrorism on American soil in the nation's history. Trained in reconnaissance and long-distance surveillance at Fort Benning, Georgia, Payne had served two deployments to Iraq as a member of the 519th Military Intelli-gence Battalion. In interviews, he alluded to engaging in at least one fierce firefight with the enemy, which nearly proved disastrous because of the military's questionable competence. It was then, he told one reporter, that he began to question what he was doing so far from home.

But being back in the United States was no bargain either for Payne, who had trouble adjusting to civilian life, losing a small business and a long-term relationship. He moved from California to Anaconda, a rural area well known for its rich mining history, its right-wing militia activity, and the presence of the sovereign-citizen "Montana Freemen." In an interview with the *Missoula Independent,* Payne alluded to a belief that "some Jews" were attempting to "control the world" and questioned whether actual slavery had ever existed in the United States. He also noted his belief that in a majority of states, a person would be within his rights to kill a police officer making an unlawful arrest. Payne found kindred spirits in camouflage in Montana and emerged in 2012 as the founder of the West Mountain Rangers militia and as a leader of an internet-based network of militia associates and patriot groups known as Operation Mutual Aid, which he described on the organization's Facebook page as "a national organization of militia and patriotic citizens who have taken a pledge to stand between tyrants and the oppressed." The group's website made its mission appear essential to the nation's security through the "defense of public and private property, lives, and liberty to exercise God-given rights, seen plainly in the laws of Nature, and codified in the Declaration of Independence and Bill of Rights, at the request of such parties in need of such defense." But it was also clear that OMA, as its members referred to Operation Mutual Aid, believed the federal government had abdicated its duty to the people:

> At such a point as the government intends to use the physical power granted it by those who implemented it against them, it then becomes the responsibility of the people themselves to defend their country from its government, and to generally revert to the process provided for in the Declaration of Independence; to absolve such government of its power, or separate from it to be freed from its oppression.

After less than three days in camp, Payne had become its outspoken liaison to the paramilitary organizations traveling to the Bundy ranch to take up arms against the federal government. Sounding like a man who had found—or regained—a sense of purpose, he claimed he had been designated by Bundy himself as the rancher's personal representative to the militias.

"When I first arrived, Cliven was just glad to see someone who wasn't afraid to carry a firearm around," Payne told a YouTube interviewer, "and he's kept me pretty close to the hip since then."

The Bundy family's embrace appealed to Payne. He had come to save them from the tyrants, and they were grateful to the Lord for his presence. He was simpatico with their cause and their constitutional views, and in the coming weeks and months he would grow especially close to Ammon Bundy, who would speak of the family's mission in spiritual terms. At one point, Payne compared the patriarchal Cliven to the father of America, George Washington.

When Payne arrived, he found a verdant meadow and a small group of contented livestock grazing in belly-deep grass. Most of the early arrivals were from Bunkerville and across the Utah state line, and were mostly related to Bundy in one fashion or another. As newspaper and television reporters began arriving, Nevada's Battle Born state flag was raised into a higher position on the pole than the Stars and Stripes. Hand-painted signs began to appear, and the ubiquitous Gadsden flag was unfurled.

On April 8, Cliven went on a national right-wing online network program called *The Blaze*, hosted by Glenn Beck. "I have raised cattle on that land, which is public land for the people of Clark County, all my life.... Who is the trespasser on this land? Is the United States trespassing on Clark County, Nevada, land? Or is it Cliven Bundy who is trespassing on Clark County, Nevada, land?"

Mainstream media circles caught on. *Fox News* and conservative talk-radio shows portrayed Cliven as a courageous man standing up to an oppressive federal government. The villain was President Obama, who was being manipulated behind the scenes by Senator Harry Reid, the Professor Moriarty of nearly every right-wing conspiracy and political mystery.

Bundy also found an animated sounding board and spokesman in California-based internet-blog radio host Peter T. Santilli Jr., a mouthy provocateur who encouraged citizens to come to Bundy Ranch and bring their guns as part of a Second Amendment protest. While news reporters asked Bundy and his followers questions, Santilli conspicuously turned his camera on the journalists when he thought their questions were too pointed.

Santilli generally walked a fine line about inciting violence, but his interview with the loudmouth Cooper revealed a growing expectation of gunplay for the militia goons. "Time we stopped all this huffing and puffing and bullshit over the microphones and computers and go down and do what we got to do." Santilli then contacted Bundy for an interview that authorities would later describe as "deceitful," since Bundy falsely claimed that BLM rangers had his house surrounded, were stealing his property, had snipers, and were "armed with assault rifles."

Santilli swelled with bravado: "If this is not the issue right now here we stand and fight to the absolute death there is no other option: the federal government must get out of the State of Nevada... if they don't want to do it peaceful it is by their choice." He implored "all Americans anywhere in the vicinity of Clark County, Nevada... if you're in Nevada and can legally carry, get weapons out there... we are going to stand and fight... they have to leave or else." The next day, he used his vehicle to attempt to block BLM rangers and contract cowboys from carrying out the impoundment—undermining his claim of being a journalist protected by the First Amendment.

Even as Bundy contended that he had not called out the militia, Payne was already doing just that. Blaine Cooper and others were on the scene to help Bundy and his family, as the rancher put it, "take our land back... we the people will put our boots down and walk over these people."

Santilli flaunted his membership in the Oath Keepers. Several others wore their "Three Percent" patches, wandering through the growing crowd with their sidearms. The patch insignia referred to the percentage of colonists who took up arms in revolt against the British during the Revolutionary War. By April 9, Santilli had fully inserted himself into Bundy's army. When the opportunity presented itself, he threatened BLM Special Agent in Charge (SAC) Dan Love, according to government allegations. "I don't believe in firing a single bullet unless in absolute self-defense and it's legal and constitutional," he told Love. Santilli crowed that as many as ten thousand armed militia associates might turn up in Bunkerville in answer to the request from OMA, the Three Percenters (sometimes styled as III Percenters), Oath Keepers, and various self-styled patriots. Intoxicated by his own self-importance, he audaciously stoked his followers: The "BLM is in violation of every God-given right of every human being."

In one internet blast, he said, "the BLM knows if they are outnumbered and outgunned...they will stand down," predicting "the standoff will occur when thousands go to repossess the rightfully owned property of the Bundys."

In a style that made some wonder whether he was suffering from delusions of grandeur, or perhaps starring in a western movie of his own making in the age of social-media celebrity, Santilli participated with the family in attempting to block a BLM convoy:

> We want BLM to always retreat because we will always outnumber them...we have all been waiting for that ultimate moment...there is so much at stake...I've got people coming from Michigan...militia members who are fully armed are here...it's good to watch the BLM with its tail between its legs.

Somewhat subtler in approach, Ryan Payne continued his internet recruitment effort with an email to OMA members. The subject line read "Bundy Objectives," followed by a message that began "Nevada Alert!" and was intended to reach the press, blogosphere, and other far-right groups. The objectives were simple: secure and protect the Bundy family, return the property to its "rightful stewards," and see the confiscated cows all come home safe.

Ricky Lovelien, regional director of the Montana State Defense Force, according to his Linkedin.com social-media site, joined Payne at the ranch. Months before Bundy and Bunkerville became household names in Patriot America, Lovelien had posted on social media that he was demanding "my country back from those who aren't fit to run it.... And if you are not willing to give it back I am prepared to take it back." With that, militia bravado became almost giddy. "I'm off to war!" posted one of Lovelien's comrades.

Gregory Burleson, a member of the Arizona militia contingent, was emblematic of those whose social-media bravado reflected their personal demons and animus against law enforcement. Burleson had a history of alcohol-fueled police encounters and arrests. If he was looking for purpose in a life spent on the margins of society, he found it in the image of defending the Bundy ranch. He also predicted a violent end to his effort, and had once written that it was time to start "killing cops."

"I see all those who have gone before me and they beg me to take my place besides them in Valhalla," he wrote. He described how federal agents were confiscating weapons from civilians, and falsely claimed "400 more BLM rangers are on their way to the Bundy Ranch.... I look forward to joining my ancestors in the afterlife." Other militia followers were more circumspect. Marine veteran Brandon Rapolla of Oregon considered himself a devout Christian who worried about the fate of the nation. "I prayed upon it very heavily," he told a reporter. "And within less than a 24-hour period, I got my gear ready and headed down there."

Militia associates continued to call Bundy and volunteer for service. Payne's loose network had closed ranks and arrived, mostly in pickups, armed, usually in camouflage, unshaven, scowling. A paramilitary air replaced much of the previously almost festive protest. Militia associates gathered in a separate section, camping among fellow travelers. What started as a campout had become an armed encampment. Bundy now enjoyed more security than some heads of state.

Neighboring Arizona was plentifully represented. Joseph O'Shaughnessy was a member of the militant Oath Keepers, a group that included current and former law-enforcement and military personnel and for several years had been a presence at the US-Mexico border. Traveling to Bunkerville was sure to raise the public profile of the group, which called itself "Guardians of the Republic" and wildly exaggerated its membership.

Santilli's crowd estimates were way off, and his self-importance was laughable. But the government took him seriously because his followers took his ranting seriously. Although he called for ten thousand militia patch-wearers, only fifty heeded the call. But he was right when he said a show of civilian force would lead the BLM and other agencies to back down out of a concern for public safety.

Santilli inflamed tensions with ominous references to "Waco and Ruby Ridge." He arrogantly approached BLM Special Agent in Charge Dan Love, himself no stranger to superciliousness, on Friday, April 11, with yet another threat of an impending "face-to-face confrontation" by "thousands of people." More confident than ever, he called the federal court corrupt and the terms of surrender "non-negotiable," and he said the militia would not retaliate against BLM officers who stood down. But "if you make the decision to go face-to-face and someone gets hurt we are going to hold you responsible," Santilli told Love.

He then fanned the flames of violence by encouraging armed militia to converge on and disrupt the court-ordered cattle roundup. He had traveled from California to Nevada, inserting himself in a case he didn't understand. "I came here to allow you to prevent a scenario where someone gets hurt."

Love, at times his own worst enemy, was increasingly becoming the target of the Bundy backers, who took potshots at him on social media and in letters to the editors of regional newspapers. To them, Love was the embodiment of federal overreach. His controversial supervision of the popular Burning Man festival on BLM land in Northern Nevada's Black Rock Desert had damaged his credibility. He would later be accused by the Department of the Interior's Office of the Inspector General (OIG) of misappropriating evidence in a native-antiquities investigation and of attempting to thwart an official inquiry into his conduct. His grating style fed theories, some of them conspiratorial, about the BLM's motives and increasingly militaristic approach.

But the beleaguered federal agency that some ranchers and many rural westerners found so easy to caricaturize as picayune and overly aggressive had been anything but that in dealing with Bundy. In fact, Bundy's long battle with the BLM clearly illustrated that the agency had shown remarkable restraint. For all its many shortcomings, the BLM was also capable of substantial nuance. Understanding that the Bundys were Mormon fundamentalists, the agency brought in a BLM agent who was a respected member of the LDS Church to attempt a peaceful resolution to the simmering dispute. The agent's recorded conversation with Ryan Bundy was filled with Old Testament allusions and lessons from the Book of Mormon. While providing insight into the religious fervor of the Bundys, the conversation was ultimately unsuccessful in reducing tensions.

With each day that passed, the scene became more demagogic. As the number of armed militia associates increased at Camp Liberty, so did their blustery talk of a shootout, despite claims that the Patriots were only there to keep the peace. In response, BLM and Forest Service safety concerns increased. The FBI escalated its efforts to gather accurate intelligence from inside the militia camp. Surveillance cameras were positioned in strategic locations, and government reconnaissance planes were put into use.

Despite Nevada ranching's long history of problems with federal control of public lands, relatively few of the armed militia were from Nevada. Many would admit that they had never heard of Bunkerville, didn't know Bundy, and knew little about his protracted legal battle. Many were unaware that most ranchers in the West were willing to pay the pittance it took to graze on sections of land as large as many counties, despite the fact that some groused about it and others were actually grateful.

In a candid moment, Idaho residents Eric Parker, O. Scott Drexler, Steven Stewart, and Todd Engel might have found themselves in that latter group. Whatever their individual concerns for the future of the American rancher might have been, they acted on limited information snared off the internet. Bundy's plight triggered their political frustrations with government. Stewart and Drexler had never heard of Bundy, but both had a friend associated with the militia. Their pal Parker was a proud official with the Three Percent of Idaho, a paramilitary group with a catchy motto: "When Tyranny Becomes Law, Rebellion Becomes Duty."

When word of the Bundy protest reached Todd Engel via news feeds, he was at home in Idaho recovering from a double-vertebrae fusion after being injured on the job at a Wyoming oil field. He knew nothing about Bundy, Bunkerville, cattle, or grazing rights, but the increasingly alarming reports on conservative media agitated him. He was especially incensed by the BLM ranger's treatment of Bundy's sister, Margaret Houston. "She's yellin' and screamin' like protesters do. And he grabs her from behind and he grabs her left arm and he literally picks her up, a grandmother, and body slams her; her feet go flyin' through the air. And I couldn't believe it," Engel later described the assault that had gone viral.

Engel caught a ride south with Parker, Drexler, and Stewart, arriving in Bunkerville on April 12. All were heavily armed and had transported hundreds of rounds of ammunition. After reaching Camp Liberty and watching Ammon give a prayer and Cliven give a speech, Engel concluded, "These folks were genuine, salt-of-the-earth people." Like most who traveled to Bunkerville, Engel had not bothered to inform himself of the legal decisions against Bundy. Those who *did* read the court orders dismissed them as the product of a "corrupt court."

New Hampshire Tea Party activist and former U.S. Marine Gerald DeLemus was among the more colorful characters to travel to the Bundy Ranch, though he arrived too late to participate in the events of April 12. Cochair of a Veterans for Trump group and the husband of a Republican state representative in the Granite State, he drove all the way from the East Coast, missing the standoff by a few hours but remaining for weeks afterward as part of Bundy's so-called security team.

Cliven repeatedly referred to his contention that Clark County Sheriff Doug Gillespie held jurisdiction over all law enforcement in the area and was the only official the rancher would answer to. The Las Vegas Metropolitan Police Department's physical presence was minimal at Camp Liberty, but while Santilli's prediction of

10,000 militia supporters had been wildly inaccurate, the estimated 60 to 150 armed men who had joined more than 400 unarmed protesters got the attention of law enforcement.

With the threat of violence increasing along with the temperature, the BLM, FBI, and other agencies made a decision on the evening of April 11 to halt the cattle impoundment. Given Bundy's continued insistence that jurisdiction lay solely with the sheriff, the group asked Gillespie to tell Bundy the following morning of the decision to stand down. The morning of April 12 was a big blue Saturday on the Nevada desert, and Cliven was dressed for showtime, wearing a white buttoned-down shirt and matching cowboy hat. If it had been a Hollywood western, there would be no confusion about the self-proclaimed good guy.

Camp Liberty bustled with activity, a nervous energy in the air. Internet-fueled rumors abounded about either a potential settlement or a real standoff with the feds. Even casual observers had seen the BLM and NPS rangers in the area wearing what appeared to be military dress. By that morning, the government had rounded up approximately 350 cows and ripped out the rancher's illegal network of water lines and troughs.

When Sheriff Gillespie, accompanied by a team of Metro officials, arrived at Camp Liberty, it appeared that tensions might at last be eased. Gillespie and Bundy were well acquainted with each other by this time. Just two years earlier, in 2012, Gillespie had watched a previous attempt to round up the rancher's cattle devolve into chaos. He had worried that the incident could turn volatile and counseled more patience. Meeting with Cliven that year, Gillespie tried to get the rancher to listen to reason and even offered attorneys willing to provide pro bono legal advice, to no avail.

Though Gillespie had been assured by federal officials that Bundy's sons, who carried out their father's orders with missionary zeal, would not be at the ranch at the time of the roundup, that turned out to be untrue.

Gillespie claimed to have tried to get the BLM to shift its schedule for a second attempted impoundment to autumn because the spring was calving season, and the delay would give the government time to better coordinate the roundup. But when the BLM rejected his idea, he withdrew his department's presence in further planning, feeling misled. Now the BLM needed bailing out of what one reporter described as an epithet-hurling crowd playing "a tense game of chicken with BLM rangers."

At Camp Liberty, the stage was set to begin.

"Good morning, citizens of Clark County, Nevada," Bundy began, with microphone in hand before a capacity crowd and a harvest of media. "Good morning, America!"

Gillespie had privately informed Bundy that the BLM was discontinuing the roundup because of safety concerns and would be releasing the cattle, telling Bundy that his call for assistance from armed militiamen had worked. The sheriff then accompanied Bundy to the makeshift platform that had been the site of many news updates and constitutional lessons in recent days. This time, the platform was fronted by a row of armed members of an Arizona militia outfit wearing camouflage uniforms. Cheers and jeers mixed amid the boisterous crowd, and the sheriff took the microphone. Understated to the point of appearing timid, Gillespie informed all within earshot of the good news, news that should have brought down the level of anxiety: the BLM was leaving. The cows were coming home. "The BLM is going to cease this operation," Gillespie told the crowd. Then, turning to Bundy, he said, "What I would hope is to sit down with you and talk about how to have this facilitated in a safe way."

Handed victory, Bundy didn't seem satisfied. He chided the sheriff for not fulfilling his constitutional duty earlier, accusing him of "trying to get some legs up under him" like a weak-kneed calf.

Catcalls mixed with cheers. "Where are the cows?" "Do your job!" Demands increased for the immediate release of Bundy's cattle, most of which were still wandering the Bunkerville allotment. "Bring the cows back! You're holding them hostage to broker a deal!" Still, Gillespie called for calm. "My intention is to keep a very emotional issue safe."

But safety seemed far from Bundy's concern. He retrieved the microphone and addressed his followers. He called for the sheriff to force the government to bulldoze "the ticket booths" outside the Red Rock Conservation Area and the Lake Mead National Recreation Area. Then he ordered Gillespie to disarm the region's federal law-enforcement contingent. "We want those arms delivered right here under these flags in one hour," Bundy said. He then called on the journalists present to bear witness to the sheriff's action—or inaction. The crowd was entertained by Cliven's antics, but rather than engage with him, Gillespie left the stage without another word.

At Toquop, the impoundment site, BLM, NPS, and FBI personnel had begun the process of breaking down their camp and packing up their gear. The agency's intelligence reports had showed a national spike of militia activity that coincided with the Bundy protest. From a defense standpoint, Toquop was a nightmare. The government had come to collect cattle, not stage a military action, and its choice of a low-lying area made BLM and park service employees vulnerable from the highway bridges above the site.

Although the command center trailers were being prepared for removal, it would later become known that Agent Love and the BLM officers under his command had only reluctantly agreed to withdraw.

Instead of relieving tensions and celebrating his victory, Bundy grew agitated and impatient, as if the crowd expected him to do something. He then came up with a plan to have the flag-carrying cowboys on horseback, his new militia friends, and the enthusiastic crowd form a posse to retrieve the cattle themselves. He no longer sounded like a peaceful rancher being harassed by the government.

Their march would take them under the bridges and across the busy interstate, but Bundy assured them it would be successful. "God is going to be with us," he said into the microphone. "We are going to get the rest of the cattle out of the compound...We're gonna... shut down the freeway.... All we got to do is open those gates and let them back on the river. We're about to take this country back by force.... Cowboys, let's go get 'er done!"

More than 250 protesters, some carrying signs, followed his orders, joining dozens of militia men and forty riders, all moving toward the impoundment site. The show of force blocked the I-15, one of the busiest highways in the nation. Within forty minutes, the interstate was backed up for miles, with Nevada Highway Patrol troopers overwhelmed. A line of vehicles from Metro responded, and more than two dozen uniformed officers positioned themselves next to the highway. Senior BLM personnel headed into Toquop Wash to help resolve the conflict before it boiled over into a blood-bath. A BLM officer could be seen marching forward, carrying a medical supply pack in anticipation of the worst.

As the wind picked up, BLM megaphones became more difficult to hear. Communication between principal parties was complicated by the presence of increasingly animated civilians tossing catcalls at government officials. Metro Undersheriff Joseph Lombardo moved to the front of the government side, along with Love and other federal officials, to attempt to get the Bundy boys to slow their march. Lombardo knew from experience that the entire scenario was set to erupt—from an accidental firearm discharge by a nervous participant on either side or even a car backfiring in the distance. It was a gloriously clear day, but the fog of chaos was rolling into Toquop Wash.

By 12:13 p.m., the barrier fence was crowded with fired-up protesters. Agent Love, wearing sunglasses with his cap turned backward and dressed in tactical gear, approached the fence between his troops and the increasingly rowdy mob. He exchanged pleasantries with Ammon Bundy, who stood on the opposite side of the fence. "Can't breach this," Love said. "This is bad." Government spotters were already sighting their long guns on the throng below. "We need you to back up. Back up."

It was too late for that.

"I'm telling you, you need to de-escalate the situation," Love said as the wind picked up. "I'm imploring upon you your responsibility to deescalate the situation. I need them back. I can't break off these guys until you get this crowd back."

"No," came the reply. "You need to leave." Ammon said. "We're staying here until they're gone. That's what we're doing."

The operation was too large to simply turn and depart the scene. Told to shelter in place where there was no shelter, the officers remained close to their vehicles, the only cover available in the potentially wide-open shooting gallery.

Then it started. The BLM agents' long scopes observed rifles in the crowd, with militiamen moving furtively and taking up strategic sniper positions. Many were using the "low ready" position with the barrels pointed down, but some pointed their scoped weapons toward the officers. In recordings and voluminous video collected by officer body cameras, vehicle dashboard cameras, civilian recording devices, and working journalists, the images and audio projected the sounds of an impending battle. Government agents sighted one, then two more riflemen moving in the wash and, far worse, positioning themselves on the northbound bridge behind concrete jersey barriers.

"Are you fucking people stupid or what?" one officer shouted.

A BLM ranger paramedic gathered his medical pack and moved toward what was anticipated to be a triage area for the wounded. Nervous laughter was heard, some crude off-color jokes were made, prayers were said.

Fearing the worst, officers positioned in the rear pulled out their cell phones and called loved ones. An NPS riot unit moved into stack position closer to the front gate. The government's preparations to defend itself took on an ominous appearance that rippled through the rowdy crowd, part of which was being used as human shields by the militia. "Go back to Washington!" crowd members yelled at the government employees, residents of Southern Nevada. "Go back to China!"

"Long guns right in front of us," agents were overheard on two-way radios. "I've got two more over here that are knelt down. There's at least 10 or 12 long guns."

Minutes passed, and more gunmen were sighted. Dave Bundy moved up through the gate where he joined his brother Ryan at what the government called Post 1. It was there and then that the brothers and Love settled on a one-hour window for the government to gather its gear and get out.

"You guys are the ones calling the shots here now," Love told Ryan.

"Yeah, I understand. It's on me," Ryan replied. "We need you guys to leave right away."

Love ordered the officers to withdraw from their positions, load up, and prepare to abandon the temporary headquarters. There wasn't time to remove all the equipment they had hauled in, and the officers, looking over their shoulders, hurriedly gathered their packs, threw their gear into their vehicles, leaving behind what couldn't be quickly hauled away. The outgunned federal government and its Metro escort hastily retreated on a dirt road, its edges lined with a gauntlet of jeering protesters flipping them off and screaming obscenities.

A red, white, and blue banner was unfurled and roped to the southbound bridge, its image flashing around the world in seconds: "The West Has Now Been Won!"

Cowboys on horseback and the cheering crowd moved toward a corral of thoroughly bewildered cattle. By 3 p.m. on April 12, Cliven Bundy had his cows back—and an international platform that stretched from the makeshift stage at Camp Liberty to the farthest reaches of the internet. His allies in the militia were back at their encampment near the Bundy Ranch, celebrating a victory over the government oppressors, some with prayer, others with beer, and many with posts on Facebook.

When a Reuters photograph went viral showing Eric Parker prone on the northbound bridge pointing his rifle down-range toward the government employees, he was immediately dubbed "the Bundy Sniper," and he didn't shy away from the nickname despite the potential legal ramifications. Other protestors took to social media to celebrate kicking the government's ass.

The events were spun into a great victory, not so much for ranchers in the West but for antigovernment extremists from New Hampshire to Washington State. Many gloated about the historic moment. On his blog, Alabama's Michael Vanderboegh, the III Percent Patriots militia leader, marked the standoff in historic terms: "It is impossible to overstate the importance of the victory won in the desert today."

"Well, for a minute there I thought I was gonna see a lot of people die today. But the feds backed down and the cows came home," wrote Arizona militiaman Micah McGuire on Facebook.

Gregory Burleson was now drunk on his participation in the standoff. "I faced off with heavily armed Federal Agents this weekend," he gloated on Facebook. "What did you do, go shopping?... Damn and all I did was go there looking for a fight." He posted a photo of himself holding an AR-15 assault weapon. "Officially an American Badass WORLDWIDE!...That right there is a True American militia." He described how he drove eight hours without sleep. "Round one is ours, gonna go back in a couple days to make sure the Fed Bastards get the message. That right there is a Real Minute Man, and I got the hat to prove it."

Many of the other "gunmen" gloated about their participation. Ryan Payne's reflections to a Montana newspaper were introspective as he claimed that a divine providence protected everyone that day. "We locked them down," he told the *Missoula Independent*. "We had counter-sniper positions on their sniper positions. We had at least one guy—sometimes two guys—per BLM agent in there. So, it was a complete tactical superiority.... If they made one wrong move, every single BLM agent in that camp would have died." Payne was obviously unconcerned about Bundy's legal dispute with the government. He compared his actions to "protecting a bank" so he could sleep peacefully at night.

The legend of saving the Bundy family grew with the telling and retelling. Its social-media sleight-of-hand had worked well—almost too well in some cases. Like celebrants at closing time calling for yet another round, some militia supporters weren't interested in returning home.

Federal and state agencies also fired off statements, and politicians took up their positions behind party lines in the standoff's immediate aftermath. New BLM Director Neil Kornze, a former public-lands specialist for Senator Reid, said the agency had tried to remove the illegal cattle from federal lands with "a safe and peaceful operation" the priority. "Based on information about conditions on the ground, and in consultation with law enforcement, we have made a decision to conclude the cattle gather because of our serious concern about the safety of employees and members of the public."

In Carson City, Governor Sandoval modified his previous wholesale defense of Bundy. "Given the circumstances, today's outcome is the best we could have hoped for."

Senator Reid, so often ridiculed in the run-up to the standoff, jabbed, "Those people who hold themselves out to be patriots are not. They're nothing more than domestic terrorists," he said, stating that he had contacted Attorney General Eric Holder to look into the matter. "It is an issue that we cannot let go, just walk away from," he told the *Las Vegas Review-Journal*, announcing that a task force was being assembled to investigate the incident.

The standoff provided a winning recruitment advertisement for militia groups. Patriot organizations, far-right extremists, white supremacists, and antigovernment sovereign citizens all found something to appreciate about the rancher who defied the feds and got away with it. The Southern Poverty Law Center (SPLC), which has tracked extremist organizations for more than a generation, drilled deep into the issue and the organizations now juiced on the victory in the desert. Second Amendment groups found reason to cheer as well. Larry Pratt, executive director of the Gun Owners of America, a group considered to the right of the National Rifle Association (NRA), enthused, "Hopefully we will look back on what happened there as a turning point in modern American history. The American people are saying 'Enough.'"

A divided nation saw the event from different vantage points. To some, Bundy was a welfare cattleman, and quite possibly a racist extremist, taking advantage of federal public land. Others weighed events and decided Bundy was a plainspoken states'-rights defender and Sagebrush Rebellion leader, a noble rancher at home on the range in the West. The *Drudge Report* and *Fox News* cheered. Tea Party Republicans in Congress and elsewhere heralded the Constitution-packing cowboy.

For the moment, Bundy was conservative America's Everyman. *Fox News* host Sean Hannity, a bellwether of the right, extrapolated the Bunkerville standoff into something larger: "I'm worried about the lies that are told to us about the IRS, about what happened in Benghazi, and the lies that sold health care. I'm concerned that the government is overreaching here." Hannity reported Richard Mack's false claims that the federal government had planned a "surprise midnight raid" on the Bundy Ranch. Mack, the former Arizona lawman and "constitutional sheriff," was a sovereign-citizen favorite. Hannity broadcast a video of Cliven flanked by his offspring wearing "Victory Over Oppression" T-shirts.

While the ready presence of militia associates from diverse regions of the nation surprised many Americans, those who study the phenomenon were not. A discernible uptick in militia, Patriot, far-right, and white-supremacist activity had been noted since the 2008 election of President Obama. The Bundy standoff also generated its own immediate impact, with the SPLC reporting a more than one-third increase (from 202 to 276) in armed militias nationally in its wake. "We believe these armed extremists have been emboldened by what they saw as a clear victory at the Cliven Bundy ranch and the fact that no one was held accountable for taking up arms against agents of the federal government," observed SPLC Intelligence Project director Heidi Beirich.

Reaction to the event also varied according to geographic location. The issue was big in the West, where 47 percent of all land is owned by the federal government (which accounts for 92 percent of all federal land in the US), and especially important in Nevada, with less than 20 percent of seventy-one million acres in private ownership. In the East, press coverage—especially that coming from conservative media—often morphed into a cheap western-movie saga. "Deadbeat on the Range," the *New York Times* headlined a Timothy Egan commentary. "Easterners, especially clueless ones in politics and the press, have always had a soft spot for a defiant white dude in a Stetson."

Bundy had allies from Nevada's ranching community who understood his frustrations with the BLM. Some made their way to Bunkerville to join the protest. Elko County commissioner and rancher Demar Dahl, who chaired a task force to study transferring title to federal land in Nevada, agreed with his friend Bundy's cause while not disputing that the federal government actually owned the land in question.

The Nevada Cattlemen's Association, long the livestock industry's voice, pointed out that most of the state's ranchers were law-abiding and not confused about federal public-lands jurisdiction. They were not surrounded by armed guards, nor hesitant to pay their grazing fees. While defending ranchers' property rights and Bundy as a man with his "back against the wall" after being harassed by federal desert-tortoise protection efforts, the Association added that it "does not condone actions that are outside the law in which citizens take the law into their own hands.... Nevada Cattlemen's Association does not feel it is our place to interfere in the process of adjudication in this matter. Additionally, NCA believes the matter is between Mr. Bundy and the Federal Courts." In a later missive, the ranching group would shrug, "Please do not judge us by one individual."

Following Bunkerville, Cliven's story ricocheted through the national news as a cause célèbre, a right-wing outrage, or a head-scratching curiosity. Then, straying off his usual topics of the dastardly federal government and divinely inspired Constitution, Bundy entered deep brush and started to give his considered opinion about "the Negro."

Captured by the *New York Times*, his words reflected much of what many outsiders thought of right-wing ranchers growing strange on the range. "Negros are enslaved by government subsidy, who abort their children and put their young men in jail because they never learned to pick cotton," Bundy said. "I've often wondered, are they better off as slaves, picking cotton and having a family life and doing things, or are they better off under government subsidy?"

Apparently oblivious to the irony that ranchers had long been recipients of financial breaks from the federal government that few others enjoyed, what the rancher may have intended as a libertarian economics lesson was considered plain racist, even by his champions and apologists on the right. Although he could still draw a big crowd at Camp Liberty, the blowback was immediate. Even Sean Hannity fell away, calling Bundy's comments "downright racist" and "beyond disturbing." And beyond embarrassing for a legion of conservatives who'd been busy painting Cliven as a hero riding off into the sunset.

As fate would have it, Bunkerville was in freshman Democratic House member Steven Horsford's congressional district. Horsford was the first black candidate elected to Congress from Nevada. "The district is a microcosm of our diverse country, and he [Bundy] is not a man who represents the American West's way of life," Horsford said with admirable restraint. "It's beyond unfortunate that from this diverse community a loud voice of intolerance has been given a megaphone."

Horsford's promising career in Congress would be sidetracked later that year when Cresent Hardy, a longtime Bundy friend, stand-off supporter, and fellow LDS Church member, defeated him. Horsford returned the favor four years later, bouncing Hardy from the House.

Bundy's impolitic racial segue put him on the outs with much of the mainstream conservative press. In a meandering attempt to explain his first comments, on April 24, 2014, he dug himself deeper into a rabbit hole of racist rhetoric, throwing out the clumsy ramblings of a true bigot: "Here's the thing, I'm a-wondering, I'm a-wondering, Cliven Bundy's a-wondering, about these people," he said, referring to himself in the third person. "Now I'm talking about the black community...are better off than they was when they was in the South with their homes, with their chickens and their gardens and their children around 'em, and their man having something to do?...I'm not saying I thought they should be slaves." He was just "a-wondering."

Long after the standoff, Sheriff Gillespie was still answering questions about how he had handled the event. While some thought he had looked weak next to Bundy, he was also credited with helping to resolve the standoff without bloodshed. Gillespie was adamant that Agent Love's dissembling with him had prompted him to pull his officers from the scene prematurely. He blamed the BLM for not handling security more professionally, and for allowing the use of snarling police dogs and Tasers to replace a more strategic and professional approach.

"I said all along to the BLM and to anyone who would listen, no drop of human blood is worth any cow," Gillespie would say.

In the aftermath of the standoff, a palpable confidence filled the air at Camp Liberty. Observers also noticed the presence of attorney

Larry Klayman, the controversial and litigious trial lawyer known as a founder of the staunchly conservative Freedom Watch and for suing the Clintons. Reporters would later see a lot more of Klayman, whose presence sparked rumors that powerful interests behind the scenes were supporting Bundy. The self-possessed Klayman was to remain involved in the Bundy legal battle.

Bundy and others had been right about the government seeing the ghosts of Ruby Ridge and Waco in Toquop Wash. Militiamen and their hangers-on lingered for days and even weeks afterward, officially to provide "security" for the family, but also to bask in the glow of victory over the government oppressor without firing a shot. They had a story they'd retell for years, everywhere from the church pulpit to the corner bar. Few acknowledged that the government had backed down not only because it was at a tactical disadvantage, but because those braggart militiamen had jeopardized the lives of hundreds of unarmed civilians and government officials. Senator Reid chided Bundy for being a "hateful racist" and strategist who endangered "the lives of women and children," and who "by denigrating the people who work hard and play by the rules while he mooches off public land he also revealed himself to be a hypocrite."

Richard Mack, the former Arizona sheriff and self-appointed militia spokesman, made it clear on *Fox News* just days after the standoff that blending Patriot gunmen among unarmed protesters was intentional: "We were actually strategizing to put all the women up front. If they're going to start shooting, it's going to be women that are going to be televised all across the world getting shot by those rogue federal officers."

Was the West really won by armed vigilantes using protesters as human shields? If not, what was the government prepared to do about it?

CHAPTER 2

You Don't Need a Reason
to Start a Revolution

As the spring of 2014 became summer, the temperatures in Southern Nevada climbed steadily toward triple digits and the Bundy Ranch standoff fell from the headlines. None of the participants in the tense showdown had been taken into custody, not even the armed volunteers who had been photographed pointing high-powered weapons at county, state, and federal law-enforcement officers. The tale of Camp Liberty grew taller with each telling.

The morning of Sunday, June 8, broke blue and mostly clear. As the sun moved toward noon and the temperature climbed to a hundred degrees, veteran Las Vegas Metro uniformed patrol officers Alyn Beck and Igor Soldo took a break from their calls in the East Valley Area Command to grab lunch in the 300 block of North Nellis Boulevard. The Cici's Pizza buffet they chose was tucked inside a careworn strip mall located approximately five miles northeast of the famous Las Vegas Strip. It was a neighborhood joint popular with families on a tight budget, and Saldo and Beck were among its early customers. It was 11:20 a.m.

At forty-one, Beck was a veteran officer well known in the department as a leader. A training instructor with Multi-assault Counter-terrorism Action Capabilities (MACTAC) and Special Weapons and Tactics (SWAT) experience, he was a mentor to younger officers like the thirty-one-year-old Saldo. Both were married with wives and children.

As they took their seats in the restaurant, they didn't notice two apparent customers coming through the door behind them, "from out of nowhere," as a witness would later recall. The young married couple had not come for lunch but were looking for the occupants of the black-and-white Metro squad car they had noticed out front.

Bent on killing the first police officers they could find, the self-styled revolutionaries later identified as Jerad and Amanda Miller went to work quickly. Drug-addled and near-psychotic with hate for governmental authority, Jerad stepped behind the seated Saldo, withdrew a semiautomatic handgun from his vest, and fired it point-blank into the back of the officer's head, killing him instantly.

Beck reacted quickly, but not before he was shot in the neck by the same weapon. As he struggled to return fire, Amanda shot him repeatedly. The officers, two of Metro's finest, lay dead or dying. Fear paralyzed customers, but someone managed to call 911.

Armed to the teeth with a pistol-gripped shotgun and two handguns with armor-piercing bullets, the Millers stripped the police officers of their weapons and ammunition. Jerad removed a bright yellow Gadsden flag, the kind favored by the Tea Party and the militia movements, and draped it over Beck's body. He added a swastika patch and pinned a note to Soldo's uniform that read, "This is the beginning of the revolution."

A poorly planned revolution, as it turned out. Although the Millers had vowed to take out as many cops as they could find, their exit strategy included a walk to a nearby Walmart for more ammunition. That's where a line of Metro officers converged on them, led by some of the SWAT team members trained by Beck himself.

Jerad Miller repeated to frightened customers, "This is the start of the revolution. The cops are coming. Get out." When a legally armed citizen named Joseph Wilcox spotted Miller waving his gun at police, he withdrew his weapon and prepared to fire, not recognizing Amanda Miller as an antagonist standing a few feet away. She shot and killed Wilcox, who was later remembered as "a man who was willing to be that person maybe some of us hope to be when danger looks us squarely in the eyes."

The Millers fired on police for fifteen minutes. As a new wave of backup officers arrived on the scene, Jerad was overheard shouting, "Stand down! I am in charge now!" But Beck and Soldo's brother and sister officers were closing in. The Millers moved to the rear of the retail store in the sporting goods section, improvising a makeshift redoubt from store shelving. Jerad grabbed a baseball bat, shattered a glass case holding ammunition, and prepared to reload.

He then went down, courtesy of his wife, who stood a short distance away. She spoke a few words to him, then completed their suicide pact with a bullet to her own head. In less than thirty minutes, the Millers' senseless revolution was over. Five persons were dead. Their Walmart battle resulted in the murder of an innocent customer and cost them their lives.

The fallen officers were honored as community heroes. The Millers would be remembered too, and not only as a "wingnut Bonnie and Clyde duo" fond of donning sadistic clown makeup and posing with weapons. They had also been spotted participating in the Bundy Ranch standoff. Reacting angrily to internet posts on the *InfoWars* website and to the Bundy family's doctored videos of their tangles with BLM rangers, the Millers had been among the patriots who loaded their guns and drove to Camp Liberty in support of the "besieged" Mormon clan. The Bundy family moved quickly to distance itself from the killers, calling them "very radical."

The Millers were at Camp Liberty for several days before Jerad's tough talk of violence finally convinced the Bundys to ask them to leave. Miller wasn't hard to spot and didn't conceal his opinions that federal law-enforcement and police officers were Nazi oppressors who deserved to be shot. In a brief interview with an NBC affiliate during the standoff, Jerad Miller wore a camouflage cap and shirt and offered, "I feel sorry for any federal agents that want to come in here and try to push us around." He had come to the camp loaded for war.

Noting the obvious—that a direct association with vicious cop killers would be bad for the family's image and cause—Ammon Bundy moved to redirect the narrative and called the Millers a "very radical" exception to the family's armed volunteers. "Not very many people were asked to leave," he said. "I think they may have been the only ones," implying that the Millers were too radical for the Bundys.

But "radical" was in the eye of the beholder. Several of the stand-off's gunmen, including Todd Engel and Gregory Burleson, also had violent revolution on their minds.

The Millers lived in squalor on the tattered lower east end of the Las Vegas Valley, financed for the most part with income from Amanda's job at Hobby Lobby. Their many internet and social-media posts painted a picture of right-wing radicals who promoted elements of white supremacy, militia action, and fundamentalist Christianity. They equated government and law enforcement, as Metro Undersheriff Kevin McMahill would put it, "with fascism and those who supported the Nazis."

They railed against government tyranny, talking often with their neighbors about killing police officers, although those neighbors did not report them to police. They posted morbid predictions and violent threats on Facebook, and Jerad's internet fingerprints were found on a range of conservative websites, some of which were aligned with the Bundys' interpretation of the role of the federal government in the management of public lands.

In one Facebook post, Miller pronounced, "I will be supporting Clive Bundy and his family from Federal Government slaughter," he wrote. "This is the next Waco! His ranch is under siege right now! The federal gov is stealing his cattle! Arresting his family and beating on them! We must do something, I will be doing something."

In his own convoluted worldview, Jerad Miller was a nihilistic American patriot who had pronounced in a post that there "is no greater cause to die for than liberty." When the Millers departed a friend's apartment on the morning of the triple homicide and double suicide, they left behind documents that included a plan to murder Nevada court officials.

Although he claimed the Bible as his favorite book, Miller would also be remembered for posting photos posing with firearms and in face makeup as "The Joker," the supervillain in *Batman*. "Either you stand with freedom, or you side with tyranny" he wrote less than a month before the Bundy standoff. "There is no middle ground."

The Millers were obviously mentally unstable. Self-styled revolutionaries, cult leaders, and outlaws commonly suffer from paranoia and delusions of grandeur. But in the wake of the Millers' killing spree, many professionals examined the role that internet influencers may have played in instigating their fears and hatreds. Did they follow right-wing hate and dog-whistle conspiracy theories out of mutual interest, or did those voices encourage them to act on their impulses?

Multiple trials in *U.S. v. Bundy* would reveal that many of the armed men, who drove hundreds of miles to provide a paramilitary presence at the ranch, were called via militia email larded with *InfoWars* misinformation and mainstream news articles taken out of context.

Jerad warned that the Second Amendment was under attack, that the U.S. Alcohol, Tobacco, and Firearms (ATF) agency was a domestic terrorist organization, and he parroted the talking points of the Three Percenters, whose founder predicted mass armed unrest. "All politics in this country now is just dress rehearsal for civil war."

"The dawn of a new day. May all of our coming sacrifices be worth it," Jerad's final Facebook post read.

On the surface, the modern militia movement bears some resemblance to its Revolutionary antecedents. In the wake of the American Revolution, militias took part in the Whiskey Rebellion tax protest and in Shay's Rebellion, a dispute over economic inequality. The John Fries Rebellion of 1799 was led by a collection of armed Pennsylvania Dutch farmers, who menaced tax collectors before being suppressed. Fries, a Revolutionary War veteran, was eventually captured, tried for treason, and sentenced to death before being pardoned by President John Adams. In those three cases, men who had fought in the War for Independence led the protests.

Following the Civil War, the Ku Klux Klan was formed in 1865 and swiftly took on the role of an antigovernment militia during Reconstruction, committing acts of domestic terrorism under the auspices of preserving the traditional southern way of life. In time, membership in the organization swelled far beyond the South with its message of white supremacy, Christian identity, and anti-Semitism.

The Silver Legion of America surfaced in 1933 as a secretive fascist organization founded in Asheville, North Carolina, by William Dudley Pelley. His "Silver Shirts" echoed Hitler's Nazi Brown Shirts and Mussolini's Black Shirts. A virulent anti-Semite and white supremacist, Pelley called for a Christian Commonwealth and a return of the country to what he considered its biblical fundamentals. He imagined a day when his followers would grow in sufficient numbers to help him take over the United States as dictator under the title "The Chief"—"Der Fuhrer" and "Il Duce" were already taken. Assured of his own importance in national affairs, in 1936 Pelley ran for president on the Christian Party ticket, a party of his own creation, and garnered 1,500 votes. The Silver Shirts returned to obscurity with America's entry into World War II.

By the 1950s and 1960s, American militias had morphed again. While the Klan was still an active presence during the heart of the civil rights movement, other militias, such as the "Minutemen," eschewed an overtly racist theme for a patriotic one during the suspected rampant rise of Communism. If the far-right-wing John Birch Society represented the intellectual argument for anti-Communist fervor, masked anti-Semitic paranoia, and the belief in an America lost to a liberal agenda, the Minutemen would play the role of army of the people, should their own worst suspicions be realized.

In the 1970s, the Posse Comitatus, or "Posse," made news with its belief that real Americans didn't need to recognize federal authority at all because they were actually governed by "Common Law," an Old English concept dating to the Magna Carta, in which the county sheriff represented legal authority. And furthermore, according to Posse logic, centuries later, in 1878, President Rutherford B. Hayes signed into law the Posse Comitatus Act, which strengthened the power of states by limiting the authority of the federal government to use the military to enforce policy within the United States.

As a group, Posse Comitatus factions have been known for anti-government and anti-Semitic conspiracies and the use of specious

Common Law courts to harass and punish perceived enemies in what are sometimes called vexatious litigations. Sentencing judges, disagreeable sheriffs, other local elected officials, members of the media, and distant Washington politicians have been sued, sentenced to prison and death by hanging, and have had liens placed on their homes and property by various Posse groups and members of the so-called Freemen. Variations of Posse Comitatus theory have echoed through the sovereign-citizen movement to justify everything from not paying federal income taxes to not recognizing the national parks system.

When Cliven Bundy, on April 14, 2014, said he would only negotiate a settlement of the standoff with Clark County Sheriff Doug Gillespie, and then demanded that Gillespie order his men to gather up all the federal government's guns and tear down the entrances to federal park and recreation facilities in the county, he sounded absurd. Even some of his supporters chuckled, and some journalists failed to make the connection as Bundy echoed common Posse and sovereign-citizen talking points.

As more information was reported about them, Jerad and Amanda Miller became easy to write off as extremist misfits, the kind of mentally ill characters who commit atrocity in the name of a twisted cause only they truly understood. But it was also true that they exhibited many of the same traits that reflected the dark antigovernment philosophy of "leaderless resistance" first promulgated in 1983 by Texas Ku Klux Klan Grand Dragon Louis Beam. Like David Duke and others, including Richard Spencer, Beam appreciated that the Klan had an image problem. Some, like Duke, eschewed the organization's haunting hood for a business suit, salesman's smile, and a brand of rhetoric that made him seem almost mainstream.

Where Duke put creases and pleats in the sheets, Beam wrote an essay defining leaderless resistance that became widely circulated among antigovernment groups. Beam attributed the idea to anti-Communist former intelligence officer Colonel Ulius Amoss, who believed that Communists had already taken over the federal government, and therefore it was the duty of informed Americans to resist it.

The idea was hardly unique. Patriots and terrorists had often acted clandestinely and independently for a common cause. But Beam was signaling to his fellow Klan members that in order to avoid infiltration by law enforcement and unwanted publicity via the mainstream press, it was time to go underground. He wrote:

> Since the entire purpose of Leaderless Resistance is to defeat state tyranny, . . . all members of phantom cells or individuals will tend to react to objective events in the same way through usual tactics of resistance. Organs of information distribution such as newspapers, leaflets, computers, etc., which are widely available to all, keep each person informed of events, allowing for a planned response that will take many variations. No one need issue an order to anyone.

This was nothing short of a domestic-terrorism game plan that came in the form of a devil's whisper and spoke to the depression, hatred, and paranoia already present in individuals who felt displaced by society and left behind by the economy. Those feelings had been keenly felt in small-town and rural America, where a single factory closure could result in a boarded-up Main Street, where a generation of family farms and ranches had gone under due to forces beyond the control of some of the hardest-working people in the nation. It was no coincidence that the insidious opioid crisis hit rural America hardest.

Dr. Glen Wallace, Oklahoma's former director of rural mental health services, chronicled a dramatic increase in antigovernment groups in that state after many of its farmers lost their land to foreclosure (in addition to a sharp rise in suicides). Wallace concluded that militias and antigovernment groups could influence "a personality that is already violent toward itself or others."

Louis Beam contended that the responsibility for action lay with the lone wolf, stoked by a common purpose against the government, to decide when to strike. He espoused leaderless resistance as the most practical way to battle the oppressor. Invoking the Founding Fathers, Beam saw leaderless resistance as "a child of necessity."

Militia associates who might never have heard of him would often repeat Beam's rhetoric, masked as patriotism, through the decades. Beam's goal was an America in which neither minorities nor Jews were deemed fit for citizenship. He was a popular speaker before a range of like-minded organizations that more or less agreed with his worldview. Among them was America's Promise Ministries, a white separatist organization aligned with the Christian Identity movement. In 2019, the SPLC tracked more than 1,600 hate and extremist groups, ranging from the notorious Ku Klux Klan to obscure white supremacist and neo-Nazi and antigovernment organizations. In a 1999 essay, Beam predicted a version of apocalypse and revolution. "Soon there will be millions in this country of every political persuasion confronting the police state in streets throughout America," he wrote. "Wake up and smell the tear gas. Freedom is calling its sons and daughters."

Beam had tapped into a malaise throughout much of an American public that felt victimized by change and left behind by progress in an increasingly complicated world. Those angry that America had lost its greatness, that society was in decline, and that government had lost its way found the message of Beam and many other facile hate-mongers persuasive.

The federal government made the job of the Louis Beams of the world much easier, inadvertently fueling the modern militia movement after its botched and bloody takedown of staggering ineptitude at Ruby Ridge, Idaho.

Army veteran Randy Weaver, who identified as a white separatist, had been on federal law-enforcement radar throughout much of the 1980s. He was the subject of an ATF investigation into illegal arms-dealing inside the Aryan Nation hate group in northern Idaho. Although not a member, Weaver associated with members and had attended its World Congress. It took a while, but Weaver was eventually persuaded by an undercover informant to shorten the barrels of two shotguns to an illegal length. He was arrested on gun charges but failed to appear in court, instead deciding to retreat in

March 1991 to his family's cabin and isolated property at Ruby Ridge. Informing the government that he would fight being taken into custody, he remained there with his wife and four children. A negotiated surrender failed.

U.S. marshals went undercover to watch his house, and shortly before noon on August 21, 1992, the family's dog spotted them. When the dog barked, the marshals quickly shot it to prevent exposing the deputies' positions. Weaver's armed fourteen-year-old son Sammy spotted Deputy U.S. Marshal William Degan and fired. A veteran of the agency since 1978, the dying Degan returned fire, fatally shooting the boy in the back as he retreated toward the cabin.

The next day, an FBI sniper wounded Weaver and killed his wife, Vicki, with a shot to the head as she stood in the doorway of the cabin, the couple's ten-month-old daughter in her arms. The second bullet wounded family friend Kevin Harris. To add to the chaotic incompetence, the number of government officers assigned to the standoff rose to nearly four hundred.

Weaver surrendered several days later and was taken into custody. With famous criminal-defense attorney Gerry Spence at his side, Weaver was acquitted on the paltry weapons charges and sentenced to eighteen months for failing to appear in court. He would eventually receive a $3.1-million settlement from the government for the deaths of his wife and son.

Ruby Ridge would rapidly come to symbolize the brazen lawlessness within federal law enforcement that extremists had been warning against for decades. Ruby Ridge proved that they were not paranoid but that there was something tangible to fear. That symbolism would be further enhanced just eight months later with another grotesquely botched federal law-enforcement effort outside Waco, Texas—an incident that would provide yet another rallying cry for antigovernment extremists.

Born Vernon Wayne Howell, David Koresh was a dyslexic from a violent broken home who sought identity and power as the leader of the Branch Davidian cult of apocalyptic Christianity long splintered from the Seventh-day Adventist Church. He had visions of becoming a professional guitar player and musician, but he gravitated toward conservative religion and in 1983 added the gift of prophesy to his playlist.

He changed his name to David Koresh to better reflect his belief that he was the Lamb of Revelation, the Christ returned in human flesh. He kept his flesh busy with his multiple wives at the Branch Davidian's Mount Carmel Center outside Waco.

Koresh wrested control of the Branch Davidians only after fellow leader George Rogen was arrested for murder—he had killed another challenger to leadership with an axe blow to the head. After Rogen was declared criminally insane, Koresh ascended as leader.

He professed peace but built an arsenal and prepared for the end of days. When an ATF investigation into suspected illegal explosives and firearms in Mount Carmel led to a 1993 raid on Koresh's sect, ten persons were killed, including four federal agents, in the shootout. Nearly two months later, with dozens of children still inside the Center and attempts to negotiate surrender having failed, the FBI moved in to end the siege. A fire of disputed origin broke out during the raid, and in the end Koresh and seventy-nine of his followers, many of whom were held hostage, were dead.

Like many people with extremist views, Jerad Miller had conflated the awful events at Mount Carmel with the concerns of a Nevada rancher in a long-standing grazing dispute with the federal government. When Miller proclaimed, "This is the next Waco!" about the Bunkerville standoff, he shared a common view among antigovernment diehards.

Images of Ruby Ridge and Waco informed the increasingly extreme beliefs of a wide variety of individuals and groups. The most infamous among them was disaffected military veteran turned right-wing extremist Timothy McVeigh, who on April 19, 1995, blew up the Alfred P. Murrah Federal Building in Oklahoma City by detonating a bomb made of ammonium nitrate, a chemical fertilizer, and diesel fuel rigged in a Ryder truck. The explosion killed 168 people, 19 of them children attending day care, and injured nearly 700 more in the deadliest act of domestic terrorism in American history.

Born in Pendleton, a small town in Niagara County, New York, McVeigh served with distinction in the U.S. Army in the Gulf War but had long harbored survivalist and racist views, stoked by such magazines as *Soldier of Fortune. The Turner Diaries*, a novel by neo-Nazi William Pierce in which the bombing of a federal building is depicted, inspired him. In his own writing, McVeigh called the deadly firefight at Ruby Ridge and the Waco assault motivations in the battle to maintain the Second Amendment. He carried out the bombing on the second anniversary of the Branch Davidian takedown.

McVeigh lived outside Kingman, Arizona, in the months prior to carrying out his bomb plot. His co-conspirators included army comrade Terry Nichols. Like McVeigh, Nichols also harbored hatred for the federal government, espoused racist views, and was obsessed with weapons. They bought and sold weapons at gun shows, and they were together as the events in Waco were broadcast on network television. Evidence would eventually show that Nichols was intimately involved in planning the act and acquiring the truck, bomb, and detonator materials.

Nichols was also from small-town America. Born in Lapeer, Michigan, he was raised on a family farm. Although an above-average student, he found success outside the classroom difficult. He served in the U.S. Army without distinction and later spent a short time in Las Vegas as a construction worker. As time passed, his personal debts worsened and his antigovernment views became more intense. He once yelled at a judge that the court lacked jurisdiction over him. Like other sovereign citizens, he attempted to renounce his American citizenship and stopped carrying a driver's license. He would be convicted on involuntary manslaughter and conspiracy charges for his role in the Murrah Building bombing and sentenced to life in prison. McVeigh would be convicted and sentenced to death by lethal injection, eventually dying in 2001.

The atrocity of the Murrah Building bombing elevated McVeigh and Nichols as domestic terrorists, and not simply as aggrieved members of an antigovernment organization. But their influences were much the same as those who guided other heavily armed militias with patriotic-sounding names.

Following the bombing of the Murrah Building, law enforcement received inquiries about McVeigh's and Nichols's suspected ties to Las Vegas and the region's reputation as a growing hotbed for extremists. Incidents involving sovereign citizens occurred there so frequently that the website of the Clark County Metro police union—the Las Vegas Police Protective Association—posted its own warning about such activity, reporting that federal law-enforcement agencies had designated the sovereign-citizen movement the greatest threat to their communities—far ahead of Islamic extremism. The FBI had long tracked the sovereign-citizen movement, but by 2014 it was charting the movement's increasingly violent tendencies as a domestic-terrorism organization and a growing threat to law enforcement:

> Sovereign citizens do not represent an anarchist group, nor are they a militia, although they sometimes use or buy illegal weapons. Rather, they operate as individuals without established leadership and only come together in loosely affiliated groups to train, help each other with paperwork, or socialize and talk about their ideology. They may refer to themselves as "constitutionalists" or "freemen," which is not necessarily a connection to a specific group, but, rather, an indication that they are free from government control.

In Nevada, sovereign-citizen white-collar crimes, referred to by law enforcement as "paper terrorism," had become commonplace. Nevada was full of examples. In 2008, the Securities and Exchange Commission (SEC) shut down a Las Vegas–based $27-million Ponzi scheme ostensibly run by a Native American tribe claiming they were sovereign citizens. In 2009, two self-described leaders—one from Arizona and the other from Idaho—were charged with laundering $1.3 million in Las Vegas. A fellow sovereign citizen, who kept a cache of grenades, weapons, and other military equipment in his home, was charged with possession of an unregistered machine gun.

Even as one of the "sovereigns" pled guilty to thirty-one felony counts, he couldn't resist portraying himself as the victim of a malicious, rights-trampling federal government that had illegally entrapped him. An elder of the "guardians of the Free Republics," he quoted the Gospel According to Matthew, along with presidents Ronald Reagan and Andrew Jackson, during his sentencing.

Few moments in the state's extremist history approach the story of Jan Lindsey, a sixty-seven-year-old retired FBI agent who committed income-tax evasion after falling into the ranks of the sovereign citizens. In 1999, he stopped filing federal income taxes, and in 2009 he pleaded guilty to evading a tax liability of $109,000 and faced a lengthy prison sentence.

But he hadn't always been a promoter of faulty tax philosophy. As a young man, Lindsey had enlisted in Vietnam and served with distinction, winning a Silver Star, Bronze Star, and two Purple Hearts. He wasn't just some scammer who hated his country. Lindsey worked as an FBI agent for twenty-six years before retiring in 1995, then spent a decade as a Bureau analyst conducting background investigations. At the time of his arrest, he was drawing a federal pension.

Later, Lindsey admitted that while in retirement he lost his sense of mission and with it his confidence. He fell in with a group of men who talked politics. Some also had military experience. All were impressed with Lindsey's FBI history. They were also followers of false tax prophet Robert Schulz, a self-proclaimed constitutional scholar whose "We the People Foundation for Constitutional Education" preached that sovereign citizens aren't required to file income tax returns or pay taxes. With the zeal of a tent preacher, and with national media attention from *Fox News*, Schulz's advice had led to misery for scores of naïve citizens.

By the time Lindsey appeared in the late Hollywood producer and libertarian political candidate Aaron Russo's 2006 film *America: Freedom to Fascism*, he was an antitax-movement celebrity. Unlike many, he wasn't in it for the book and CD sales. No matter how misguided, he said he believed that his new role was a chance to get back in the fight for justice.

He stood before sentencing Judge James Mahan a broken man whose misguided beliefs had cost him his home, his reputation, and his family relationships. His court-appointed public defender pleaded for leniency in his sentencing. "He found people who made him feel important," she told the court. "They used him. They convinced him, slowly, that he did not have to pay taxes." Tempering justice with mercy, the judge sentenced Lindsey to probation and $109,000 in restitution.

Other Las Vegas characters were convicted of brokering false credentials and license plates, and some filed phony real-estate paperwork to take control of empty homes in the Las Vegas Valley. It was little wonder that Nevada Attorney General Aaron Ford echoed the FBI and other law enforcement when he called the sovereign-citizen movement the state's largest terrorist threat.

While sovereign citizens often threatened violence and retribution, and increasingly acted on such impulses against law-enforcement authorities, they were in stark contrast with the plainspoken Old-West image cut by Cliven Bundy and his sons. The God-fearing constitutional cattlemen were rarely armed and reminded doubters that they kept few firearms around the ranch.

Of course, with their armed allies in the militia movement, they didn't need to wear six guns. The Bundys proved that the propaganda-generating ability of Facebook, cleverly edited YouTube videos, far-right news sites and blogs, and online podcasts were far more effective weapons in delivering their revolutionary message.

As 2015 came to a close, not a single charge had been filed in connection with the Bunkerville standoff. With rancher nemesis Harry Reid having announced his retirement from the Senate—"ahead of the posse," to hear his detractors tell it—the Bundy family struggled for opportunities to stay in the limelight.

Various Bundys spoke at gatherings of ranchers and like-minded conservatives in the region. Their participation in the desecration-by-ATV of Native American pueblo ruins and burial grounds in Utah's San Juan County generated decidedly mixed publicity after BLM rangers and local police failed to take the bait and stoke a confrontation.

Near the end of the year, rumors abounded that the FBI's investigation of the Bunkerville standoff was heading toward indictments. With federal charges looming, the Bundys turned their attention to—and brought to the attention of their militia allies—the case of eastern Oregon ranchers Dwight Hammond Jr. and his son Steven. The Hammonds had been convicted on federal arson and conspiracy charges. Their decades-long, well-documented history of ignoring BLM and Forest Service warnings about lighting fires to clear brush and timber finally appeared to have reached its conclusion. The felony convictions not only meant a loss of freedom but their disqualification from maintaining their federal grazing permits.

The case had nothing to do with Cliven Bundy, and the Hammond family hadn't sought his counsel, but Bundy seized the opportunity to weigh in on the matter. He started with media interviews and a press release on January 1, 2015, on the family's popular blog, bundyranch.blogspot.com: "I, Cliven D. Bundy, have been…striving to understand and comprehend your dilemmas in Harney County, Oregon…. The United States Justice Department has NO jurisdiction or authority within the State of Oregon, County of Harney over this type of ranch management."

He sounded like a self-appointed attorney. But while the Hammonds already had professional legal representation, along with the support of much of their community, Cliven decided the Bundy family would ride to the rescue.

Family-owned Hammond Ranches, Inc. had grazed cattle on BLM land in Burns County, Oregon, since 1964. They ran approximately a thousand cows in the early years, and in the first decade of the twenty-first century their federal grazing permits logged nine hundred cattle feeding almost exclusively on public land.

To understand how the Hammonds came to face prison sentences for what they claimed was a prescribed burn gone awry, it is important to appreciate the ranchers' own history. The brushfire that spread from their ranch onto the 188,000-acre Malheur National Wildlife Refuge was far from the first time they had set federal public land ablaze. Although their friends considered them "the salt of the earth," they'd been getting away with arson for decades. A nineteen-count federal indictment in 2010 cited at least eight late-summer fires on public lands. Many were small and contained, but one they were suspected of igniting burned 46,000 acres. "For more than twenty years, Hammond family members have been responsible for multiple fires in the Steens Mountain area," then–U.S. Attorney Dwight C. Holton wrote.

A jury convicted the pair of starting the 2001 Hardie-Hammond Fire that burned 139 acres of BLM land. Steven Hammond was also convicted of intentionally starting another fire in 2006, and in 2014 the Hammonds' grazing-permit renewal was denied because of criminal activity that "endangered the lives of numerous individuals including firefighters." The most egregious documented violation occurred on September 30, 2001, the first day of deer-hunting season. The Hammonds took Dwight's thirteen-year-old grandson hunting and, according to another hunting party, the Hammond group fired into a herd of deer, wounding several bucks. At another stop, members of the Hammonds' hunting party were given matches and instructed to fan out and "light up the whole country on fire," according to the grandson, who testified truthfully under oath despite orders from his grandfather to keep quiet about the arson.

Although the president of the Oregon Cattlemen's Association called the Hammonds "really, really good folks," they were undeniably comfortable with fire. The Hammonds' defense that lightning started the fires created reasonable doubt that the ranchers weren't malicious, and a jury declined to convict on most of the charges. But court testimony made clear that "good folks" aside, the Hammonds had little regard for the BLM and other federal personnel managing the area. Their refusal to follow regulations, such as prescribed burns designed to protect not only public lands but also their own ranching interests, threatened the safety of wildland firefighters and federal personnel. Steven Hammond was also accused of threatening the safety and career of a BLM ranger in connection with the explosive 2006 Grandad Fire—a blaze that consumed 46,000 acres.

Found guilty in June 2012, the Hammonds faced mandatory minimum prison sentences of five years, with up to $250,000 in fines, but they caught a break at sentencing when U.S. District Judge Michael Hogan ignored the federal sentencing guidelines and gave the father a three-month sentence and the son a year and a day.

They appealed that lenient sentence, only to have the original five-year minimum reinstated.

By December 2015, the Hammonds were packing for prison and rumors of a Bunkerville-like action in support of the ranchers were taking on a life of their own. In an attempt to stave off unrest and prevent violence, Acting U.S. Attorney Billy J. Williams in Oregon implored the community to pause and get a better understanding of the facts of the case. "I understand that there are some individuals and organizations who object to the Hammonds returning to prison to serve the remainder of their sentences mandated by statute," Williams wrote in a commentary for the *Burns Times Herald*. "I respect their right to peacefully disagree with the prison terms imposed. However, any criminal behavior contemplated by those who may object to the court's mandate that harms someone will not be tolerated and will result in serious consequences."

But Ammon Bundy had his own legal theory, and he called upon family, friends, and like-minded followers—including his fellow sovereign citizens and armed militia associates—to help him test it in snowy Harney County. Assembling in Burns, a quiet town of fewer than six hundred residents, Bundy's armed posse looked more like a ragged army unit than cowboys. Burns gets its share of hunters in season, but locals were unaccustomed to armed strangers on their streets and frequenting the Pine Room, Juniper Cookhouse, and El Toreo Mexican restaurant. Some, even those who supported the Hammonds, felt intimidated by the new strangers in town. Whether out of fear or solidarity, a few residents even started packing their own weapons. Among those who answered Ammon's call to arms was Ryan Payne, whose bearded face was familiar to those who had followed the Bunkerville standoff.

For his part, Ammon's presence in Burns was no secret. With Iraq War veteran Payne at his side, Ammon met with David Ward, sheriff of Oregon's Harney County, in early November 2015 to implore him to protect the Hammonds from being taken into custody. When Ward responded that he lacked authority and jurisdiction and would be committing a crime, Payne's and Ammon's calm demeanor quickly shifted. Ammon began his usual preaching about the Constitution and common law and how the sheriff was the only law enforcement with authority. He then threatened that thousands of armed militia members would converge on Burns to protect the embattled ranchers if Ward didn't intercede.

In preparation, Fish and Wildlife officials circulated a photograph of Ammon to staff. Like Bunkerville redux, militia associates made their way to Burns, some camping on the edge of town. The Idaho Three Percenters came, along with members of a group calling itself the Pacific Patriots Network, whose website described its mission as "first responders" serving communities through "mitigation, preparedness." The federal agencies were poorly positioned to police the area themselves, and Harney County law enforcement was clearly outgunned by men who claimed they had come to help.

As 2015 drew to a close, it was clear even to casual observers that the Bundys and their band were preparing to stage a larger action. At the Harney County Fairgrounds, their rhetoric about justice and liberty included shout-outs to the American Revolution with the creation of a "Committee of Safety" consisting of well-armed militia associates and a few ranchers from out of state. They vowed to protect the Hammonds, but they were also preparing to take control of the government's headquarters at the Malheur National Wildlife Refuge.

After his January 2, 2016, speech, Ammon led a group of armed men to the largely unoccupied refuge headquarters. In short order, their numbers would swell to more than two dozen, with as many reporters in tow. The refuge made a better backdrop than the Safeway parking lot and the fairgrounds where they had previously congregated. Ammon's argument, endorsed on the scene by brother Ryan, echoed their father's mantra that federal agencies—in this case the BLM, Forest Service, and U.S. Fish and Wildlife Service—didn't have jurisdiction over the Malheur Refuge. Located thirty miles south of Burns, the Malheur sanctuary is a 293-square-mile oasis and home to 320 species of birds and 58 species of mammals. It is a stop on the Pacific Flyway, the airway traveled by migrating ducks, swans, and geese, and it annually draws visitors from around the world.

Ryan Bundy wasn't there to play tour guide. He told a Las Vegas radio audience from the refuge headquarters, "We realize that they are abusing the land and rights of the people all around…so that's why we're here…this wildlife refuge here has been an instrument of tyranny." The refuge had been carved out of land once used by the region's cattle ranchers, Bundy said, neglecting to mention that the region's indigenous population had inhabited it for many generations before that. He also failed to point out that the refuge was more than a hundred years old, having been founded in 1908.

The Bundys and Payne, it seemed to some observers, were positioning themselves in a higher profile to deflect from their impending indictment in connection with the Bunkerville standoff.

The Hammonds apparently preferred that the Bundys kept their theories to themselves. "Neither Ammon Bundy nor anyone within his group/organization speak for the Hammond Family," attorney W. Alan Schroeder wrote to Sheriff Ward, who pleaded publicly with the paramilitary types to "go home." But Ammon and Ryan Bundy, in their new capacity as public-lands prophets, doubled down in the support of their fellow ranchers, with Ammon chiding the sheriff for failing to step in and protect the Hammonds.

Undeterred, Ammon claimed that the father and son, who had admitted to starting the fires that led to their convictions, should be exonerated. At a news conference that attracted national reporters to what was becoming a media circus, Ammon accused the federal government of trying to steal the Hammond ranch. "The Hammond family have refused to sell it because they want to pass on the ranching heritage to their children and to their grandchildren. Because of that refusal to sell their ranch, those agencies began an attack on this family."

With his acolytes hanging on each word, Ammon added, "There comes a time when people are ignored to the point they're frustrated, they don't know what else to do—they see an injustice but all levels of government are ignoring it…. That is when the people have a right to take a hard stand, and that is what we did."

Regardless of the facts of the criminal case, Ammon portrayed the Hammonds as victims of an overreaching government, echoing the narrative well known to the sovereign citizens. Visiting with the press from under a brown cowboy hat while flanked by men in combat gear, Ammon had the calm demeanor of a Sunday school teacher.

On January 4, 2016, Ammon announced that the occupiers of the refuge would henceforth be called the "Citizens for Constitutional Freedom." The "Ammonites," as his followers were now called, were seldom far away from high-caliber weapons. "Our purpose as we have shown is to restore and defend the Constitution that each person in this country can be protected by, and that prosperity can continue," he said. An image of Thomas Jefferson on a Skousen-printed Constitution peered from the breast pocket of his overshirt. "We love our country. We love the people in it. We know that we are struggling to be able to know what to do as a nation and in many ways we are divided." The Hammond family had been "put under duress by multiple federal agencies," he said, and he had been compelled by the Almighty to act on their behalf. Taking on a messianic air, Ammon had three days earlier proclaimed that the "Lord was not pleased with what was happening to the Hammonds," and a failure to aid them would lead to "accountability" from on high.

For their part, the Hammonds warmed up to the idea of having such high-profile advocates, and although they reported to prison that same day, they announced that they would seek clemency from newly elected President Donald Trump.

An abandoned federal office on the edge of a dormant wildlife refuge in the middle of a frosty eastern Oregon winter was not an optimum venue to instigate a massive armed response from the federal government. But the mainstream press kept the story alive, despite the freezing locale, for fear of being scooped by the conservative media in an incendiary presidential election year.

Disparate militia groups eager to make news elbowed for position as Ammon Bundy's most loyal lieutenants. A fistfight that ended in a black eye and a trip to the hospital for one occupier made headlines. Another was picked up while driving a stolen vehicle. The Burns Paiute Tribe called the occupiers and asked them to pack up and go home, a news-making reminder of the little-mentioned and long-ignored Native Americans' ancestral claim to the land.

In less than a week, Oregon Governor Kate Brown weighed in, requesting that the occupiers vacate the refuge immediately. But Ammon refused to decamp.

Suddenly, a new voice gained clarity in the occupation. It belonged to Arizona rancher Robert LaVoy Finicum. A devout Mormon, father of twelve, grandfather of twenty-five, and aspiring martyr for the cause, Finicum was a vocal devotee of the by-then executed Timothy McVeigh. Finicum was well versed in the sovereign citizens' patriotic vernacular of states' rights at all costs.

The self-styled libertarian rancher talked about freedom and independence while taking advantage of government programs that had helped keep his family ranch afloat for years. He made more money rounding up strays as a foster parent in tandem with his wife, Jeanette, than bringing Hereford steers to market. After he embarked on his mission to Malheur, Arizona authorities removed four foster children from his ranch. His contract with Catholic Charities Community Services paid him $115,343 in 2009 alone. That's a daily average of approximately $30 per child under his custody. He estimated that the family had fostered fifty children, apparently all boys, through the years.

"That was my main source of income," he told a reporter. "My ranch, well, the cows just cover the costs of the ranch." He claimed the ranch had been "a great tool for these boys," prompting speculation that the free labor provided by those fifty boys had been a great tool for the ranch. When he learned that the four remaining foster children had been removed in his absence, Finicum claimed the government was victimizing him for his politics and participation in the Bunkerville and Malheur standoffs. He seemed tone-deaf to the fact that going on national television with a pistol in his belt and a deer rifle across his lap might be bad optics for his image as a foster parent.

In fact, Finicum's foundering ranch was tottering on insolvency. He'd been falling behind on his grazing fees and, following a fantasy perhaps born of desperation, he had chosen to follow the Bunkerville boys down the rabbit hole. After the Bundys' protest, Finicum said he "had to do a lot of soul-searching. I realized Cliven Bundy was standing on a very strong constitutional principle—and yet, here I was continuing to pay a grazing fee to the BLM."

Finicum played to the press, who dubbed him "tarp man" and the "blue blob" for his appearance guarding the entrance to the Bunkerville compound under a blue tarp. He had conducted media tours of the grounds under control of the armed militants. But for all of his expressions of love for the land, family, and his maker, he had decided to risk everything. He set loose his cattle in a federal area not approved for grazing, and in an August 2015 letter to the BLM he declared his independence from the agency. "I sent a letter to the BLM saying, 'Thank you so much for your help in managing my ranch. I shall no longer need your help. I shall manage it myself,'" he revealed in a YouTube video.

In the heartfelt video, he lectured viewers on the Constitution and extolled his love of the land. "I do not have a speeding ticket. So it's not in my nature to go out and poke my finger in people's eyes." He liked to say he was raised in the country and liked to feel the "wind on my face and see the sunrise, to see the moon in the night. And so I have no intention of spending any of my days in a concrete box." He gave an interview to MSNBC on January 6 while sitting in a camp chair guarding the protest site long after dark. With a sleeping bag draped over his lap for warmth and to obscure a high-powered weapon, Finicum said he was waiting for the possible arrival of the FBI. Asked what he was prepared to do if faced with arrest, he played coy.

"I'm telling them right now," he said. "Don't point guns at me."

"So you're prepared to die?" the interviewer asked. "Better dead than in a cell?"

"Absolutely," Finicum replied.

The paranoia and propaganda increased after the refuge occupiers stole government surveillance cameras, and while some social-media and right-wing websites still fanned the flames of their cause, few ranchers were willing to join the protest or stop paying their nominal grazing fees. The occupiers alluded to an exit strategy, but the most obvious one—abandoning the refuge—was not considered, even after the governor revealed that she had requested the FBI to bring a swift resolution to the standoff. Ammon met with FBI agents on January 22, but he rebuffed them by dismissing their authority in Harney County.

But the government's patience was wearing thin. On the afternoon of January 26, two pickups carrying the protest's leaders left Malheur on icy U.S. 395 headed for a meeting with Grant County Sheriff Glenn Palmer in the town of John Day. Oregon State Police, who were joined by FBI agents, stopped them in an attempt to take them into custody.

What happened next was recorded by FBI aerial surveillance and, in what had become standard procedure for participants in the Bundy family agenda, cell phone video from inside the pickup driven by Finicum.

Troopers ordered him to exit the vehicle and he refused.

"Just shoot me," he said. "I'm going to meet the sheriff. The sheriff is waiting for us. So you do what you damn well please. But I'm not going anywhere. Here I am. Right there. Right there. Put a bullet through it. You understand. I'm going to meet the sheriff.... Go ahead, put a bullet through me." His words were eerily reminiscent of John D. Lee, the Mormon scapegoat for the infamous Mountain Meadows Massacre of 1857 who instructed his executioner firing squad to "center my heart, boys."

With the country song "Hold Each Other" blasting from Finicum's truck radio speakers, he accelerated to an estimated seventy miles per hour. Encountering a roadblock with heavy snow on either side of the two-lane highway, he attempted to steer clear, nearly struck an FBI agent, and buried the vehicle in a snow bank.

What briefly had the appearance of an old black-and-white movie, complete with voiceover narrative by Shawna Cox—a Bundy family friend and devotee who accompanied Finicum in the car— and cowboy bravado from Finicum swiftly returned to grim reality.

As Ryan Bundy and Shawna Cox crouched down in the vehicle, Finicum climbed out of the truck, ignoring law-enforcement orders to keep his hands in plain sight.

"You're gonna have to shoot me," Finicum yelled, apparently believing his was a righteous mission to end his life story as a constitutional cowboy. After he reached repeatedly toward his coat, under which was a 9mm Ruger, two SWAT officers with the state police fired six shots. Finicum fell dead onto the January snow. He was fifty-four years old, leaving his wife to run the family ranch.

Ripples of protest flowed in the wake of the shooting, especially after FBI agents were accused of dissembling about whether they had discharged their weapons. To Finicum's family, he was a patri-archal hero whose

> life was cut short in an ambush set up by government offi-cials sworn to serve and protect. With his hands in the air, he sealed his testimony with his blood and gave his all to stand for and protect the freedoms of the American people. When he answers before God at that judgment seat, he will do so with a clear conscience, knowing that he stood with convic-tion for the cause of liberty.

Shawna Cox widely distributed her video, which was meant to cap-ture the government's overreaction, but instead it clearly depicted Finicum's refusal to follow orders from the state police, daring them to shoot him. Even to untrained eyes, it was clear that Finicum never intended to be taken alive as he hankered for martyrdom. His self-published novel, *Only By Blood and Suffering*, was an eerie predictor of events and his death wish. He didn't pull the semiautomatic fire-arm he carried under his camouflage jacket, which would have made him appear more of an outlaw and less of a victim, but his repeated furtive moves toward the weapon justified the police response.

Still, though the fatal shooting was swiftly ruled not only justi-fied but "in fact, necessary," by the Deschutes County district attor-ney, to antigovernment protesters Finicum was instantly elevated as a selfless folk hero shot in the back by government assassins. Sup-porters of the protesters seized on the presence of an unexplained bullet hole as evidence of a "deep-state" cover-up.

CHAPTER 3

Ghost Dancing Through Deseret

Two years earlier, in the spring of 2014, before BLM and NPS officials had finalized their plans to impound the Bundy Ranch's wayward cattle, they strategized one last-ditch effort to reach out to the
family and find a peaceful solution. In mid-March of that year, the
BLM decided to send rangers Robert Shilaikis and Michael Johnson
to personally serve papers and mediate the best way to proceed
without incident. The two were carefully selected for their personal
knowledge and background with the LDS faith and the fundamentalist views of the Bundys. But when they arrived, Cliven was not
available and they were left to speak by cell phone to Ryan Bundy,
who upbraided them, angrily blending his constitutional and spiritual beliefs. He claimed that the case should go before a state court,
and when asked if his family would recognize the BLM's authority
when the time came, Ryan made clear they would not.

The rangers attempted to calm Ryan with references to their
mutual faith, but he only became more agitated when he spoke of
his religious beliefs, "scripture," and his family's long ties to the land.

"You will not take one single cow that belongs to us," Bundy
said. "I'm putting you on notice...I will come after you personally
and legally.... We've been here a lot longer than the BLM has been
in existence...We the people did not give the federal government
authority to own these lands."

When the attempted intercession for an amicable settlement was
clearly unsuccessful, one of the rangers gave Ryan notice. "We are
coming," the ranger replied. "Let us be clear on that."

Cliven Bundy had long claimed that his defiance of the federal government was not a desperate attempt to avoid paying his grazing fees by citing a phony legal theory, as many suspected, but a divinely inspired act of constitutional protest. In interviews, he regularly positioned himself as a spiritual cowboy on a mission far greater than his own self-interest. He left out of his zealous rhetoric the fact that doing the Lord's work also figured to dramatically expand his ranch, while also advancing the goals of those who sought to privatize public land for their own interests.

After the April 2014 standoff, Cliven would tell a radio interviewer, "If the standoff with the Bundys was wrong, would the Lord have been with us? Could those people that stood without fear and went through that spiritual experience have done that without the Lord being there? No, they couldn't."

The rancher also attributed to God's will his call to disarm the federal agents. He believed that, without like-minded sheriffs throughout the country seizing weapons from federal agents, there would be mass bloodshed. The message he was conveying was that "this is our chance, America, to straighten this problem up. If we don't solve this problem this way, we will face these same guns in a civil war."

Bundy's libertarian spiritual view echoed a staunchly conservative interpretation of Mormonism, one defined in the twentieth century by its thirteenth president, Ezra Taft Benson, and popularly promoted by Mormon author W. Cleon Skousen. Skousen was a rabid supporter of the far-right John Birch Society—the same organization that in the 1960s called for small government and considered the civil rights movement a Communist plot. After serving as secretary of agriculture under President Dwight Eisenhower, Benson claimed the administration was riddled with Communist infiltrators. Benson's own son, Brigham Young University religion professor Reed Benson, later emerged as a Birch Society leader.

Skousen influenced a generation of Saints, taking a most conservative view of the Church's teachings on the Constitution and the definition of the "free agency" of man. To Skousen, anything that stood in the way of a man's freedom was antithetical to God's will and the essence of liberty. Not surprisingly, Skousen opposed the existence of all federal regulatory agencies, with which Bundy wholeheartedly agreed as he advocated the elimination of the BLM and Forest Service. As a founder of the ultra-right All-American Society, which later became known as the Freeman Institute dedicated to "born-again constitutionalism," Skousen espoused the elimination of environmental-protection laws, the national parks, social security, and the income tax. This supposedly strict constitutionalist also wanted to eliminate the separation of church and state, which Bundy also vociferously supported. "Nearly every problem facing America today could be solved by going back to the principles of the founding fathers," Skousen had said in 1982. It was that kind of rhetoric that led Moral Majority leader Reverend Jerry Falwell to call Skousen's Freeman Institute "the conservative answer to the Brookings Institute."

Skousen compared the early Mormon Church to an idealized communal society. His views were extreme but not unusual for the Church, which had been slow to accept the authority of the federal government, renounce polygamy, and accept African Americans into its membership priesthood. Bundy's bizarre public comments "about the Negroes," whom he said were better off as slaves, echoed Skousen's own view that "American slave children were freer than white non-slaves."

Skousen's Freeman Institute was essentially the John Birch Society with a new label, its founder a man who reduced the Constitution to a brand of snake oil he could package and sell in the form of incendiary books and tapes. He not only opposed the civil rights movement, he called for the end of federal minority protections and unionism, along with the minimum wage. He was also responsible for printing the ubiquitous booklet Constitutions, so often seen poking from the breast pocket of the shirts worn by Cliven Bundy and his followers.

Cliven Bundy's own talk of doing God's work brought context to his son Ammon's confident comments in 2016 in Oregon that he "clearly understood that the Lord was not pleased with what was happening to the Hammonds. It was exactly like it was happening at the Bundy ranch, when we were guided and directed as to what we were supposed to do." In an internet post prior to the Malheur takeover, Ammon had written, "Come to Harney County and see the wonderful thing the Lord is about to accomplish."

By 2018, the Lord was telling Ammon Bundy other things. Bundy said there were "infiltrators" in the form of socialists, environmentalists, and globalists not only in the federal government and American society generally, but even in his own church. He would tell a gathering in Smithfield, Utah, organized by a Republican Party Central Committee, that his family's fight was a "battle of high priests" pitting the righteous Bundys and their attorney on one side and LDS members from the U.S. Attorney's Office in Las Vegas, a federal judge in Oregon, and former Nevada U.S. Senator Harry Reid on the other. Ammon's reduction of the public-land dispute to white hats and black hats and good and bad Mormons caused a stir in the largely LDS crowd. Quoting scripture and linking his family's actions with biblical references, he implored, "Why would I come in here and testify to you that I truly believe The Church of Jesus Christ of Latter-day Saints is the true church and that the Book of Mormon is true and that we're being prosecuted by a high priest of The Church of Jesus Christ of Latter-day Saints?...Why would I tell you these things? Because the truth matters."

The truth was, LDS Church officials had not supported the Bundys' divinely inspired armed takeover of the Oregon wildlife refuge. Just two days after the siege began, the Church issued its unequivocal rebuke: "While the disagreement occurring in Oregon about the use of federal lands is not a Church matter, Church leaders strongly condemn the armed seizure of the facility and are deeply troubled by the reports that those who have seized the facility suggest that they are doing so based on scriptural principles. This armed occupation can in no way be justified on a scriptural basis. We are privileged to live in a nation where conflicts with government or private groups can—and should—be settled using peaceful means, according to the laws of the land."

Religious interpretation aside, it was also true that the Bundy family's view of the Constitution was relatively common in the rural West, where politics were often inspired by other prophets, such as *Atlas Shrugged* author Ayn Rand and Austrian economist Ludwig von Mises. Historian and author Matthew Bowman observed in his *The Mormon People: The Making of an American Faith*: "We can talk about the Bundys as Mormon, but their beliefs are very Western as well—it's not a mistake that you see this happening in the West. There is a pervasive Libertarianism in the region."

This was also the rhetoric commonly used by white separatists and supremacists who gravitated toward the "Redoubt" region that encompassed parts of Oregon and Washington and all of Idaho, Montana, and Wyoming, blending fundamentalist Christian beliefs with End Times and revolution themes. Although separatists and fundamentalists had been moving to the region for generations and often centered around Sand Point, Idaho, more recently the "American Redoubt" region was proposed by survivalist novelist James Wesley Rawles as a conservative and libertarian stronghold. When the end came, they'd have their last stand locked and loaded.

For its part, the LDS Church had come a long way in its relatively short history, but like religions of old its story is one of patriarchal prophets, acolytes, and supplicants. Although the faith would flourish in the West, it began in the East at Palmyra, New York, with the soul-searching of a fourteen-year-old named Joseph Smith, son of a failed farmer. A revelation came to him in 1829 when an angel named Moroni visited Joseph and assigned him the challenge of restoring God's church on earth.

Smith would recall Moroni telling him "that God had a work for me to do; and that my name should be had for good and evil among all nations, kindreds, and tongues." The work was a book inscribed on golden plates and would be found, Moroni explained, buried inside a mound nearby at Cumorah, where they'd been placed some

1,400 years earlier. Young Smith would be tasked with transcribing the work to the written page with the aid of the Urim and Thummim, "seer stones" capable of translating the ancient symbols. The angel would visit him multiple times, but by then such experiences were fairly regular events in his life, even as he continued to read and relate to the voices of the Bible and in his spare time hunt treasure in the countryside around Palmyra. The plowman's son had no shortage of "Doubting Thomases" in his circle of friends.

Smith was notably moved by references to the persecution of the Apostles for their spiritual insights and beliefs. "It would be the first of hundreds of mythical persecutions that would mark Smith's life and death," author Sally Denton observed, "and portend a future of oppression and vengeance unlike anything America had seen."

After repeated visits, as Smith recounted it, Moroni provided him with access to the golden plates on which were inscribed the history and teachings of ancient American prophets and peoples. From the plates, he said, came the story of the Book of Mormon, a 275,000-word tale that he dictated in a fevered dream in the course of a few weeks. Promoted as an addition to the New Testament, the book became a mysterious sensation despite its density, dizzying plot, and torpid style, and the new religion propelled the then-twenty-four-year-old Smith to international celebrity.

From the outset, the Book of Mormon had no shortage of critics. Few can rival Mark Twain for satiric bite. Although Twain spent precious little time among the Mormons, he thought little of the faith and less of its holy book, calling it "an insipid mess" and "merely a prosy detail of imaginary history, with the Old Testament for a model; followed by a tedious plagiarism of the New Testament."

Twain has been quoted so often by skeptics of the faith that some may conclude there can be no writing about the LDS Church without first consulting "the Lincoln of our Literature." Twain cut his sharp literary teeth as a correspondent and reporter for the *Territorial Enterprise* of Virginia City, back when Nevada was on the cusp of statehood and great change. He scribbled fewer than three years in the territory, from 1861 to 1864, but he later recounted part of his misadventures in his 1872 travelogue *Roughing It*. It's there we first discover Twain's terse view of the Mormons under the leadership of Brigham Young, following a two-day visit to the heart of Deseret in Salt Lake City. Twain was writing about what was then a new, mysterious, and highly controversial religion that promoted polygamy and an almost commune-like strategy of shared resources. The religion was considered mysterious by many and no more than a cult to many God-fearing Christians.

The wilderness has always been a good place for prophets and panderers to wander, whether in search of prophesy, paradise, or a place to hide. Smith was a bit of both. By 1830, the "Church of Christ" (one of several names Smith tried) was born, and Smith's best-selling tome was an overnight sensation.

His church began moving West almost from its inception, in search of an American Zion where a system of beliefs that included the priesthood for qualifying males and pluralistic marriage could be practiced with impunity in a kind of communally libertarian society of the faithful. The Saints stopped first in Kirtland, Ohio, where they built a temple that nearly bankrupted the Church and resulted in Smith being accused of banking fraud. Although he preached purity and piety of body and spirit, he also took spirits internally and was a womanizer not shy about making cuckolds of followers, friends, and family members.

With Kirtland in disarray, the Saints traveled on to Missouri and a town called Far West, where Smith grew increasingly authoritarian, expelling fellow Church founders and assembling a fiercely loyal armed militia known as the Danites. From that point on, dissenters and non-Mormon Missourians blasphemed the Church and its famous elder at their peril. Mormons were often harassed, forbidden from voting, and persecuted, and some saw their farms burned. Others retaliated against nonbelievers, whom they called Gentiles.

Seldom short of revelation, Smith changed the name of his church several times in its first decade of existence, perhaps to avoid confusion with other religious organizations. Not long after Smith led his rapidly growing flock to Far West in 1838, his creation became officially known as the Church of Jesus Christ of Latter-day Saints. But many people would continue to call them Mormons, in a sometimes-derisive reference to the book and its backstory, which remained controversial even as it inspired converts from as far away as Europe.

But the Danites and other Mormon militia men gave as good as they got, ransacking non-Mormon towns, assaulting the Missouri state militia, and taking casualties in what would become known as the Haun's Mill Massacre. Smith himself would eventually be charged with treason in the state. By the time Governor Lilburn Boggs signed Missouri Executive Order 44—which declared Smith and his followers "enemies" who "must be exterminated or driven from the state if necessary for the public peace—their outrages are beyond all description"—the Saints had worn out their tenuous welcome in the "Show-Me" State.

Although they had invited much of the trouble they'd received, in a sense the Saints were also religious refugees, even if their religion was little respected by others. They found brief respite in Commerce, Illinois, which Smith would rename "Nauvoo," after the Hebrew word meaning "beautiful." It was a hard-won beauty that included more controversy after Smith's reputation for sexual rapacity and the practice of polygamy began to spread. Although he had condemned the practice, the Church's leaders had already begun adding "celestial wives" to their singular marital unions.

Undaunted by his increasing characterization as a religious charlatan, with no shortage of the criticism coming from the flock itself, Smith embarked on a presidential campaign in 1844, running as commander in chief of an "Army of God" and advocating the overthrow of the federal government for a Mormon-ruled "theodemocracy." From the beginning, Smith flirted with martyrdom, and in the middle of his campaign he was murdered by an anti-Mormon mob in Illinois.

The first tumultuous chapter in the history of the Church had ended in violence, but the second had already begun. Without a codified plan of succession, chaos, intrigue, and paranoia increased as hundreds of the faithful splintered into offshoot congregations that headed south to Texas and north to Wisconsin. Joseph's suffering widow remained in Illinois "to run her dead husband's tavern in

Nauvoo," as Wallace Stegner wrote. "But the whole structure did not disintegrate with Joseph's passing. He had left it too well organized, and he had left behind him a Quorum of Apostles and Brigham Young, their president."

Born in 1801 in Whitingham, Vermont, Young was inspired by an 1830 reading of the Book of Mormon, and three years later he followed Smith to Kirtland. A gifted intellect, Young was a member of the first Quorum of Twelve Apostles.

Mormons had endured hardship and religious discrimination, the violent deaths of their prophet and scores of the faithful, their ranks broadened by zealous converts and thinned by disease. By the time they headed west from Nauvoo, they moved en-masse as a persecuted people, many believed, wandering toward Zion in preparation for the End Times with each handcart-pushing wave "like a new flight out of Egypt," as Stegner observed. "The Old Testament parallel was like a bugle in the brain; some of them probably even hoped for a pursuing Pharaoh and a dividing of the waters." Their collective strength "was the herd strength and the cunning of the tough bulls who ran the show."

Where the prophet Smith had excelled at prolific revelation and had been suspiciously unsuccessful at managing the flock's finances, Young was eminently pragmatic and possessed a genius for organization. It was surpassingly fitting that Young's singular revelation produced a brilliant strategy, a math-principled template for the business of migration and colony, which would become an admired hallmark of the Church. "The secretary had taken over the administration of the business," Stegner wrote. "If it didn't sound like blasphemy, one might say that he proved a better executive than his former employer."

Under Young's visionary leadership, the gathering faithful endured great hardship in their western migration across the Rocky Mountains before arriving at the shores of the Great Salt Lake in 1848. In less than two decades of existence, the Church's sense of persecution and defiance of federal authority was already well established. So was its soon-to-be famous shared use of irrigation and development of precious riparian resources, first at City Creek

Canyon in the Salt Lake Valley, and eventually across the West. Their "group dream," as Stegner called it, would put down roots for the ages as part of Young's plan of empire through the implementation of a united order of agrarian communalism and the further practice of polygamy. At a time when others might have been satisfied just to find a bountiful land free of religious persecution, Young had far bigger ideas. He sent missionaries across the continent and into Europe to attract skilled workers of every craft. Under Young, "Mormonism had been conceived on a grandiose scale," Stegner observed. "It was meant to cover and inherit the world in the great and terrible last days. Under Brigham Young it became in fact a world-wide movement." Although the prophet Smith had referred to all of America and every stop along the way as Zion in the early years, the Mormons had found their place in a part of the West that only a short time earlier had been part of Mexico.

The journey to the Mormon Zion was more than a thousand miles, but here again Young's planning paid off by dividing parties into groups of a hundred led by a captain. Cattle were herded and a group of intrepid planters first tilled the soil of the Salt Lake Valley ahead of the pack. Cutting a steep trail that kept them from suffering the fate of many travelers who tried to cross the Great Basin's deserts, Young's army of believers crossed through verdant valleys where the Ute and other indigenous peoples irrigated with available water and grew abundant crops that helped ensure their winter survival. This was a lesson no eastern college could teach.

The first 1,533 Mormon pioneers arrived in the Salt Lake Valley with 2,313 cattle. A long cold season of suffering at the foot of the Wasatch Range failed to shake their faith, and by spring Young's call to "come immediately and prepare to go West" echoed far beyond the Rockies.

But the great Mormon migration was unlike others in important ways. Young wasn't simply moving people. He was attempting to create a society, an audacious utopia of spiritual discipline and communal agricultural cooperation. He envisioned a place that would position the faithful outside the reach of the Gentiles and away from a federal government that threatened their religious existence.

Although the origin of Young's often-quoted lines are in some dispute, he is credited with offering his followers this credo: "No man can buy land here, for no man has any land to sell. But every man shall have his land measured out to him, which he must cultivate in order to keep it. Besides, there shall be no private ownership of the streams that come out of the canyons, nor the timber that grows on the hills. These belong to the people: all the people."

The authenticity of Young's remarks has been challenged, but Mormons considered his wisdom divinely inspired. Generations later, its message was long lost on the Bundys and others who looked at the West's vast public common and attempted to own it all.

Next to faith, water was the pioneers' most precious commodity. It was zealously and bureaucratically monitored. "Rigid controls governed the use of water," Stegner noted. "Each main irrigation ditch was supervised by a church committee which saw to it that farmers received just enough precious fluid for efficient agriculture." Young's great communal experiment worked well on paper. The productive fields, profitable cattle herds, and wide streets were impressive successes, but like all other religions the pews of the Mormons' temples were filled with flawed human beings. As Stegner put it, "The Saints were, in one sense, typical of all pioneers, who were less individualistic than opportunistic."

While he was busy constructing a new society, one he imagined would become its own nation, Young added to his wealth and built up his power base. He was a grand example of prophet-as-business tycoon and set a template that helped strengthen the Church in spiritual and financial ways. He was also devoted to the practice of polygamy, keeping fifty-five wives and fathering fifty-six children.

His genius and vision for the business of community were genuine. "Young organized the mass movement with a brilliance and compulsion never before seen in the annals of the American experience," Sally Denton wrote. Utah-born historian Bernard DeVoto noted that Young's headquarters buzzed with activity from "an immense bookkeeping, a constant dispatch and arrival of couriers, an almost nightly convocation of the counselors, the Prophet's fingers on the controls of an organization that stretched from the

Missouri River all the way eastward across America and half way across Europe."

As the Utah Territory's first governor, Young found his political skill tested from within as the Church's ranks grew and from without as authorities in Washington looked with increasing skepticism at his Mormon-dominated governmental structure. He assembled a militia led by his fiercest acolytes. Young's missionary outreach to the region's Indian tribes was in part his responsibility as the territory's superintendent of Indian affairs and in part an element of the faith's belief that the indigenous people were their long-lost "Lamanite" relatives.

Although the Mormons attracted much suspicion and were commonly vilified in the press, especially on the subject of polygamy, they were also known for great acts of humanity. In February 1854, legendary pathfinder John C. Frémont led a mapmaking expedition through the West that found itself rapidly running out of supplies. Frémont was no fan of the Mormons but, when in the wilds of the Utah Territory, his party exhausted the last of its food and was forced to travel for two days before arriving in Parowan, where hungry members were received with open arms. "The kindness of these Mormons completely altered the explorer's views of the sect," Pulitzer Prize–winning historian Allan Nevins observed. Frémont himself remarked that "the Mormons saved me and mine from death by starvation in '54."

Nor was everyone Young's critic. The adventurer and prolific author Richard Burton wrote of Young in *City of Saints*, "He has been called a hypocrite, swindler, forger and murderer; no one looked it less. His want of pretension contrasts favorably with certain pseudo-prophets that I have seen."

As a world traveler and translator of the *Arabian Nights*, Burton was no stranger to mysterious religions and exotic marriage practices. While Twain would play Young's enormous "Mormon bed" for laughs, Burton was more thoughtful.

"When conversation began to flag, we rose up, shook hands, as is the custom here, all round, and took leave," Burton wrote. "The first impression left upon my mind by this short seance, and it was subsequently confirmed, was, that the prophet is no common man, and that he has none of the weakness and vanity which characterize the common uncommon man."

More appreciative still was poet-philosopher Ralph Waldo Emerson, who lauded Young's genius "for the creation of Salt Lake City—an inestimable hospitality to the Overland Emigrants, and an efficient example to all men in the vast desert, teaching how to subdue and turn it to a habitable garden."

But when President James Buchanan moved to replace Young with a non-Mormon as territorial governor, in an effort to make Utah less of a theocracy, Young's followers took up arms in anticipation of a great battle with the federal government. This was a setback in Young's push to expand the geographic reach of the faith into parts of what would become the state of Nevada.

Historian Richard Lillard reflected, "The Mormons could have made Nevada into an agricultural wonderland. They started the job but did not get to finish it. In 1854 President Brigham Young ordered many Mormon families into the Carson, Walker, Washoe, and Truckee valleys, where they at once established stable farming communities by the conservation practices that had recently made Deseret an immediate success at the foot of the Wasatch Range. But a few years later, Colonel Albert Johnson was advancing with an army on Salt Lake City, and other trouble with federal authorities was brewing. As a matter of theocratic defense, Young contracted the Mormon empire. He called the Nevada settlers back to Salt Lake."

Although the so-called Utah War in 1857 produced no large-scale battles with the federal government, it stoked a collective sense of persecution in the End-Times believers that manifested in extreme violence in September with the massacre by Young's men of a wagon train of immigrants passing through Utah. When the slaughter ceased, 140 unarmed men, women, and children were dead in what would become known as the Mountain Meadows Massacre. Young's loyal lieutenant John D. Lee served himself up as a scapegoat and would be remembered as the only man held accountable for the carnage. He was executed by firing squad.

The year 1857 was pivotal in many ways for the Church as it spread its message and membership into the Great Basin. This was also the year a group of Mormon pioneers settled along the Virgin River in the southeast part of the territory and found surprisingly rich bottom land suitable for growing crops and watering livestock. Nevada's 1864 statehood and multiple border revisions would eventually place the settlement called Bunkerville in the Battle-Born State.

Bunkerville was located on the southern edge of Utah's "Dixie Country," so named by a Mormon convert and former Mississippi plantation boss dispatched in 1857 by Young on a "Cotton Mission" to the Virgin River Basin. The region was also home to former Confederate soldiers who moved their kin West following the Civil War, in part in protest of Reconstruction and its free black men. Although LDS leaders more than a century later would argue that the "Dixie" title was based more on climate than Confederate sympathies, many former slaveowners and Rebel sympathizers flocked to the Mormon Church. In light of continued controversies over the use of Dixie and Rebel imagery in the twenty-first century, and the Church's reluctance to acknowledge the long shadow of the Confederacy over the region, clear-eyed Utah historian Will Bagley noted that facts about the Mississippian put "the skids to this happy fantasy that [Utah's Dixie has] no connection to the Confederacy. The name Dixie reflects the sympathy that the southern Utah and the Mormon people felt for the Confederacy." Indeed, the two had been linked together publicly since the 1856 presidential race, when the platform of the newly founded Republican Party—with John C. Frémont as its candidate—called Mormon polygamy and slavery the "twin relics of barbarism."

The Church officially discontinued polygamy in 1890—in no small part to gain its 1896 statehood—and excommunicated many members who practiced it. The Church would gain growing measures of acceptance and respect following statehood because of the undeniable outreach and industry of the faithful. "I have witnessed their devotion to public service and their support of charitable efforts over our country and in foreign lands during all these years,"

President Herbert Hoover said. "I have witnessed the growth of the church's communities over the world where self-reliance, devotion, resolution and integrity are a light to all mankind. Surely a great message of Christian faith has been given by the church—and it must continue."

Three decades later, President John F. Kennedy, a Catholic who'd experienced scrutiny for his religion during the 1960 campaign for the White House, stood in the Tabernacle and lauded the faith: "Tonight I speak for all Americans in expressing our gratitude to the Mormon people—for their pioneer spirit, their devotion to culture and learning, their example of industry and self-reliance. But I am particularly in their debt tonight for their successful battle to make religious liberty a living reality—for having proven to the world that different faiths of different views could flourish harmoniously in our midst."

But the Dixie region remained a fundamentalist hotbed and polygamist backwater. Polygamist communities at Short Creek, Arizona; Hilldale, Utah; and in rural Lincoln County in Nevada were well known for the practice, which rarely resulted in government and law-enforcement action—and even then with decidedly mixed results.

A 1953 raid on Short Creek and its shrewd fundamentalists by Arizona State Police and the National Guard resulted in the detaining of the entire town's population of 400, including more than 250 children. The town was renamed Colorado City in 1960, but it remained a center of polygamy, eventually under the leadership of Fundamentalist Church of Jesus Christ of Latter-day Saints President Warren Jeffs, who had at least eighteen wives (some reports registered as many as eighty-seven wives) and eighty children. Jeffs would ultimately be convicted of rape and child sexual assault, and in 2011 he was sentenced to ten years to life in state prison.

Jeffs's prosecution revealed another ugly truth: that young males of Colorado City and elsewhere were strongly encouraged to leave the sect and find their own footholds in communities that were strange to them. The so-called lost boys often found themselves going north to St. George and Cedar City or south to the Sin City itself, Las Vegas. But, as ever, whether they identified as Saints or sinners, the sin was in the eye of the beholder.

Painting in decidedly broad strokes, Stegner wrote a generation ago that his Mormon Country hadn't seen an influx of "outsiders," in no small part because "there is no place for them to come. Mormon farmers long ago owned all the suitable land and home sites, as well as all the water, and Mormon farmers are of a breed that does not sell out.... Brigham's dream of settling up the empire so solidly that a Gentile couldn't get in with a shoehorn has completely come to pass." But Utah's reputation as a place where church and state are inseparable belies more complex truths. Two decades into the new century, Utah's population reached three million, with just under 63 percent identifying as members of the Church. In Salt Lake County, where Young's dream first took shape, the population continued to diversify, with approximately 50 percent of residents identifying themselves as followers of the Church.

Even as LDS fundamentalists decry the "infiltration" of "environ-mentalists" and "socialists" into the Church, travel and tourism in Utah generated a record $8.54 billion, with much of it attributable to unprecedented visits to the state's five national parks, eleven national monuments, two national recreation areas, and one national historic site. The federally managed facilities that the Bundys and their followers so scorned were an integral and irreplaceable part of Utah's economic model. As environmental historian Sara Dant observes, that "the new westerners sought out the environmental amenities that Old West industries threatened—open spaces, public lands, unmarred views, abundant wildlife, clean air, and free-flowing rivers—only exacerbated enmity."

In keeping with the patience of the modern LDS faith, the Saints appear to have developed a better sense of humor about Twain's zingers than some writers who suspect the Church is behind every boulder and patch of sagebrush in the Great Basin. With the satiric needling of *South Park* and the smash Broadway musical *The Book of Mormon*, Twain's efforts appear as quaint as an ice-cream suit by comparison.

As a Mormon patriarchal blessing reminds the faithful, "Seek truth always. Be not afraid to learn the truth of anything, for no truth will be revealed to you as such that will be in conflict with God's kingdom." When it came to the Bundy saga and the emergence of sovereign-citizen politics in the West, the truth was in the telling and often hard to come by, even under oath.

No matter their opinion of the righteousness of his cause, all who met Cliven Bundy would be compelled to admit he took great pride in his ranching family's historic ties to Bunkerville and the Gold Butte area where his cattle roamed. His relatives, he said, were among the first Mormon pioneer families to arrive at the Virgin River in 1857—the year of the nearby Mountain Meadows Massacre. Although he was born in 1946 in Las Vegas, and his father and mother established a 160-acre homestead on the ranch in 1948, even a critical reader of his biography couldn't help but appreciate that a keen sense of place in the West seemed self-evident.

Less well appreciated, and rarely mentioned by the rancher or his followers, was the fact that indigenous people had called the Virgin River home for multiple generations before Anglo settlers set the first stake. Whether it was the Mohave to the south along the Colorado River, or the Paiute throughout the region, Native Americans had long called the area home. Like other tribes whose knowledge of the land was put to good use by passing settlers, Mohave farms made efficient use of water resources. Even when forced onto reservations immediately after the Civil War, the Mohave maintained water rights still in use today.

The Mohave were made up of several bands with distinct dialects and languages. Their religious and social customs were as complex as anything prophesied by Joseph Smith. Matevilya, their Creator, gave the people commandments to live by long before they were first sighted by Christian Europeans in the late 1700s. Franciscan missionary and explorer Francisco Garces in 1776 estimated their numbers at more than three thousand. The Mohave didn't know Jesus, but they gave thanks to Mastamho, son of their creator, for the river that gave them life—but ultimately also attracted the whites.

The Southern Paiute knew every inch of the Virgin River. Their people had roamed the Colorado River Basin for centuries in what is now part of Nevada, Utah, and Arizona. By the time the first Franciscan friars noted their seemingly savage appearance, which included facial hair uncommon in the religious men's experience with the continent's indigenous peoples, they also glimpsed the social structure of the tribe. Like the Mohave, the Paiute were also capable farmers who understood the priceless value of the Virgin River to their way of life.

So imagine their surprise when those resources were placed out of reach to them by the first Mormon pioneers who passed through the area in the early 1850s. By shortstopping the flow that fed Paiute crops, Mormon missionary Jacob Hamblin and his fellow travelers put the natives in the awkward position of relying on the strangers for water to which they had long had unfettered access. The presence of the whites in the area had an upside: tribes such as the Navajo and Western Ute no longer raided their camps and kidnapped their women and children for use in the slave trade. Among bad actors, the marauding Western Ute leader Waccara, "The Hawk of the Mountains," was most notorious of all. His band of violent thieves commonly demanded not only Paiute ponies, but their women and children as well. Mixing near the Mormons of Provo, the Ute were commonly sighted with "some Indian children for sale," as Daniel W. Jones recalled in a nineteenth-century oral history. "They offered them to the Mormons, who declined buying. Arapine, Waccara's brother, became enraged saying that the Mormons had stopped the Mexicans from buying these children; that they had no right to do so unless they bought them themselves. Several of us were present when they took one of these children by the heels and dashed its brains out on the hard ground, after which he threw the body towards us, telling us we had no hearts, or we would have bought it and saved its life."

Although the slaving discontinued, the endless swelling of the white population meant a change in the way of life of the Paiute, who were skilled basketweavers, desert farmers, and small-game hunters. With a keen understanding of survival in arid country, they kept their population organized into small groups to better facilitate living off the land.

Once the route along the Virgin River was used for immigrant travel and cattle and horse herds, the Paiute lost not only their garden spot but also the game that browsed and drank along the riverbank.

Most egregious of all, the Paiute were wrongfully blamed for participating in the Mountain Meadows Massacre as part of the cover-up of the 1857 slaughter. Tribal elders worked well into the twentieth century to have the facts heard.

The Paiute didn't leave their sacred land quietly. They fought near the Virgin River and north to Pioche to prevent the spread of the strangers. Settlers and mining operators attempted to civilize the Paiute and use them as cheap labor, compelling their children to attend school, but the Paiute failed to thrive in a new setting.

The tribe eventually settled onto two main reservations in Southern Nevada: one at Moapa Valley not far from Bunkerville, and the other on a careworn end of Main Street in downtown Las Vegas. If there was any solace for the Paiute, the Moapa band excelled in facilitating a site for solar-energy production, and the Las Vegas Paiute in 2018 opened an enormous legal recreational marijuana dispensary.

Either out of ignorance of the deeper history of the region or from an arrogance born of white privilege, sagebrush rebels and sovereign citizens rarely mentioned their second position to the real Native Americans of the West. While they readily touted their own ties to the land, they declined to add this simple truth during the Malheur Refuge takeover, even with the presence of Indian artifacts all around them. Although precious Indian petroglyphs were visible in the slot canyons of Gold Butte, the Bundys rarely referenced them.

But the rebellion in the West has never been about fairness or historical accuracy. It has always been about control.

For his part, Cliven Bundy and his followers missed a bet when he declined to acknowledge the long fight of cattle and horse ranchers Mary and Carrie Dann of Nevada's Western Shoshone tribe. To those who knew the Dann sisters' story, the so-called rebels were windy buffoons with big hats and buckles to match who were "clad

in sackcloth of injured innocence and professing to be the beleaguered natives of the Great Basin's high desert," as law professor and
public-lands specialist John W. Ragsdale stated in a blistering assessment. Bundy and his followers "announce rebellion against the evil
federal Sheriff of Nottingham. In truth, only the Western Shoshone
could legitimately make this claim and, indeed, the Dann sisters are
true American heroes. These characters at Bunkerville and Malheur
are most decidedly not the like of the Dann Sisters."

Whether holding forth for his followers or answering questions
from pesky reporters, Cliven Bundy has often spoken with pride
about his historical ties to the land near Bunkerville. He counted
his ancestors among the town's plucky Mormon founders, settlers
who drew from the Virgin River to grow abundant crops and water
livestock. Although his father didn't buy the ranch until 1948, Cliven
repeatedly boasted that his ancestors had called Bunkerville home
since 1877.

Still, that made Bundy no better than a wet-behind-the-ears
newcomer to Nevada in comparison to the Dann sisters, and his
dispute with the federal government was a Sunday school dustup
compared to the roots of the Western Shoshones' struggle with
the white fathers from Washington. Long before the West was settled and boundaries were drawn, the Shoshone roamed enormous
stretches of what would eventually become Idaho, Utah, and Nevada,
in a region they referred to as Newe Segobia, or "the people's earth
mother." According to tribal lore, Coyote, the trickster assigned to
carry them in a closed basket, brought the first Shoshone to the
Great Basin. But the famously curious dog spirit couldn't resist and
opened the lid, enabling the Shoshone to escape into the desert
wilderness.

Coyote was a playful pup compared to the tricks the white man
would play on the Shoshone through the years, first in the 1800s
through a series of armed confrontations and treaties that were
audaciously unfair, and in the twentieth century as the Indians
attempted to organize and seek reparations while the federal gov-

ernment crafted laws that enabled cattle ranchers and large-scale gold-mining outfits to encroach on traditional tribal lands.

Back when the notion of statehood for the region must have seemed a laughable dream, the Shoshone moved with the seasons through the breadth of the Great Basin and beyond, living off pine nuts and other native plants, insects, birds, small animals such as rabbit and squirrel, and the occasional deer and pronghorn. The tribe was generally divided into Western, Eastern, and Northern groups. While outsiders traveled *through* the land, the Western Shoshone were *of* it, and their numbers reached from modern-day Idaho as far south as the Mojave Desert and the eastern slopes of the Sierra in California. Whether known as Tukuaduka ("sheep-eaters"), Goshute or Toi Ticutta ("cattail-eaters"), or Agaidika ("salmon-eaters"), theirs was an ancestral territory that encompassed more than 93,750 square miles, or approximately 60 million acres.

The discovery of gold on January 24, 1848, at Sutter's Mill on the American River at the base of the Sierra near Coloma, California, shaped the nation's destiny in many ways, but initially the most noticeable impact it had on the indigenous population was in creating a dramatic increase in traffic across their ancestral lands. Fur-trapping mountain men had cut the first trail, and "The Pathfinder," Army Captain John C. Frémont, had produced the first widely circulated map of the region. By the early 1850s, traditional Indian game and water sources were under stress. Along with the Paiute and Bannock tribes, the Shoshone initially met the strangers in peace, but in time tensions flared and violence erupted. When whites took game that fed the Shoshone, the Shoshone felt comfortable taking horses and cattle from the newcomers. Trouble was inevitable.

Eventually, a series of treaties followed. Acting on behalf of the federal government, Utah Territory Indian Agent Garland Hurt crafted an agreement in 1855 with the "Sho-Sho-nee" in the Humboldt River region, intended to "amicably" settle "all former disputes and hostility between our people and the People of the United States" by guaranteeing the settlers and prospectors "perfect safety to life and property at all times when peacefully sojourning in, or traveling through our country." The treaty also allowed those travelers to settle in Indian Country "as brothers and friends, and not as enemies." In exchange for peace in the valley, the Shoshone chiefs who signed the treaty with their Xs would receive $3,000 in presents in the form of provisions and clothing, including farm implements.

Blending cultures so different would have been difficult in the best of circumstances, but the Shoshone knew something the white newcomers could only learn through bitter experience: living in their world and balancing survival with the lean seasons was a challenge far more complex than merely killing more game to eat. And so the troubles continued.

A treaty between the Paiute and whites signed in 1858 called for peaceful coexistence and the protection of Indian game, but the agreement was broken in a single hard winter. With game over-hunted, the Indians scrambled to survive, and many suffered starvation. Although newspapers such as Virginia City's *Territorial Enterprise* would report citizens taking up the case of the desperate natives, tribes were ravaged by hunger.

The murder of a white settler by a renegade band of Northern Paiute not under the control of tribal chieftains Numaga and Truckee increased tensions further. Numaga also understood that Paiute land, with silver reserves beneath the surface of millions of acres, held far more value to the whites than they were willing to admit. Numaga was not above cutting a deal with the newcomers for some of their cattle or coin in exchange for helping to keep the peace, but a showdown was coming that would take dozens of settlers' lives and an uncounted number of Indian warriors.

Encroachment by white ranchers and settlers forced the Paiutes' hand at Pyramid Lake and nearly two decades later at a lush high-desert oasis in eastern Oregon called Malheur, where even designated reservation land wasn't safe from the gradual expansion of the ranchers. When the Indians, driven by hunger, once again took up arms in the 1878 Bannock War, they purchased some of their weapons from Mormon merchants.

Led by Chief Numaga, the Paiute War of 1860 was brief but bloody. The history of the Pony Express (April 1860–October 1861) is replete with tales of intrepid riders and stalwart station tenders who delivered the mail while taking arrows from bands of Paiute warriors enraged by the endless march of often destructive and disrespectful white settlers across their land. Numaga, sometimes called "Young Winnemucca," and his forces were brave and notched their successes, but Numaga was also wise enough to know when to play for peace.

"My brothers," he said,

> you would make war upon the whites. I ask you to pause and think of what that would mean to our People. The white men are like the stars over your heads. You have wrongs, great wrongs, that rise up like those mountains before you; but can you, from the mountaintops, reach and blot out those stars?... Could you defeat the whites in our own home, from over the mountains in California would come to help them an army of white men that would cover your country like a blanket.... They will come like sand in a whirlwind and drive you from your homes.

By the time the Paiute War ended, life for the region's tribes was forever changed. As a statement of peaceful coexistence, in 1863 Ruby Valley Shoshone leader Te-meok and Nevada territorial governor and Indian agent James W. Nye signed a treaty that called for the protection of native rights and safe passage for emigrants and the military.

But this wasn't the end of armed conflict between the tribes and against the US government in the region. The Bear River Massacre of 1863 saw American cavalry slaughter more than four hundred northwestern Shoshone men, women, and children. The Shoshone and Bannock tribes combined to battle US troops from 1864 to 1868 in the Snake War, and the Shoshone and U.S. Army allied in the 1876 Battle of the Rosebud in Montana against members of the Lakota and Cheyenne nations.

The "Treaty of Peace and Friendship made at Ruby Valley, in the Territory of Nevada," as the agreement began, was signed on October 1 in the name of ending the violence. Both sides agreed "that hostilities and all depredations upon the emigrant trains, the mail and telegraph lines, and upon the citizens of the United States within their country, shall cease." The tribes guaranteed that several routes through Shoshone country used by emigrants, the army, and others were to remain open and unobstructed and "without molestation or injury" from the Indians. The treaty also cleared the way for the construction and maintenance of military posts and station houses of the kind used by the Pony Express and overland stage lines. Telegraph lines and the coming railroad system were included as well.

Article 4 of the treaty would reverberate with meaning for decades to come. It gave blanket approval to prospecting and mining gold, silver, and other minerals throughout Shoshone country, approved the establishment of farms and ranches, and allowed the cutting and milling of timber whenever necessary for mining or building.

The treaty defined the Shoshones' territory and went further to constrict their movement and compel them to "become herdsmen or agriculturalists" on an authorized reservation at a time to be determined by the president of the United States, "and they do also hereby agree to remove their camps to such reservations as he may indicate, and to reside and remain therein."

The agreement wasn't entirely bereft of consideration for the sacrifices the Shoshone were making in the name of peace. The treaty duly noted that the United States was "aware of the inconvenience resulting to the Indians in consequence of the driving away and destruction of game along the routes traveled by white men and around the new developments being built."

So what did the Shoshone receive for agreeing to become peaceful and compliant subjects? The equivalent of $5,000 worth of "articles, including cattle for herding or other purposes," for a period of twenty years. By signing the treaty, they agreed that the annuity would constitute "full compensation" for the loss of game, their rights, and other privileges they may have enjoyed. And the government kept its promise of compensation—for one year.

The treaty not only redefined the Western Shoshones' expansive territory but allowed miners to develop the region's silver and gold deposits without further compensation, in keeping with other sleight-of-hand agreements between the US and Native Americans. And the deal changed over time. As Nevada grew following statehood and the discovery of gold and silver, there was pressure to what was euphemistically termed "revisit the terms of the agreement." A century later, the Shoshone and the federal government would still be arguing over the issue of tribal sovereignty. Thanks to congressional action a long way from the windy deserts and mountains of Northern Nevada, the official shape of Shoshone country shifted right beneath the Shoshones' feet.

It was into this tribal, ranching, and political tradition that sisters Mary and Carrie Dann were born. In addition to running hundreds of head of horses and cattle, the Danns battled the federal government over control of their grazing land for half a century, with the definition of Shoshone sovereignty often hanging in the balance. In time, they would be honored as respected elders and spiritual leaders among their people. They defined tireless activism against unfathomable odds: when the decision was made to donate the archive of their legal struggle to the University of Nevada, Reno (UNR), after Mary's death in 2005, the Dann collection filled 120 boxes.

Long before achieving a kind of national celebrity status, the Danns were young Indian girls playing under a poplar tree on the family's Crescent Valley Ranch in sparsely populated Eureka County. Carrie Dann recalled her grandfather, who had been their age when the Treaty of Ruby Valley was signed, telling her, "This land is yours. When you learn to read and write and to move in the white man's world, there is a paper held by a white judge and there is a book with writing in red that tells that the land is yours to do with as you will." The book, Mary Dann recalled, was last seen around the time Dewey Dann homesteaded the ranch. That long-lost book, which explained the Shoshones' intentions when they signed the treaty, was sometimes alluded to when the Danns argued that the slender agreement signed by illiterate Indian leaders was never intended to give up the rights to millions of acres of Shoshone land.

The sisters' father, Dewey Dann, was no activist. He had raised cattle on the family's ranch since homesteading 160 acres in the 1920s. Years later, the ranch was described as an 800-acre spread, which still amounted to a small piece of one of the largest and least-populated places in the contiguous United States. He may have taken notice of the passage of the Indian Reorganization Act in June 1934, or the "Indian New Deal" as it was popularly known, with its goals of halting forced assimilation and encouraging tribal histories and traditions, but the Taylor Grazing Act passed that year was of far more immediate importance in his life. Although he protested payment, Dewey Dann followed the new rules when notified of the requirement of small fees per animal for the responsible use of federal public lands that had long been roamed by the Shoshone. Carrie Dann said her father followed the rules out of ignorance "of what these white man laws meant. He felt he had to or he would be run off the land."

But he did pay, if only in an effort to keep the peace. Other members of the tribe also went along with changing times. In the 1930s, some were included in training programs for road crews. When federal dollars trickled into the Public Works Administration during the Great Depression to fund small hospitals on Indian land, the Shoshone were among the tribes included.

The Shoshone faced poverty and prejudice, but they were motivated to organize and exercise their sovereignty and civil rights, as evidenced by a meeting of tribal elders that took place in Elko in 1937. Representing the Shoshone from Washington State was one of their own, a tribal member named George LaVatta, who had been educated at Fort Hall. The gathering was held, they said, "in order to establish a tribal organization for ourselves and for the other groups and members of the Temoak bands of Western Shoshone Indians in northwestern Nevada, to conserve our tribal property, to develop our resources, to administer justice and to promote the welfare of ourselves and our descendants." With a constitution and by-laws, they hoped their desires would be understood and articulated in the white world.

By the end of World War II, the inequity of taking of so much from the Shoshone for so little in return wasn't in doubt in Washington. An Indian Claims Commission was created under the direction of President Harry S. Truman, and lengthy hearings were held to consider approximately six hundred cases. The claims of the Western Shoshone were among the more egregious on a list of tragedy and inequity that gave new meaning to a "trail of tears."

What confounded Congress was the challenge of determining what doing the right thing by the Indians was worth. As it turned out, not very much.

The figure reached by the commission made for an impressive headline: approximately $1.5 billion, all told. But that meant an average check of under $1,000 to tribal members. While it beat blankets and farm implements, it wasn't likely to change many lives. With the exception of a few success stories, most notably the efforts of the Apache to pool their resources and invest their slice of the pie in tribal-owned cattle ranches, logging companies, and even a ski resort, the small money was spent quickly.

Although they lived hand-to-mouth on reservations, the Shoshone and other tribes were often faulted for their supposed lost pride and spendthrift ways.

During the Cold War of the 1950s, a time of American trepidation over the suspected rise of Communism and socialism on domestic soil, the plight of the Shoshone and other native tribes was sometimes used to illustrate the point that Indian sovereignty and reparations were little more than socialist Petri dishes. Western Shoshone Mission Reverend R.J. Rushdoony of Owhyee, Nevada, fed green wood into the political fire, proclaiming in a widely circulated missive,

> One of the surest consequences of a government of "welfare" and "security" is the rapid decline and death of responsibility and character. Whatever the pre-reservation Indian was, and his faults were real, he was able to take care of himself and had a character becoming to his culture and religion. He was a responsible person. Today he is far from that. The wretched security he has had, beginning with the food and clothing dole of early years, designed to enforce the reservation system and destroy Indian resistance, has sapped him of his character. Too often they impede the man of character.

Only the Sioux nations could match the Shoshone when it came to spurning the government's largesse to cover past grievances and close the books. In the new century, more than half a billion dollars in claims money lay untouched by Sioux tribal members who, despite their very real needs, still saw the government through the lens of the massacre of three hundred men, women, and children in 1890 at Wounded Knee, South Dakota, on the Lakota Pine Ridge Indian Reservation. Activists and followers of the American Indian Movement raised the grievances of the Sioux on behalf of a new generation with the occupation of the Wounded Knee Massacre site for seventy-one days in early 1973.

The Shoshone kept fighting for their land rights long after they agreed to set aside their weapons. Although its designers had only intended the Indian Claims Commission to exist for a decade, after ten years much work was left undone and another decade was added. Although the Western Shoshone filed their grievance in the early 1950s, it wasn't until 1959 that the final testimony of witnesses, historians, and anthropologists was heard. Among the experts to testify were anthropologists Omar C. Stewart and Edward Adamson. The journal entries and remembrances of trappers and writers from the 1800s were taken into account by the commission, which relied heavily on the prolific research and writing of Western Shoshone chronicler Julian Steward.

In November 1962, approaching a century after the signing of the Treaty at Ruby Valley, the Claims Commission announced its decision that the Shoshone had indeed lost their land and deserved compensation for it. But there was a catch: the land would be appraised at the price it was worth at the time they lost it. They would get approximately $26 million for the loss of millions of acres of territory.

The Indian Claims Commission Act created a government forum to hear land claims brought by Native American tribes. The commission's stated intention was to finally resolve land-confiscation issues that in some cases had festered for nearly a century. The commission was also given the power to decide the land claims brought against the United States and, when deemed appropriate, to provide a final payoff to the Indians. The act also made clear that "payment of any claim…shall be a full discharge of the United States of all claims and demands touching any of the matters involved in the controversy."

Into that field of legal fire walked the Te-Moak Band of Western Shoshone, who sued for the return of a massive swath of Indian land. The commission heard evidence and concluded that the Shoshone claim of title was extinguished "by gradual encroachment by whites, settlers and others, and the acquisition, disposition or taking of their lands by the United States." The commission valued the land lost at $26 million and ordered that amount issued to the tribe.

After the award was confirmed by the Court of Claims and certified by the General Accounting Office, it was deposited for the tribe in an interest-bearing account in the U.S. Treasury, with the intention of having the Department of the Interior process the distribution to Shoshone members.

The tribe had other ideas. It rejected the commission's decision and refused to accept the payment. And when government agents alleged that the Dann sisters' and other ranchers' grazing livestock were trespassing without a permit, the Shoshone countered that they were the land's true owners—and went on the offensive. The Dann sisters sued in U.S. District Court to halt the confiscation of their livestock and their own eviction from land their family had worked for three generations. The Danns argued with logic, if not legal standing, that they hadn't accepted any payment for their land, and because it was still their land, they didn't owe the government any Taylor Grazing fees.

With the passing years, the plight of the Shoshone gradually transformed from occasional media curiosity to cause célèbre and caught the attention of actor Robert Redford, a supporter of the movement to secure American Indian rights and an environmental activist. Redford used his considerable celebrity to bring attention to the cause. His friend, filmmaker Joel L. Freedman, produced three documentaries on the Danns' struggle over a three-decade period, including the Redford-narrated *Broken Treaty at Battle Mountain* in 1975, at a time of heightened awareness of the challenges the

Indians faced. The sisters were featured in an endless number of newspapers, magazines, academic studies, and political polemics.

About the time President Jimmy Carter was ending his term in office, the Department of the Interior carved out what was believed to be a final payment to the Shoshone in exchange for their land: $26.1 million. This came out to as little as fifteen cents per acre for land that had long been in multiple use for mineral extraction and cattle- and sheep-grazing.

Although the court of public opinion was in their favor, the court of standing was not as sympathetic to the Danns. When they sued in U.S. District Court to halt the government's actions against them, they were rebuffed by a determination that their so-called aboriginal title had been extinguished by the Claims Commission and the $26-million payment.

Undaunted, they pressed on to the U.S. Ninth Circuit Court of Appeals. There, they found fleeting hope in the court's reversal and opinion that actual payment, growing steadily thanks to accruing interest, hadn't occurred because the tribe had refused to accept it.

Along the way, the Danns picked up another powerful media ally in Washington investigative columnist Jack Anderson, whose ability to illuminate issues and intimidate public actors was well established. In an April 1984 column that ran in hundreds of newspapers, Anderson ripped into the government for its treatment of the Western Shoshone and the Dann sisters. The Mormon columnist argued with irony, "If the government wins, the Danns will be transformed into trespassers on their own ancestral land, and will have to turn to the government for help."

Dann attorney Thomas Luebben, who clearly had the columnist's ear, observed, "The Justice Department is trying to make them into dependent Indians."

Legally speaking, it was a slender reed the Western Shoshone grasped as thirty-five tribal elders traveled to Washington, some spending as much as five days on buses, to listen in person to a legal argument that would determine their future. On November 5, 1984, *U.S. v. Dann* was argued before the U.S. Supreme Court with Assistant Attorney General Robert McConnell speaking on behalf of the government and John D. O'Connell representing the sisters.

Some of the Shoshone had come expecting a legal and historical showdown, but they were disappointed. Over the course of one hour, they listened to a spirited debate, not about the rights of their cheated ancestors but about the technical truths of aboriginal titles and grazing laws. The tribal elders went away shaking their heads.

O'Connell argued in part, "The Danns shouldn't need a permit on their own property. The payment has not been made.... The Danns were born on this land and have used these lands for three generations. Now the government seeks to eject them from their property." The Indians hadn't signed up for government grazing permits for a simple reason, he argued—they already owned the land.

Not so, McConnell countered. There was an account with the tribe's name on it containing $26 million, plus interest.

"This has been litigated, the money has been paid, and that forecloses any individual claims," McConnell told the justices, adding that the only step remaining was for Congress to authorize a plan to distribute the money.

The justices weren't moved by the Shoshones' arguments. "Aren't we spinning our wheels?" Justice Harry Blackmun chided, and Justice William Rehnquist asked why the case hadn't been dismissed at the lower-court level.

Outside the nation's highest court, Carrie Dann continued the argument. "If you sell your property," she said, "the other person doesn't own it until he has paid for it." But by then, only news reporters were listening.

On February 20, 1985, the U.S. Supreme Court unanimously reversed the appeals court and remanded the case, writing in part, "To construe the word 'payment,' as the Court of Appeals did gives the word a markedly different meaning than it has under the general common law rule.... Once the money was deposited into the trust account, payment was effected."

Calling on the strength of their spirit elders and allies, the Danns persisted. At the time of the high court's decision, it was believed that as much as 80 percent of the tribe was willing to leave the pay-out untouched. Tribal attorney Michael Lieder would observe, "You can't just snap your fingers and resurrect an entire culture. We have been fighting that issue, and we will keep on fighting it."

Led by the Dann sisters and other activists in Nevada and as far away as Washington, DC, the tribe assembled the Western Shoshone Tribal Coalition and Western Shoshone Defense Project to do legal and rhetorical battle with the federal government. The impressive effort had mixed results and suffered a jarring setback in 1998, when the BLM issued trespass notices, ordered the removal of hundreds of head of cattle and horses, and fined the sisters and the tribe some $3 million. Nevada Senator Harry Reid attempted to intervene on their behalf and to arrange a distribution of $20,000 to each tribal member, but even that proposal failed to come to fruition.

But as time passed, that fierce resolve began to weaken. By the turn of the new century, many of the Western Shoshone who believed in the cause of the Dann sisters had tired of the endless battle with the government. Others, some of them economically disadvantaged, were simply interested in finally enjoying some of the settlement money that had been accruing interest for so long. Even a little would go a long way in careworn Crescent Valley.

Weathered by time and the challenges of living in an arid and wind-swept land, where temperatures were commonly below freezing in winter and occasionally topped a hundred degrees in summer, the Danns were often described as rough and wrinkled. They were "hidebound ranchers who live without electricity, hot water or furnace." At a time their city counterparts might have been long retired, Mary and younger sister Carrie still cooked with a wood stove, ran their livestock, broke horses, and mended their own fences, while keeping the metaphorical fences broken with the government with whom they battled.

Less dramatic, and far less likely to garner much media sympathy, was the BLM's position. The highest court in the land had ruled that the Danns' land was part of the BLM's jurisdiction and therefore under the Taylor Grazing Act of 1934. The Danns' compelling struggle and quotable style aside, they were increasingly perceived in the mainstream press as recalcitrant ranchers who refused to cooperate with the BLM and make even the pretense of following the law.

Exasperated BLM officials, who said they had tried to work with the Danns and local interests in every possible fashion over a number of years to resolve their unauthorized use of public lands, moved forward with a last-resort plan they knew would be unpopular with many rural Nevadans: the roundup of hundreds of the sisters' trespassing cattle. Helen Hankins, a frustrated BLM Elko office manager, said the gather came after nearly thirty years of patience and legal arguments and only after the Danns' overgrazing cattle had caused "severe degradation of the public range lands," and restoration of the pummeled allotment area would take "years and likely millions of dollars."

Although it wasn't often a hot topic of discussion in the press, the Nevada BLM office issued nearly seven hundred grazing permits to ranchers throughout the state, with what state director Bob Abbey estimated was a 99-percent compliance rate. "They pay their fees and they're good stewards of the public lands," career civil servant Abbey said. It was the Dann sisters and a few others, he said, who garnered most of the attention.

Part of the challenge for the press came in separating the rough-hewn imagery of the American cowboy from the federal bureaucracy's mundane rules. Ranchers were often more than happy to use their iconic occupations amid scenic settings to best effect in the media, and it was clear that BLM rangers in their bland uniforms would be hard-pressed to compete in the public-relations roundup.

Although the government repeatedly pointed to a "99-percent" compliance rate by ranchers, the Danns weren't the only members of the Western Shoshone who ran into trouble with the BLM over stray cattle. Rancher Raymond Yowell, a Western Shoshone leader and a member of the Te-Moak Band south of Elko, failed to comply with grazing regulations and saw more than 150 of his cattle rounded up and sold by the government at auction for approximately $27,000. Unlike the Danns, who welcomed the curious media and placard-waving protesters, Yowell didn't appear excited to see activist groups come to his aid. Only thirty or so protesters turned out at the cattle gather in Palomino Valley. The American Indian Movement failed to attract much tribal interest from neighboring states, and Yowell also ignored the Nevada Committee for Full Statehood, which didn't believe in federal land ownership. The Committee's leader reflected, "At some point you have to let the owner do what he wants, and he didn't call us or ask us."

It would be understandable if the longtime Te-Moak leader was exhausted by the endless conflict of the Danns and others with the BLM. It was Yowell a decade earlier who had suggested that the sisters and tribe "have a meeting on the land. It is not the way we choose to go. Who would? But it may be the only way we have left."

They didn't listen.

By September 2002, the Danns were reminded of that fact when forty armed BLM agents and rangers converged on their ranch and collected 232 head of cattle, which were later sold at auction to offset a fraction of what the government claimed the sisters owed—$50,000 in unpaid grazing fees and penalties, and $3 million in fines for willful trespass. As one *New York Times* reporter put it, "Depending on who is asked, the Danns are either modern-day Geronimos, common rabble-rousers or scofflaws." Others came to view them as "intransigent old-timers pursuing a quest so far-fetched it amounts to folly."

While the Danns and some of their followers remained steadfast, members of their own tribe were no longer up for a fight that stretched back more than 130 years. Even their ancestors would have tired by now.

It was also true that despite their status as quotable and weatherworn darlings of the press, the Danns had long since been outflanked in the US federal courts and the halls of Congress. And the $26-million award with interest had grown to $130 million. This meant that Western Shoshone of at least one-quarter blood would receive more than $20,000 each—real money for people often living on the brink of poverty. Some saw it as little more than a bribe in exchange for land worth billions to big gold-mining corporations. Duckwater Shoshone tribal official and longtime activist Ian Zabarte called the effort to pass legislation that would begin the distribution process "a money-waving campaign. It feeds the perception that justice is being served and that the Indians have been paid. In fact, justice has not been done."

But the Nevada delegation, led by Nevada Senators Reid and John Ensign and Congressmen Jim Gibbons and Jon Porter, had wisely developed its own allies on the ground in Indian Country through the Western Shoshone Steering Committee, which participated in helping to craft the bill. Its members also provided a positive spin on a contentious issue that had some critics accusing the elected officials of throwing money to bury a historically complex and racially shaded issue. "We need it [the money] very badly," steering committee member Larry Piffero pleaded. He would emerge as a vocal ally of Reid's effort to resolve the dispute once and for all.

In another comment, Piffero sounded like a member of the Nevada congressional delegation's press office:

> The majority of the Western Shoshone people are grateful to our Nevada congressional delegation.... Without their help the voice of the silent majority of Western Shoshones would never be heard in Congress.... The Western Shoshone Claims Distribution Act is a bill that belongs to the majority of the Western Shoshone people. Our Nevada congressional delegation did only what the Shoshone people asked them to do and nothing else.

Reid's stated purpose was unambiguous. The tribe had argued its case to the highest court in the land and lost. A straw poll in 2000 showed that by a wide margin—1,230 to 53—those Western Shoshone surveyed supported receiving the payment. "To come back now and say it's not fair doesn't really ring true to me," Reid said after learning of yet another challenge by the Danns and their allies. "Everything was covered. This is all sour grapes. I'm used to close elections and that's not even close."

Two more polls would produce similar results: a majority of tribal members understood the historical argument but wanted the money. Undeterred, the Danns and tribal leaders Corbin Harney and Kevin and Marie Brady pursued relief, at least in a spiritual sense, from the United Nations Working Group on Indigenous Populations. The Ely and Yomba tribes complained to the UN's Committee on the Elimination of Racial Discrimination, in addition to a previous objection to the Inter-American Commission on Human Rights.

Appeals to the United Nations, including another complaint filed in 2006, would yield sympathy, righteous indignation, and great umbrage in the tribal interest, but not an ounce of legal authority. But as the years passed, the arguments made less and less practical sense in a changing state. And by 2006 the funds with interest were reported to have risen to more than $145 million. One exasperated Reid spokesman offered, "The tribe twice has voted decisively in favor of the distribution. The senator will continue to work with the interior department to assure a fair and expeditious distribution under the law."

With the law on its side, its patience exhausted, and the Danns' refusal to pay nominal grazing fees growing into a debt they'd never be able to pay even if they were willing, the BLM began a series of roundups of the sisters' horses and cattle. Each confiscation had the feel of a military tactical exercise with armed rangers in uniform, a swift-moving strategy, and helicopters knifing through the desert air above Crescent Valley.

Even those gatherings made with little notice managed to draw dozens of protesters. Some were fueled by the public release of a confidential report by the Inter-American Commission on Human Rights that accused the US government of historical violations of international human-rights laws in its treatment of the Dann sisters—namely, for failing to respect their ancestral property rights. But a report wasn't going to halt any roundup, or stop the wheels from turning in Washington in the effort to begin distributing the government's payment to the tribe.

As the BLM's spring 2003 horse roundup began at dawn, one particularly passionate chronicler observed that it was foaling season, and some mares gave birth prematurely. By the end of the day, hundreds of horses were taken and auctioned to a local rancher.

Another fifty animals had starved to death and were disposed of without ceremony. "Indians love horses," Carrie Dann told an interviewer, laying partial blame for her sister's faltering health at the government's feet.

The Danns found an ally in Buellton, California, rancher Slick Gardner, who volunteered to herd hundreds of the sisters' horses to his bucolic 60,000 spread in the Santa Ynez Valley northwest of Santa Barbara. The Danns signed over ownership of their animals, confounding the authorities in the process. They had already lost 227 head of cattle to government confiscation.

By now, only the Danns' closest followers repeated their mantra that the BLM was trespassing on Western Shoshone land. "I believe government officials lied to our people," former tribal chairman Felix Ike charged, but there was little to be done "After the Supreme Court ruled against the Danns, what hope was there?... They took the land away from us. It was over." Ike helped to organize a vote of tribal members, a strong majority of whom supported taking money that could be used for needed things.

"Our tribe has decided we want our money. It's time. We're never going to get the land. Let's get what we can for our older folks," Diana Buckner, Ely tribal chairwoman, said in 2004. There was much more at stake that a few hundred cows and horses—a 100,000-acre land sale by the BLM to Canadian gold-mining company Placer Dome Inc., a plan made public in 2004 in legislation sponsored by Congressman Jim Gibbons. At the time, the amount of gold believed to be contained on the land at Mount Tenobo was believed to be worth billions.

Mary Dann died in April 2005 after an ATV accident on her family ranch in Crescent Valley. In her early eighties (she never publicly revealed her precise age), she had been repairing ranch fence at the time of the accident. As her niece Patricia Paul would reflect, her Aunt Mary died "with her boots on and hay in her pocket." To her supporters, she was a timeless part of Shoshone history. To others, even some within the tribe, the Danns' recalcitrance in paying their nominal federal grazing fees made them adversaries because they allowed their legal battle and the fallout from the mass of publicity they received to interfere with the distribution of millions of dollars from a government settlement of the land claims.

For her part, Carrie Dann carried on alone, in part because it was a cause that defined her life. And it was what her big sister would want her to do.

"This was Mary's life's work," she said. To another interviewer she would add, "The earth is our mother and we can't give up on our mother. No way in hell."

Two years after Mary Dann's death, the Shoshone continued to plead their case and use the land issue as a means of legally challenging a plan by the Department of Energy to develop a massive nuclear-waste repository at Yucca Mountain, approximately ninety miles north of Las Vegas and on their ancestral territory. It gave reporters an opportunity to recount the Danns' tale, with Western Shoshone leader Allen Moss uttering a familiar phrase: "Our land is not for sale.... The whole things boils down to, 'How many times can you break the law or twist the law in your favor?' That's what the government has done."

As of spring 2019, Carrie Dann continued to live on her family's ranch in Crescent Valley with the spirit of her big sister. To those who would stop to listen, she called the government's actions over three decades "mind terrorism," asserting, "We've lived under constant threat of being rounded up, almost thirty years. I want us to be free. All I ask of the United States is the opportunity to sit across the table and talk.... Is it in the Constitution? Is it an amendment to the Constitution? Is it an act of Congress? Gradual encroachment is not a law of the United States as far as I know. I certainly don't want people saying, 'I gradually encroached on you, and took your rights away.' Either I am a human being, or I am not a human being."

But by then she was talking to the wind. However, her words about observing a strict adherence to the Constitution echoed those from years earlier outside Bunkerville. The difference between the tribe's aboriginal-rights argument and the ranchers' constitutional case would often be conflated as time passed, but both had something in common: federal courts, with few and fleeting exceptions, ruled against them. They might win a round, but even during the vaunted Sagebrush Rebellion era the results were essentially the same: federal public lands were available to all, but to some more than others. And those others were inevitably large mining corporations and developers with the political clout to force rural water out of the ground and into developing urban areas, no matter how steep the grade.

CHAPTER 4

Saddle Born

A few months before Ronald Reagan scored a landslide victory in the 1980 presidential race, he made a campaign stop in Salt Lake City and addressed a group of Republican supporters. At the time, legislatures across the West had either passed or were entertaining laws calling for the transfer of millions of acres of public lands from federal to state control as part of the Sagebrush Rebellion.

"I happen to be one who cheers and supports the sagebrush rebellion," Reagan said. "Count me in as a rebel."

Although wildly applauded for his support, in reality Reagan was many years late to the fight. Ranching, mining, and timber interests, long reliant on cheap federal land for grazing, hard-rock extraction, and logging, had howled for decades about what they called overregulation by the federal government and especially the Department of the Interior. Even a cursory glance at the history of the development of the West shows they've had little to complain about.

It's no wonder that Interior has been called "the Department of Everything Else." Since its inception on the last day of the Thirtieth Congress in 1849, it has been tasked with the nation's "internal affairs." From the construction of the Washington, DC, water system and the operation of its jail, to the management of public lands, patents, parks, universities, Indian tribes, and territories in the ever-expanding West, Interior's original mission was almost as vast as the country itself. "In one way or another," its official website enthuses, "all of these had to do with the internal development of the Nation or the welfare of its people." In the early decades of its existence, the Department of the Interior played what was considered a custodial and even passive role. That would change as the West's untold riches were better understood.

From the beginning, Interior served as facilitator and gatekeeper, its history a blend of commerce, conservation, and occasional corruption. Following the Mexican-American War, it established the international boundary with Mexico, a nation neutralized and no longer a threat to the flood of gold-seekers pouring into California and pre-statehood Nevada. With the help of John C. Frémont's maps, Interior improved emigrant trails. When Yellowstone National Park was created in 1872—the same year the passage of the General Mining Act made gold-prospecting a free-for-all for everyone but the Native American tribes—Interior was in charge of its management.

Thanks to allies in Congress, railroad barons received 150 million acres in the name of the transcontinental track. Mining magnates extracted vast fortunes in gold and silver in the West, coal and iron for steel in the East, and built castles from San Francisco to London without paying a royalty to the government. The tycoons were wealthy beyond most imaginations, rising in no small part through greed, corruption, a lack of government regulation, and workforce exploitation. They leased Congress, spun their own myths with the help of a lapdog press, and defined what Mark Twain coined "the Gilded Age." Although at times he'd fallen under the spell of the affliction himself, Twain saw the danger of the idolization of wealth to a nation controlled by the limitless greed of the ruling class. In an 1869 letter to Cornelius Vanderbilt, he wrote, "You seem to be the idol of only a crawling swarm of small souls, who love to glorify your most flagrant unworthiness in print or praise your vast possessions worshippingly; or sing of your unimportant private habits and sayings and doings, as if your millions gave them dignity." There's no record of whether Vanderbilt lost a single hour of sleep over Twain's rebuke.

The damage wrought by the rapid expansion of the nation didn't go unnoticed. Clear-cutting in old-growth forests and overgrazing from the Great Plains to California led President Theodore

Roosevelt to emphasize orderly conservation with the creation in 1902 of the Bureau of Reclamation, which established a federal system of dams and aqueducts in the West. When President Woodrow Wilson established the National Park Service in 1916, Interior's mission grew once more.

Interior's history has been marked by landmark protections of federal public lands but also marred by corruption. During the Warren G. Harding administration, a bribery scandal called Teapot Dome became a euphemism for scandal. Teapot Dome was significant because of the integral role that Interior Secretary Albert Fall played in issuing bid-free oil leases on public lands worth billions at the Elk Hills field in Kern County, California, and at Teapot Dome, Wyoming. Fall eventually became the first presidential cabinet member in the nation's history to go to prison, convicted of soliciting bribes and receiving more than $400,000 in cash and gifts. Although oil baron Harry Sinclair was found guilty of jury-tampering, neither he nor Edward Doheny was convicted of bribery. Both kept their legal leases and, beyond becoming characters in Upton Sinclair's novel *Oil!*, barely skipped a beat on the way to building Sinclair Oil and the Pan American Petroleum and Transport Company into multibillion-dollar enterprises. Ensuing decades would have their share of rapacious behavior under Interior's watch, with private interests seeking everything from the diversion of precious water resources, to the exploitation of oil, gas, and coal extraction on Native American lands, to lucrative contracts for politically favored builders.

But contrast Fall's shamelessness with Harold LeClair Ickes's remarkable thirteen-year tenure as Secretary of the Interior, and you'll discover one of the better angels of the federal government's nature. Ickes served throughout President Franklin Delano Roosevelt's New Deal administration from 1933 to 1946. He simultaneously headed Interior and the Public Works Administration. The progressive former Republican, known to allies as "Honest Harold" and to enemies as the spoiler of many an inside deal, mixed his dedication to helping FDR repair an ailing country by putting it back to work with a devotion to environmentalism seldom before seen. Although some of the power plants approved by Ickes would prove problematic, he was also largely responsible for implementing the Taylor Grazing Act of 1934, battling the political corruption associated with the Hetch Hetchy Dam located inside Yosemite National Park, promoting soil and water conservation in some areas of the arid West, and ramming through the Pacific Remote Islands Marine National Monument and the Kings Canyon National Park.

In keeping with the great pendulum swing of American political history, many of Ickes's attempts to compel conservation and set controls on unrestricted development that resulted in harm to the environment, indigenous peoples, and the nation's cultural and natural heritage almost immediately began to erode after FDR's death. First under Democratic President Harry S. Truman and then under Republican President Dwight Eisenhower, use of federal public lands was steadily fed to private interests.

The pendulum swung again following the election of John F. Kennedy. In September 1963, just weeks before his assassination, Kennedy embarked on a five-day cross-country swing to raise the issue of conservation. He started in Pennsylvania, where he dedicated the home of conservationist and former chief of the U.S. Division of Forestry Gifford Pinchot. The president's whirlwind tour ended on September 28 at the Las Vegas Convention Center, before a capacity crowd inside the rotunda. With Governor Grant Sawyer, U.S. Senators Alan Bible and Howard Cannon, and Department of the Interior Secretary Stewart Udall in the audience, Kennedy offered a prescient reminder of the importance of protecting the country's natural resources from exploitation while balancing the interests of environment and industry. Taking the trip, he said, enabled him to better understand the essential necessity of conserving natural resources and using them wisely. Getting out from behind his desk and seeing the West's water issues for himself transcended statistics.

Crisis-tested in his third year in office, Kennedy touched on maintaining a strong defense while simultaneously seeking peace where it was possible, and he called the education and care of the nation's children a top "conservation" priority. Second, he said, we should resolve "to use what nature's given us, and wherever we can to improve it. There is no state in the Union where these two twin concepts of conservation, to conserve and to develop, can be more clearly seen than here in the state of Nevada."

The swing back toward greater conservation and the vigorous renewed embrace of environmentalism was illustrated by the passage of the Wilderness Act of 1964 under the administration of President Lyndon Johnson and Stewart Udall's leadership at Interior. The act itself was the result of nine years of effort that included sixty-five rewrites and eighteen public hearings. The legislation created a legal definition of wilderness and protected more than nine million acres of federal public land from development under the National Wilderness Preservation System. Drafted by Wilderness Society executive Howard Zahniser, the act represented a public declaration of the interdependence of humankind and nature. Far beyond the millions of acres set aside for future generations, the act amounted to an audacious declaration that there was something that even the farthest reaches of crony capitalism in the name of "Manifest Destiny" couldn't despoil.

"A wilderness, in contrast with those areas where man and his own works dominate the landscape, is hereby recognized as an area where the earth and its community of life are untrammeled by man, where man himself is a visitor who does not remain," Zahniser wrote. Like Aldo Leopold, Arthur Carhart, and Bob Marshall, all of whom toiled for the U.S. Forest Service, Zahniser also worked for many years as a federal employee with the Fish and Wildlife Service, and later with the Department of Agriculture.

In his speech "The Need for Wilderness Areas," Zahniser observed that "The idea of wilderness as an area without man's influence is man's own concept. Its values are human values. Its preservation is a purpose that arises out of man's own sense of his fundamental needs."

The rise of the modern environmental movement, and its successful use of the courts and Congress, only increased the anxiety of ranchers and miners. Following the passage of the Wilderness Act, a flurry of environmental legislation served as a sore reminder that use of federal public lands didn't constitute a transfer of ownership.

Although Ronald Reagan superficially appeared to take up the mantle of the West's ranchers, miners, and loggers, he could already count on their votes. But his cowboy image clearly appealed to him. Fond of riding a trusty Arabian around his 688-acre Rancho del Cielo in the Santa Ynez mountains twenty-five miles northwest of Santa Barbara—even when the cameras weren't capturing his tall-in-the-saddle image—Reagan could tell his political allies in the West that the Sagebrush Rebellion agenda had almost made it into the platform at the 1980 Republican National Convention in Detroit. He would be less inclined to add that it had been his own campaign chairman Paul Laxalt, the U.S. senator from Nevada, who had downplayed the states'-rights agenda for fear it would cost Reagan important votes in the East. Laxalt's name was later placed on the short list of potential Interior secretaries in an era that was defined by Reagan's eventual choice, the brusque James Watt.

In the end, it wouldn't matter much. Reagan won a staggering 489 electoral votes and every state in the contiguous West. Although there was talk in the press that the sagebrush rebel-in-chief might name Laxalt as Secretary of the Interior, it never happened. In fact, a lot of what states'-rights activists and ranchers envisioned might occur in their interest under a Reagan presidency never really materialized.

But Reagan's rhetorical embrace of western ranchers had two effects. It helped craft the actor's reputation as a bootstrap libertarian, and it further painted the beleaguered BLM as a meddling federal interloper out to hamstring and even put out of business America's icons on horseback.

The BLM was created in 1946 when Interior merged the venerable General Land Office (started by President James Madison in 1812) and the Grazing Service (as in Taylor) in an effort to dispose of some public lands while simultaneously keeping watch over vast federally designated expanses used by western cattlemen and increasingly powerful mining concerns.

The BLM's relationship with stakeholders was mixed from the outset. Whether berated as the "Bureau of Livestock and Mines" or the "Bureau of Land Mismanagement," it was charged with enforcing rules over ranchers and hard-rock mining outfits that traditionally hadn't had many—and didn't appreciate being told what to do.

Nevada's own history with the BLM was fated to be complicated. It begins long before statehood or the agency's creation with the signing by the United States and New Mexico of the Treaty of Guadalupe Hidalgo, which marked the end of the Mexican-American War. The treaty transferred all land previously under control of Mexico to the United States, including the land that on October 31, 1864, would become Nevada. As a condition of statehood, Nevada ceded all rights to its vast ranges and deserts to the federal government.

The Nevada constitution makes clear that the state won't claim any undesignated public land. That meant most of the state was technically "in the public estate" and managed by the federal government through the General Land Office, which parceled out 160-acre slices under the Homestead Act. For the most part, Nevada was wide-open rent-free country for cattle-grazing, sheepherding, and mining following the discovery of gold and silver in the late 1850s. The General Mining Act of 1872 set the foundation of federal oversight, such as it was, of hard-rock mineral extraction.

In time, cattle ranchers and sheepherders found that grazing in arid country prone to drought was more difficult than it looked. Large swaths of overgrazed desert and mountainsides led to soil erosion and the eventual need for the Taylor Grazing Act of 1934 and increased oversight, starting in 1936 with the federal Grazing Service.

At first managed from San Francisco, Nevada's BLM contingent moved to Reno in 1950 with Edmund "Tiny" Greenslet eventually in charge until his retirement in 1958. The cigar-smoking Greenslet was a BLM legend who began his career in government service in 1918 with the U.S. Geological Survey, eventually becoming one of seven persons to transfer to the newly created Grazing Service. An expert in arid-land soil management, his advice was sought in nearly every state west of the Missouri River.

In Nevada, he led an office that managed 57 million acres of Taylor Grazing land and another 3 million acres under lease. During the New Deal era, he supervised one hundred Civilian Conservation

Corps camps while simultaneously serving as grazing expert in Nevada, California, New Mexico, and Wyoming. In time, he would become noted for his ability to bring together ranching and wildlife interests for a common purpose of respectful use and conservation of public lands.

Greenslet also set a template in Nevada as a wielder of outsized power on the behalf of the BLM and sometimes to the benefit of private interest. He battled the U.S. Navy's attempt to carve out 3 million acres for military use, eventually reducing its request to 700,000 acres. He later helped negotiate the Curtiss-Wright land swap in the early 1950s, which eventually gave the New Jersey–based aircraft manufacturer the space it required for a planned rocket-engine testing area. At one time, the New Jersey–based company owned nearly three hundred square miles and a fortune in water rights in western Nevada near Reno. In a state with the vast majority of its land owned by the federal government, the Curtiss-Wright swap put diminutive Storey County almost entirely in private hands.

Future BLM directors would be pressured on multiple fronts, from traditional sources, such as mining and ranching, and increasingly by politically active wildlife conservationists and progressive environmentalists. In some ways, the agency's frustration would be defined by its attempt to manage Nevada's largest-in-the-nation wild horse and burro population. The tireless publicity efforts over two decades by self-styled mustang-defender Velma "Wild Horse Annie" Johnston helped lead to the creation of the Wild Free-Roaming Horses and Burros Act of 1971. The campaign made her the enemy of so-called mustangers—depicted in John Huston's 1960 film, *The Misfits*—who rounded up wild horses for resale, often to slaughterhouses. Johnston became a hero to the animals' advocates—and created an unending headache for the BLM as it searched for ways to manage ever-expanding herds.

Increased use and a burgeoning interest in wildlife, hunting, and fishing led to new challenges for the BLM and other federal agencies. In 1964, the same year that saw passage of the Wilderness Act, the Public Land Law Review Commission convened, with an emphasis on considering the effectiveness of prevailing-use policies in a changing society. When the commission disbanded in 1970, it concluded the obvious: that increasingly stressed federal lands were inadequately managed and suffered from a lack of regulatory enforcement. The commissioners recommended substantial revisions to federal large-scale land-disposal policy, so that in the future, sales "should be of only those lands that will achieve maximum benefit for the general public in non-federal ownership while retaining federal ownership [of] those whose values must be preserved so that they can be used and enjoyed by All Americans."

It was actually President Richard Nixon's administration that proposed broadening the authority and enforcement power of the BLM while emphasizing a philosophy calling for cooperation and multiple use of the people's property. In 1973 Nixon signed the Endangered Species Act, which sought to define and protect endangered and threatened species and habitats. The Republican's adherence to consensus at the cost of hardcore conservatism earned him the scorn of many of the captains of industry who'd supported him. The Endangered Species Act would be vilified as an example of a flagrantly liberal, even socialist, trend in federal government, and it would be waved like a battle flag many times on the road to Bunkerville.

While Nixon's second term was shortened by his resignation, stand-in President Gerald R. Ford signed a sweeping revamp of federal public-land use and the BLM's role in administering it. The Federal Land Policy and Management Act (FLPMA) of 1976 would eclipse the Taylor Grazing Act and provide all the fuel that western ranchers would need to energize their sagebrush revolution.

The act itself was historic, its fifty pages cementing federal authority over public lands under the philosophy of "multiple use and sustained yield." Its declaration of policy was clarion: "the public lands be retained in Federal ownership, unless as a result of the land use planning procedure provided for in this Act, it is determined that disposal of a particular parcel will serve the national interest."

As to management, the act appeared to side with the land itself, ordering that it "be managed in a manner that will protect the quality of scientific, scenic, historical, ecological, environmental, air and atmospheric, water resource and archeological values." Not only would management be compelled to err on the side of preserving certain lands in their natural condition, but it was required to ensure that habitat for fish and wildlife as well as domestic animals be maintained, and that the government maintain and protect the land for outdoor recreation, occupancy, and use.

The "management of the public lands and their various resource values so that they are utilized in the combination that will best meet the present and future needs of the American people," as the FLPMA defined "multiple use," must have sounded reassuring to a generation of outdoors enthusiasts. But the expansion of federal preeminence and sovereignty and the expansion of wilderness-area study and designation set off alarms with ranchers across the West.

And all that change came in the same year that saw the election to the presidency of Georgia governor and peanut farmer Jimmy Carter. The Carter administration pressed the Surface Mining Control and Reclamation Act of 1977, which required the restoration of mined land to its original condition, and the Public Rangelands Improvement Act of 1978, which set restoration goals on depleted federal grazing range—the latter only serving to stoke suspicions and motivate a voting bloc already disinclined to support Carter. (The former Georgia governor won zero contiguous states west of Texas in 1976 and just as many four years later.)

Voters found Carter's clean living and candor refreshing in the wake of the Nixon-Watergate morass, but he entered the White House almost painfully naïve about the politics in regions outside the South. He alienated the West almost immediately.

In an attempt to keep a campaign promise to shake up Washington and eliminate wasteful spending, upon taking office Carter immediately proposed to cancel a slate of thirty western water projects that cost taxpayers billions, threatened the environment, and appeared to offer the public little in return. He even attempted to have funding impounded for projects already budgeted. The exercise was met not with cheers for his fiscal sobriety but with pushback from inside the federal bureaucracy and from outside corporations that had long relied on cheap or free infrastructure-development assistance, courtesy of the government.

By mid-April, the "hit list," as it was termed, had been cut to seventeen with Interior Secretary Cecil Andrus, the popular former governor of Idaho, taking heat from ally and enemy alike across the West. Andrus took over a department that had morphed into a facilitator for a growing corporate state in the decades following Ickes's departure. Even a devoted conservationist like Stewart Udall, whom historians would later laud as a protector of the national-parks system, was also responsible for enabling the Navajo power plant, Black Mesa coal strip mines, and the Central Arizona Water Project, the latter considered "the last of the big federal water projects" that came to symbolize the New Deal's government-subsidized engineering feats.

Andrus, considered one of Carter's most loyal soldiers, declared that the president had "canceled the blank check" at Interior. Andrus announced plans that not only emphasized a new fiscal sobriety at the department but renewed Interior's environmental mission. Among the changes announced were a revision of the General Mining Law of 1872, expanding Alaskan wilderness designations, and promoting a strip-mine reclamation bill. "We intend to exercise our stewardship of public lands and natural resources in a manner that will make the 'three Rs—rape, ruin, and run—a thing of the past," Andrus told a meeting of the National Wildlife Federation in March, earning a standing ovation.

Outside the environmental community, the applause ceased—especially in the West. While Andrus touted Carter as a man with "a deep personal commitment to end the waste and misuse of America's natural resources," his ambitious plan and principled stance came at a high cost in Congress. For a generation of corporate lobbyists who had cut the lucrative deals for dirt-cheap development; gold, silver, and copper mining; easy coal-extraction; forest clear-cutting; and endless miles of Taylor grazing land, Carter's policy was nothing less than a political call to arms.

The West wasn't Carter country to begin with, but the administration's plan to cut back lucrative federal water projects alienated him in states he'd won the previous November. His hit list took a beating and steadily shrank. Far from being lauded as a fiscally focused conservative Democrat, Carter was described as weakening. Then another announcement slashed the hit list to ten and expressed support for two dozen projects previously thought to be expendable. Andrus persuaded Carter to soften his grip on the issue, even to the extent of acknowledging that the states themselves knew best when it came to managing their water resources.

But the damage was done. The sagebrush rebels, no friends of most Democrats in the best of times, had found their villain in the Georgia peanut farmer.

Although ranchers often complained about the BLM's confounding and costly red tape, the fact was that their grazing fees didn't come even close to covering the price taxpayers paid for the government to administer them. Grazing administration by the start of the 1980s cost well in excess of $100 million a year, at a time ranchers in the West paid just $25 million in fees. Even that figure was deceptive: approximately half the revenue generated was used to directly benefit the ranchers through the BLM's Range Improvement Fund. Ranchers who espoused their libertarian ethic in reality rarely pulled their own weight.

"The old interests which have for so long dictated public land policies have lost control," said Carter's Undersecretary for the Interior James Joseph. He continued:

Many of you have been saying for years that more than stockmen have a stake in how the public lands are grazed; more than miners have a right to suggest how, when and where mining will be done on the public lands; more than loggers care—and may rightfully comment on how our timber resources are managed.

There is nothing particularly mysterious, I now believe, in what is being called the "Sagebrush Rebellion." Indeed, it is

the time-honored response of the fellow who upon finding
he can no longer dictate the rules of the game decided to take
his ball and go home.

In Nevada and throughout the arid West, this statement was tantamount to heresy.

Andrus's critics were many, but he also found allies in western
Democrats who appreciated the nuances of Interior's evolving mission and the needs of their own growing states. Popular Nevada
Governor Mike O'Callaghan appreciated the secretary's accessibility
and willingness to listen. "As long as there's room for negotiation,
it's not all that bad."

House member Morris Udall of Arizona chaired the Interior
Committee. He was no friend of Carter's, having been defeated by
him in 1976 and later aligning himself with Ted Kennedy in an unsuccessful challenge at the 1980 Democratic National Convention that
damaged the president's campaign. But Udall appreciated Andrus,
observing in 1977 that the secretary had ruffled the "Western types
who are used to having someone favor the timber, cattle and mining
people, the people who run big irrigation systems.... But it's all part
of the Interior Department coming of age. It isn't a little public land
company anymore."

Carter's advocacy for increased competition and regulation of
offshore oil-leasing policies alarmed oil companies. Coal-production
outfits were angered by the administration's strip-mining bill.
Timber companies became incensed by Interior's call to discon-
tinue logging close to California's Redwood National Park. It was
all anathema to the corporate status quo in which Interior had for
so long played the role of facilitator. Andrus proclaimed, "We have
begun to make sweeping institutional and policy changes to end
the domination of the department by mining, oil and other special
interests.... Business as usual has been put out of business."

He stumped for the administration's policies week after week,
losing twenty pounds in the process, generating bruising headlines,
and making clear the direction in which Carter was heading. While
some oil, gas, and coal executives expressed nervous apprehension

and even said they were "doing a lot of praying these days," they were doing more than wringing their hands. They rallied lobbying forces and called in congressional markers as never before.

No matter its impact on the environment, big mining had never been short of friends in the Nevada press. In the wake of Andrus's rhetorical onslaught, the *Reno Gazette-Journal* opined, "In two centuries, the mining industry has disturbed only a fraction of one percent of the land area of the United States. Here in Nevada, one of the most heavily mined states in the nation, it is difficult to find bona fide examples of rape and ruin.... The rip-and-tear attitude of pioneer days has settled down. Most mining firms would not rape and ruin if they were of a mind to. They fear public opinion and government regulation too much."

Had Interior not been a glorified welfare agency for industry, many of Andrus's comments might have been lauded. He compared Interior's organizational chart, so riddled with special-interest considerations, to the wiring diagram of an intercontinental ballistic missile. He vowed to break up "the little fiefdoms" and advocated controlled growth. In short order, the policies forwarded by Andrus quickly "alienated virtually every powerful constituency in the West." Carter's environmental positions and call for cutbacks in lucrative federal water-development projects made him an ideal target. The blowback was immediate and ceaseless.

It is within this maelstrom that we see the framework of what would later be marketed as the Sagebrush Rebellion.

In reality, movements were already in motion to battle the environmentalist agenda on multiple fronts. Both movements had something in common: seed-money investment and the right-wing, anti-environmentalist political philosophy of beer-brewing titan Joseph Coors of Colorado. Although suspicion and distrust between ranchers and the federal government ran deep, the actual Sagebrush Rebellion was championed by Coors, whose anti-environmental politics found ideal mascots in the West's cattlemen. Large mining corporations and big timber-milling companies left enormous scars on the land, but the ranchers had long been symbols of libertarian independence in American popular culture. The fact that many were given a leg up in the saddle thanks to the Taylor Grazing Act, or that much of the BLM's funding was devoted to helping them maintain habitat for their herds, wasn't often mentioned in this melodrama.

In the wake of the passage of the Horse and Burro Act and the alarming call for changes at the Department of the Interior by the Carter administration, Coors ponied up $250,000 in 1976 to open the doors of the Mountain States Legal Foundation as an outspoken voice on behalf of "constitutional liberties and the rule of law." Attorney James Watt served as the foundation's first president. The fight was on.

The foundation's mission was seldom in doubt. It filed lawsuits and amicus curiae briefs that attacked a long list of conservative bugaboos. Through the years, the office would provide a training ground for like-minded lawyers, and it filed a wide range of legal actions. Among many: an attempt to force the federal roundup of wild horses on public land, a move to block the Nuclear Regulatory Commission from forcing rocket-fuel manufacturer Kerr-McGee Corp. to clean up uranium-tailings piles from its Oklahoma mill, and even school-desegregation efforts in Detroit. On its official website, the foundation's Statement of Purpose was to "provide an effective voice for the rights of private property ownership and freedom of enterprise in the development of law by the courts, administrative agencies, and elsewhere."

Some of the sharpest criticism of Carter and Andrus came from the Heritage Foundation. This neoconservative think tank, founded in 1973, also with a financial boost from Joseph Coors, determined that the Democratic administration was under the alarming influence of the "Environmental Complex," a collaboration of nonprofits led by the Sierra Club, Natural Resources Defense Council, Friends of the Earth, Environmental Defense Fund, National Audubon Society, Izaak Walton League of America, Energy Action Committee, and Wilderness Society, among many. Even Zero Population Growth and Planned Parenthood were considered part of the agenda-setters at work to undermine the influence of the oil, gas, logging, mining, and ranching industries. To Heritage, Interior's hiring of Joseph Browder of the Environmental Policy Center and Cynthia Wilson of the Audubon Society was a dangerous sign of trouble ahead for industries used to having the run of the house on federal public lands. The conservation groups' intentions, attorneys, memberships, and funding were officially under suspicion.

"The environmental movement," one Heritage report unintentionally deadpanned, "is probably far more widespread than is generally appreciated." From a standpoint of political stagecraft, the Sagebrush Rebellion was ideal for Reagan's image-makers and hard to beat as a campaign issue. Government overregulation of federal public lands hurt the already stagnant economy, he argued, and was tantamount to an assault on states' rights.

Reagan, the made-for-TV sagebrush rebel, won by a landslide in November 1980, to the cheers of ranchers throughout the West. Even Andrus had admitted that the out-of-date Taylor Grazing Act was "primarily for livestock, often to the detriment of livestock." Reagan loyalists eagerly pointed to some of his early cabinet appointments as signs of his devotion to the Sagebrush Rebellion, but what was not in doubt was his devotion to his supporter and confidant, Joseph Coors. Reagan's appointment of the Mountain States Legal Foundation president and rabid anti-environmentalism attorney James Watt as Secretary of the Interior was one example of several administration appointees whom critics called members of Coors's "Colorado Mafia."

Reagan followed the Heritage Mandate for Leadership playbook assiduously in what would later be touted as the "Reagan Doctrine," while critics labeled the conservative foundation as the president's shadow cabinet. In addition to Watt, Reagan tapped Anne Gorsuch Burford as the controversial first female administrator of the Environmental Protection Agency, and rancher Robert Burford as director of the Bureau of Land Management.

All this pleased ranchers in the West—for a time. But a funny thing happened on the way to revolutionizing federal land policy and returning control of 400 million acres of public lands to the states. With some carved-out exceptions, it didn't happen. Instead of returning millions of acres of federal public land to the states, Watt established what was labeled as the "Good Neighbor Policy" as a way of placating ranchers and making the BLM more user-friendly. Despite all the buildup, Watt was a traitor to the ranching rebellion he'd stirred up. He favored privatization over returning federal land to the states.

Watt also believed in a dispensationist Christian philosophy that read prophetic scripture passages literally and saw distinct roles for Israel and the Pentecostal church in God's plan. He clearly appeared to see his role in the Interior Department as part of his stewardship of America's natural resources. "I do not know how many future generations we can count on before the Lord returns," he said in a statement before Congress. "Whatever it is we have to manage with a skill to leave the resources needed for future generations."

For some reason, God was always on the side of oil, gas, logging, and mining corporations. Although Watt invoked the future, he represented a return to the Interior of the past, one marked by scandal and embarrassment—almost all of it self-inflicted by the secretary. Watt compared environmentalists to Nazis, and in an echo of John Birchers of a previous generation, he labeled Indian sovereignty as socialism. He equated the criticism he received from the press to the persecution of the Jews under Hitler. "He cannot speak without reminding us of his bizarre vision of American society," one of those print persecutors observed, noting Watt's jaw-dropping statement that the Beach Boys were the "wrong element" for a Fourth of July concert on the Washington Mall.

The challenge for those who sought his ouster was simple: he brought with him his own constituency, led by Coors and Reagan's born-again Christian base. As Wilderness Society chairman Gaylord Nelson jabbed, "Watt only has two constituents—Reagan and the Lord. If you've got both of them on your side, you don't have to worry about anyone else."

Watt's Pentecostal zealotry when it came to using the Department of the Interior to assist industry was evident from the start. In an openly antagonistic anti-environmental agenda, he rapidly sped up and expanded coal-mine leasing on federal land and set the stage for expanded oil-drilling on the outer continental shelf. He sometimes alluded to religious symbolism to justify his signature policies, and he was noted for dividing citizens into "liberals and Americans." When he was quoted at a Chamber of Commerce breakfast describing members of a coal-leasing policy board as "a black, a woman, two Jews and a cripple," even his ally and defender Reagan couldn't ignore the damage being done. Watt resigned in 1983 and was later ranked in the "Top 10 Worst Cabinet Members" in the nation's history by *Time* magazine.

Without Watt, there was no one at Interior to stir the pot. His successor, William P. Clark, was one of Reagan's closest advisors. Donald P. Hodel, who was considered a consensus builder who attempted to balance the interests of industry and the environment, followed Clark. Watt's departure followed the exit under pressure of his protégé, Anne Gorsuch Burford, at the Environmental Protection Agency. Replaced by moderate William Ruckelshaus, the changes signaled a shift in the administration away from its obsession with rapid development of federal land. Before Reagan's second term ended, following a flood of legal defeats and losses in the court of public opinion, Mountain States director David Flitner lamented, "Things were going well at first but the bureaucracy is so entrenched. It's almost immaterial in the end which administration gets in."

But in Nevada, times were good for the sagebrush rebels. At the height of the movement's political strength, just weeks before Watt finally imploded and was rushed out of the Reagan cabinet, it appeared to some observers that the public goals of the Sagebrush Rebellion were within reach. But those goals had shifted in an important way, from a push to transition federal land into state control to a desire to privatize the vast real estate altogether into the hands of ranching and mining interests.

Not surprisingly, this was an idea that suited men like Elko rancher and Nevada legislator Dean Rhoads just fine. Tall and square-jawed, described by one admiring journalist as "ruggedly handsome in the James Garner 'Maverick' mold," Rhoads was a high-profile spokesman for the sagebrush rebels and was proud of his membership on Reagan's Presidential Advisory Committee on Federalism. After helping to press a pro-ranching agenda in the state senate for many years, and finding allies in the brief rebellion era, Rhoads shifted directions after meeting with Reagan and Watt. "Most of us who spearheaded the drive felt private ownership is better than government control," he admitted in a candid moment. Of course, the cost of the land at its current-market value would be exorbitant, and purchase would be impossible for most ranchers, who couldn't even afford to pay the government what the government had been willing to pay the Dann sisters and other Native American ranchers being forced off their ancestral land.

Rhoads found a growing chorus of critics from what most ranchers wrote off as the environmentalist crowd, which increasingly included a wide variety of campers, hikers, hunters, and anglers who were enthusiastic supporters of the preservation of federal public land. One of those critics was Charles Watson of the Nevada Outdoor Recreation Association, who saw the anger of the rebels as a cover for something else: "It is the land grab of all time and makes Teapot Dome look like a parlor game. They don't want wilderness or natural areas or anything that conflicts with giving them a pre-emptive right to public lands. They had special privileges, entrenched privileges, over and above everyone else. They don't have that anymore and it is disturbing to them."

The fact that the transfer of public land to private ownership would constitute the largest land grab in modern United States history didn't faze Rhoads or his fellow ranchers. Although the legislator did allow, "If I said the land should go to the highest bidder, I would never get re-elected. It would be political suicide." To little surprise, the ranchers wanted the land to go to those currently using it, either as deeded or through the assignment of permanent specific rights, such as grazing or hard-rock mineral extraction. Operator of a 100,000-acre spread located sixty miles north of Elko, Rhoads painted a grim picture of federal overreach and meddling in the minutiae of ranching life while simultaneously declaring victory for the rebellion: "If it ended today, it would be more successful than I ever expected. But it's not over. It's just begun." Although some of his fellow ranchers admitted that the land at times had been overgrazed, they groused that they had been made to play the villain by environmentalists who worked the courts and Congress. Reagan's presidency, they believed, represented an opportunity to see 49 million acres of federal land in Nevada returned to their rightful owners.

By that, they did not mean that the land should be turned over to its original owners, Nevada's Western Shoshone and Paiute tribes.

There was life after the Reagan White House for Watt. After leaving office, Watt followed the path taken by so many former public servants who called for smaller government and reduced restrictions on industry: he began to milk the federal system as a consultant. Joined by his son, the Reverend Eric Watt, he also maintained his standing in the fundamentalist community by joining the board of the PTL televangelism network, a position from which he later resigned following a scandal involving teary TV preacher Jim Bakker. Watt also sought Housing and Urban Development (HUD) financing for clients pursuing low-cost housing projects in three states, Puerto Rico, and the Virgin Islands. In 1995, he was indicted on twenty-five felony counts, including obstruction of justice, perjury, and hiding subpoenaed documents; he eventually pleaded guilty to a single misdemeanor. At the time of his indictment, he resumed his religious posture and promised, "I am trusting God that justice can arise and will prevail." With more than 70 percent of westerners living in urban settings, and a majority favoring environmental protections over rampant development, the fundamentalist Watt found himself an eccentric heretic among many of his own fellow believers.

A decade after leaving office under a cloud of controversy, and finally out in the open as an advocate of the pro-industry wise-use movement, Watt could still draw an enthusiastic following in Elko by railing against Clinton administration Interior Secretary Bruce Babbitt and telling his audience to "Never, never trust your government. It is there to serve you, not to rule you."

Other Nevada ranchers predated Cliven Bundy in challenging the federal government, some of whom emboldened Bundy to follow in their footsteps. One was Ben Colvin, who ran his cattle in central Nevada's Esmeralda County. One of the least-populated places in

America, in 2017 the county had just 850 residents scattered over thirty-six thousand square miles. One longtime resident echoed the sentiments of many when he encapsulated Esmeralda's mixed history with the BLM and others from the outside world: "I don't think the federal government really cares about us out here at all. Like I say, we don't carry enough votes. We're kind of like the crazy folks who live out back."

Established in November 1861 by the Nevada Territorial Legislature, during its early years Esmeralda County was known for the discovery of gold at Aurora, a boomtown that at one time was claimed by both California and Nevada. After statehood, a series of roaring camps sprang up across the desert expanse with the greatest of them in 1903 at Goldfield—the county seat and largest town.

Ben Colvin didn't come for the gold or silver but for the opportunity to do the work he knew best. Colvin was born of pioneer stock in 1938 in Pendleton, Oregon, where his father, Bud Colvin, ran cattle on federal land near the John Day River. Ben's grandfather had worked on a cattle ranch in New Mexico. By their count, the Colvins had been running cows since 1860.

In 1968, Ben followed ranching relatives who paid $400,000 for the Hip-O ranch in central Nevada. The country looked wide open, but by then it had been pored over for a quarter century by government surveyors in association with its potential use as a military bombing range. The military's increasing presence in the region led to the redesignation of hundreds of thousands of acres of rangeland and many productive wells for the Nevada Test Site and military purposes.

When the opportunity arose, Colvin purchased the 40 Bar spread outside Goldfield, approximately 190 miles from Las Vegas. With abundant feed of Indian rice grass, Guyetta grass, and white sage, but little water near the surface, Colvin could run several hundred head of cattle. And when he subleased land run by ranchers Jim Daniels and Andy Anderson that included all-important water rights and grazing leases, Colvin controlled 520 acres of deeded property and a range of 550,000 acres at an annual cost of $4,000 dollars.

Ranching in that region of Nevada in those years was open-range—
that is, not fenced. Colvin recalled his father's elation after so many
years spent relatively penned up in Oregon. In central Nevada, a
herd rarely strayed more than a few miles from available water.

Ranching was hard work in the best of years, but it was in the
Colvins' blood. For a time, Ben believed he was up for any challenge.
"All the Colvins have always been involved in cattle," he said. "I'll
keep learning till the day they pat me in the face with a shovel."

But like many Nevada ranchers, he failed to adjust to changing times and the complications of the Wild Horse and Burro Act.
Colvin eventually found himself at odds with the BLM over grazing
rights in a dry land. The horses and burros dined at the expense of
Colvin's cattle. Once the grasses were eaten, the BLM prohibited the
land's use for grazing.

"They were running horses on my range, and they wouldn't
reduce the number," he said. "I tried to get along with them. I've
paid my dues, paid my grazing fees, and as far as I knew I was doing
everything right, trying to be a good guy. And they came up with
this thing…this range management plan."

Colvin cut his herd from 900 to 750 in 1987 due to a lack of sufficient forage. By 1990, he cut hundreds more, and his herd numbered
under a hundred. "From the time that damn Wild Horse and Burro
Act went into effect until 1990," Colvin said, "they never removed
one horse or burro off of my ranch."

He complained of the ever-breeding horses and burros and
sought reimbursement for the water and forage they consumed. He
did not consider BLM employees as bad people, just incapable of
controlling the mustang stampede on land he considered his.

When he stopped paying his paltry $1.35-per-month, per-animal
grazing fees in 1995, he made the government's case a relatively
simple matter. Eventually, they would come for his animals.

In 1999, Colvin shipped his last fifty cows out of state, returning
them two years later in order to legally maintain his water rights. But
the BLM was waiting for him, and in July of that year the government
seized his cattle. An auction was quickly scheduled, and the owner

of the auction business received an estimated fifty threats, which he believed came from Colvin supporters.

Colvin's dilemma spotlighted the government's inability to manage the horse and burro population, while also highlighting the obvious: it made no good sense to graze large animals on sparse rangeland that existed in a region that by definition was in a constant state of drought. Still, Colvin found support from strict constitutionalists, states'-rights activists, and conservative Mormons.

After dealing with Colvin and other recalcitrant ranchers, government officials were in no mood to sympathize. "I don't really even care to characterize these people as ranchers," BLM Nevada Director Bob Abbey said. "They are trespassers."

Undaunted, Colvin filed a lawsuit against the BLM in November 2001, claiming that through its incompetent management the agency had allowed 1,300 horses and burros to ravage the precious feed on his federal allotment to the detriment of his herd, which had once numbered 900. He charged that the BLM had not removed the horses and burros until after he had drastically reduced the number of his cattle on the range. A federal judge dismissed Colvin's lawsuit later that year, and 62 head of his cattle were auctioned off. At the time, he owed $73,000 in fines and unpaid grazing fees.

Colvin had allies in his fight. Fifty friends and family members turned out, despite tight security at the BLM's National Wild Horse and Burro Center in Palomino Valley north of Reno, to protest the action. But the law was clear. "Grazing on public land is a good deal for a rancher. In order for a rancher to get that good deal, they have to pay a nominal fee and follow some rules," a BLM official pointed out the obvious.

Colvin seethed. "I'd still be paying my fees if the BLM had managed those horses as they're supposed to," he said. "Those horses ate me out of house and home."

With the Sagebrush Rebellion fully faded from the headlines, Colvin emerged as a leader of the Nevada Livestock Association and the Nevada Committee for Full Statehood, a states'-rights organization that argued for the return of federal land to state control. Rancher Wayne Hage and his wife, former Idaho Congresswoman

Helen Chenoweth-Hage, led the group. Although unsuccessful in court, the group managed in December 2003 to encourage then-state attorney general and future Nevada governor Brian Sandoval to request a legal opinion to clarify the state's role in the BLM's seizure of Colvin's increasingly famous sixty-two cows. Colvin filed a $30-million lawsuit against the BLM in U.S. Claims Court after losing his grazing-fee protest. He accused the state's brand inspector of conspiring with the BLM over the confiscation, and he sought a grand jury investigation in Esmeralda County. Sandoval determined that the brand inspector had acted appropriately, and Colvin felt thwarted once more.

More than a decade after he'd begun waging his own range war with the BLM, Colvin remained cynical about his experience and saw greater forces at work:

> The way the bureaucrats in the government are working, I think they're putting all the ranchers out of business. Fifty or sixty years ago, I think the bureaucrats who worked for the Forest Service and the BLM were more on, I'd say, the livestock people's side. But here in the last twenty to thirty years, they've turned. One reason is there are so many environmentalists out there that are running the show; they outnumber the ranchers ten to one, twenty to one, or whatever it is. So the bureaucrats listen to them because this is where their money is coming from, where the votes are coming from.

Years before Cliven Bundy emerged in the bipolar American consciousness as either a revolutionary states'-rights wrangler or a fee-scofflaw and welfare cowboy, Pine Creek rancher Wayne Hage rode point in the political territory of the Sagebrush Rebellion. Born in 1936 in Elko, Hage grew up in ranching, having persuaded his parents to let him drop out of eighth grade to help other cattlemen caught in the harsh winter of 1952. The image of a young Hage on horseback riding to the rescue of his fellow ranchers was endearing and hard to beat. After that, as friends and family would attest, he was not to be corralled. Hage could say with justification that he was born to the saddle: "My family, in one way or the other, was either involved in mining or ranching from the time they first came into that part of the country, which was in the very early days of settlement."

As a rancher and leader of the Sagebrush Rebellion, Hage brought authentic experience to the discussion of independent cattlemen battling federal overreach. The image was valuable for ranchers and Ronald Reagan alike, and Hage often recalled that snow-covered winter season when he was just a teenager.

The irony of Wayne Hage's winter's tale was lost on most. As much as he wanted people to think that Nevada ranchers were just fine before the federal government began meddling into their lives, that's not what Elko's ranchers thought in the 1950s. Back then, they prayed for federal assistance and cheered when it arrived by air and across the icy land. With ranchers and sheepherders at risk of losing an estimated 200,000 cows and 400,000 sheep, Nevadans from U.S. Senate powerhouse Pat McCarran to Governor Charles Russell rode metaphorically to assist frostbitten ranchers from Elko to Nye counties who were clamoring for assistance from Uncle Sam. President Harry S. Truman declared Elko and five other northeastern and central Nevada counties a disaster area and freed up federal money for the emergency. While Hage's ranch tales recalled halcyon days of hard work and adventure, he had been too young to quit school in 1949 when C-124 "flying boxcars" hauled tons of hay from Northern California into the backcountry of Elko County in an effort to rescue livestock. "Operation Haylift," as the rescue became known, was welcomed by the governor and Elko political powerhouse Newton Crumley. Hotelier Crumley helped coordinate the flights, which used U.S. Air Force pilots from California and heavy-equipment operators and twenty army bulldozers from Utah. Tons of hay were shipped down from Idaho as lambing season approached in the spring, and state and federal officials prepared to counter the flooding expected with the snowmelt.

"The big cattle outfits would put out a roundup wagon and they'd just stay out on the range for maybe 10 months of the year," Hage wrote in 2002, romanticizing the cowboy life. "For a teenage boy, that kind of life—riding horseback on the open range—was an adventure that made school pretty dull and uninteresting by comparison, so I just stayed with it."

When he wasn't chasing cows, like many Nevada ranchers Hage made money rounding up wild horses for sale and slaughter, "before they passed the Wild and Free Roaming Horse and Burro Act in Congress and made outlaws of all the mustangers. If you weren't handling cattle, you were running mustangs."

The image of the born-in-the-saddle rancher served Hage well, but in reality he cracked more than a few books growing up. He received his high-school equivalency while serving in the U.S. Air Force and used his G.I. Bill benefits to study first at Boise (Idaho) Junior College, then at the University of Nevada in Reno and at Colorado State, where he majored in animal science and minored in chemistry. He studied animal nutrition and bought a ranch in Northern California. The 1965 passage of the California Land Conservation Act was Hage's first entry into the political fray over the tax status of ranchers. He formed a committee and wrote a plea on the ranchers' behalf. He was a member of the California Chamber of Commerce land-use subcommittee for several years before moving back to Nevada and, in 1978, taking control of the massive Pine Creek Ranch in northern Nye County, a spread of patented and permitted grazing land stretching over 760,000 acres, or approximately 1,100 square miles. He understood from the outset that although he had more than $1 million in cattle grazing, the real value of the land lay in the water rights he obtained along with the federal grazing permits.

Hage's candor on that issue is a key to understanding some of the underlying politics of the Sagebrush Rebellion and its direct line to the Bundy Ranch controversy. Where arid ranching is the subject, cows are important, but the water rights are by far the most valuable asset.

For his part, Hage saw attempts by federal agencies to tighten their grip on his range as part of a greater conspiracy to control water, not just for development but for something larger. "The main value right today like with most ranches in the West, the main value is water," he told an interviewer. "There has been an ongoing effort for years and it's an international effort, to gain control of fresh water supplies. And, of course, in the western United States the ranchers are the ones who own the majority of the fresh water out here." Between stress on supply, burgeoning population, and growing pollution, "a barrel of freshwater is worth more than a barrel of oil. So you can see the intensity with which many entities are trying to control it."

By the late 1970s, Hage was an outspoken sagebrush rebel and a sharp critic of the Carter administration's promotion of the gargantuan MX Missile project in Nevada and part of Utah. With its wide-open arid spaces and sparse population, Nevada had long been a popular site for everything from atomic weapons tests to war games on land and in the air, air bases to munitions dumps, and even a submarine training center. However, the MX Missile project was not going to be just another government construction job.

The $33-billion behemoth would be capable of secretly moving warheads on underground railroad tracks over miles of desert as a way of playing hide-and-seek with the Soviet Union at the height of the Cold War. When the Soviets demonstrated the high accuracy of their SS-18 and SS-19 missiles, beginning in 1979, Carter knew the American nuclear arsenal was at risk and expedited the MX plan. With two hundred mobile missile launchers and four thousand concrete bunkers, each protected by 2.5-acre secured sites, it would be the most costly government construction project in the history of the Republic, surpassing the nation's federal highway system and the Panama Canal. During its five-year construction, it was estimated to employ thirty thousand workers—more people than lived in Nye County.

The MX raised concerns common in small towns across the rural West that had survived previous boom-and-bust cycles—the best of times often left the worst hangovers. The prospect of the MX was a cause for celebration in some circles but a source of consternation in others. As authors Peter Wiley and Robert Gottlieb observed, "In this instance, a small number of Mormon towns on both sides of the Nevada-Utah border were involved. Prominent Mormon politicians tried to balance their conservative pro-military and pro-growth point of view with the belief that the MX would devastate those communities." Some of these fears were bolstered by the very real strain such a project would place on available water and power resources. In an era before the dawn of renewable-energy solar fields, ranchers believed that the missile construction giant would use scads of power and drink dry much of the aquifer available for grazing lands.

Hage saw the project as an attempt by the federal government to carve out yet another piece of Nevada's rangeland, and his argument found allies across the rural part of the state. Bumper stickers on pickups along U.S. 95 read, "Might Xplode," "Misplaced Xpectations," and "More Xcrement." On a route that passes not far from the front gates of the sprawling Nevada Test Site, where hundreds of atomic weapons were exploded during the height of the nuclear-arms race, the stickers berated the proposed MX project.

As a member of the Nevada Cattlemen's Association, Hage expressed offense at the lack of respect that MX backers were showing residents and ranchers. "This isn't Kansas, and it's not the central valley of California," he chided the opposition in an open meeting. "This is Nevada, and it's range country."

His protestation aside, the fee-grazing land belonged to the federal government, not to the ranchers. While the history appeared clear, the issue was a public-relations nightmare for the military and the Carter administration. It also provided a genuine opportunity for those desiring to use the issue for political gain as the 1980 election approached. When the military engineers mapping the area exploded "simulated nuclear blasts" not far from the Test Site, Hage took the stage. "I have $1 million worth of cattle out there and another $1.5 million in improvements, and I don't even rate a letter to tell me what they're doing," he complained. His two thousand cows couldn't vote, but he'd make sure their interests were heard. When Hage talked about the need to preserve the state's ability to produce "renewable resources," he was talking about range-fed beef. He argued that any grazing land taken by the massive construction job should be replaced with other suitable lands. He found a well-sourced ally in Richard Blakemore, a state legislator and trucking-company owner from Tonopah who was considered one of the founders of the Sagebrush Rebellion.

Air Force Brigadier General Gary Hecker proved an unlikely but effective salesman for the MX as the government took its show on the road to Tonopah and elsewhere in rural Nevada. A slow-talking Alabaman with a country sensibility, Hecker spoke of the affection he had for the West and the state, despite his short acquaintance. "I've grown to love and admire the people out here," he told a meeting of the Tonopah Rotary Club. "To me, that has really become heartland America—independent spirit, patriotic spirit—just the things you all stand for. I wish we could get all of the bureaucrats out of Washington and out here to see what the real America is all about. I really mean that."

And perhaps he did. But that didn't stop the rising protest, which fed into Reagan's own campaign narrative about Carter, who had opposed the project before reluctantly signing on. Although Carter forwarded the mobile "shell game" MX plan in September 1979, he wasn't around to guide it to fruition. Under Reagan, the well-known defense hawk, the project was dramatically scaled back. Reagan, who had criticized the MX, once elected declared himself enthusiastically in favor of it. A modified version would be tried before the program would eventually be scrapped during Reagan's second term.

Given the depressed economic condition of the communities most affected by the MX project and the area's long history of environmental exploitation, some Nevada historians and journalists found the vehemence of the protest odd. "For many years, because their land was so poor and their economy so unstable, Nevadans welcomed federal projects of this kind," historian James Hulse observed. "When the federal government eventually scrapped the plan in the wake of a strong public protest, these communities returned to the obscurity that had been the standard with them for decades."

The plan lived for fifteen years past the fall of the Soviet Union and the Cold War, eventually being cancelled by President George H. W. Bush in September 1991. But the real turning point for the Nevada-Utah MX Missile project had come way back on May 5, 1981, from the Mormon Church in a statement issued by President Spencer W. Kimball and his two counselors, N. Eldon Tanner and

Marion G. Romney. At the time, there were more than 1 million Mormons out of Utah's 1.5 million population and another 56,000 among Nevada's 800,000 residents. The message was eloquent and adamant: the Church of Jesus Christ of Latter-day Saints opposed a nuclear missile project carved out of its Promised Land. It read in part:

> Our fathers came to this western area to establish a base from which to carry the gospel of peace to the peoples of the earth. It is ironic, and a denial of the very essence of that gospel, that in this same general area there should be constructed a mammoth weapons system potentially capable of destroying much of civilization.
>
> With the most serious concern over the pressing moral question of possible nuclear conflict, we plead with our national leaders to marshal the genius of the nation to find viable alternatives, which will secure at an earlier date and with fewer hazards the protection from possible enemy aggression, which is our common concern.

The message from the Church hierarchy sent a political chill through Congress that reached the Reagan White House, and even the missile project's firmest advocates began to lose confidence in the odds that it would be built—which made the 1988 Nevada desert–Florida swampland exchange all the more intriguing.

Under Reagan, Hage shifted his focus to the administration's plan to swap 34 million acres of western public land between the BLM and the Forest Service—an exchange dubbed by conservationists as the "Great Terrain Robbery." Nevada would see 5.1 million acres of Forest Service land redesignated for management by the BLM, which would allow easier access to grazing cattle and mineral extraction. Hage supported the plan, thinking it would "save a lot of duplication" between the two agencies. He also welcomed the decreased scrutiny of the public lands on which his cattle grazed that would result from the transfer.

Despite his independent-rancher image, Hage had powerful friends. One was Ron Arnold, considered a founder of the wise-use movement backed by logging, ranching, and mining interests. Arnold headed the Center for the Defense of Free Enterprise and would assist Hage's legal battle with the government. He later published Hage's 1994 book, *Storm over Rangelands: Private Rights in Federal Lands.*

When Nevada Secretary of State Frankie Sue Del Papa aligned her office with the federal government in the Hage lawsuit and retained a lawyer who had represented the National Wildlife Federation, she incurred the ire of Arnold and ranching state senator Dean Rhoads, then chairman of the legislature's committee on public lands. Arnold's Center filed an ethics complaint: "The linkage is clear: Del Papa is attempting to give the Hage ranch and its water rights to her pet environmental group by intervening in this case." Del Papa's terse response was that Hage was a "bad rancher" who didn't pay his fees and exploited land and water to the detriment of the state. Hage became ever more active in the pushback against what his like-minded colleagues considered an environmentalist, anticapitalist agenda, and what some conspiracists saw as part of an effort to usher in a New World Order.

For many years, Hage had followed the rules. He applied for and received federal grazing rights in 1978 after he paid $2 million for the Pine Creek Ranch north of Tonopah. The ranch not only included 752,000 acres of private and public grazing land but long-established access to available water as well. He watered hundreds of cattle on private and public range and timberland, but over time he increasingly bristled at the presence of the BLM and Forest Service. Years earlier, he'd made his political views clear that the federal government had no business in the Nevada land business. The proper owner was the state—preferably the county—and himself, ideally. Legal precedents notwithstanding, he'd rather do it himself.

In time, his disputes with the government increased. He was angered when nonindigenous elk were released onto federal land and claimed that the large animals harmed his livestock's grazing area. Officials fenced off a spring to prevent his cattle from ruining it. When it became necessary for Hage to repair fence and maintain a 28-mile-long ditch used for decades to move water to a meadow on private land, officials ordered him to use only hand tools instead of heavier equipment. The government offered to buy the portion of the ranch that Hage actually owned, but he rejected the offer.

When the government increased restrictions on the environmentally sensitive Humboldt-Toiyabe National Forest where Hage grazed his cattle, eventually confiscating more than a hundred head of cattle and revoking his permits, he sued for $28 million in damages to his ranching. In 1993, his application for renewal of his BLM grazing permit was rejected on a technicality. A range war of attrition was on.

Hage found some success arguing about his water rights in federal court. "If you don't have the water rights, you don't have a ranch," he said in a 2004 hearing. A judge ruled that Hage deserved to be compensated—$4.2 million plus prejudgment interest, which doubled that figure—for the taking of some of his water rights and for his range improvements. "The potential ramifications of this decision are enormous," Hage boasted. "Thousands of ranchers now have good hope for redress against harassment and abuse by federal agencies."

That same year, Hage and fellow central-Nevada rancher Ben Colvin were fighting new federal trespass charges after they grazed their cattle without permits for three years on BLM and Forest Service land. Although the facts weren't in their favor, Hage and Colvin experienced something rarely seen in federal court—a judge in their corner.

U.S. District Judge Robert C. Jones had already gained a reputation as an outspoken, controversial, and occasionally overturned jurist when *U.S. v. Hage* came before him. The trespass matter would only add to that reputation. In pretrial hearings, Jones not only allowed wide latitude to the ranchers' claims but at times appeared to offer his own legal advice. An appeals court would later determine that Jones had used what at best could be called an "idiosyncratic view that Defendants' water rights—perfected by Defendants' predecessors-in-interest in the late 1800s and early 1900s—provided a defense to the government's action." Jones had then more than hinted that he'd be amenable to hearing their counterclaim for damages against the government. The "court invites them to try," Jones said.

The just-add-water counterclaim was filed the next day and granted.

The twenty-one-day bench trial that followed produced more of the same for the government. Jones started the 2012 trial by accusing the BLM of entering his courtroom "with the standard arrogant, arbitrary, capricious attitude that I recognize in many of these cases.... [I]t's my experience that the Forest Service and the BLM is very arbitrary and capricious.... Your insistence upon a trespass violation, unwillful—your arbitrary determination of unwillfulness [sic: willfulness] is undoubtedly going to fail in this court."

Jones repeatedly ruled almost exclusively in Hage's favor. The judge shot from the lip and ruled from the saddle, holding two federal officials in contempt and awarding the government a measly $165.88 in damages. "The government's actions over the past two decades shocks the conscience of the court," he wrote in his decision. He held that Hage had proven a procedural due-process violation and invoked a broad injunction against the government.

This was not only a thorough rebuke of the federal government's long-established preeminence over the management of public land, but it was begging to be overturned on appeal. When that appeal came, the U.S. Ninth Circuit gutted the case and Jones as well. Hage's folly would eventually cost his estate $578,000 in fines and overdue fees. "Defendants openly trespassed on federal lands," wrote Ninth Circuit Judge Susan Graber on behalf of the court. "Rather than simply resolving the fact-specific inquiries as to when and where the cattle grazed illegally, the district court applied an 'easement by necessity' theory that plainly contravenes the law. The district court also encouraged defendants to file a counterclaim that was clearly time-barred.... Moreover, as discussed more fully in a separate disposition filed today, the court grossly abused the power of contempt by holding two federal agency officials in contempt of court for taking ordinary, lawful actions that had no effect whatsoever on this case."

The judge turned a simple trespass case into a redress of grievances in Hage's long battle to evade paying grazing fees and avoid government control of public land that he considered his. "A dispassionate observer would conclude the district judge harbored animus toward the federal agencies," Graber wrote in considerable understatement. "Unfortunately, the judge's bias and prejudgment are a matter of public record."

By then, Hage was deceased, but his son, Wayne Hage Jr., expressed his disappointment for himself, his family, and the cattle industry. Then he said something to a reporter that to some might have sounded like a threat: "It looks to me like the Ninth Circuit just swelled the ranks of the militias."

Nye County Commissioner and Big Smoky Valley rancher Dick Carver proved to be a particular burr under the government saddle. Before he became nationally known as the leader of "Sagebrush Rebellion II," Carver was an outspoken member of the county commission and a staunch advocate for dramatically reducing government oversight of his cattle grazing on federal land—those rules were bad for his business. Although he professed a love of the land, as late as October 1993 Carver was still predicting that the Big Smoky Valley would one day "become a retirement community. It's a difficult country to make a living in."

As both a commissioner and member of the State Land Use Advisory Council, Carver put BLM officials through their paces during 1994. According to his reading of the Constitution, law, and history, the federal government lacked jurisdiction over federal lands. He set in motion a plan to transfer federal land located in Nye County into the county's control. "There is no such thing as a United States Forest Service," Carver proclaimed, citing the lack of its mention in the pocket Constitution prominently displayed in his shirt pocket.

The rebellion was rekindled.

It caught fire a few months later when, on July 4, 1995, at a gathering of like-minded folks, some of them armed, in Jefferson Canyon, Carver mounted an old bulldozer and plowed open a dirt road in the Toiyabe-National Forest. The road had been closed years earlier to prevent cattle overgrazing in that area. Carver announced to cheers that he and his supporters were taking their land back from government interlopers, whose No Trespassing sign meant nothing because they claimed the government lacked jurisdiction there. The lone federal employee on duty, U.S. Forest Service agent David Young, was himself threatened with arrest and forced to move out of the way or get run over by Carver's bulldozer and the rowdy crowd. With the advantage of hindsight months later, Carver expressed relief that the federal man wasn't murdered by one of his followers. "My friends would have drilled him," he told the *Los Angeles Times* in a statement echoed in future armed conflicts. "I didn't want that."

News of Carver's actions, which some called brave despite the fact that he'd been accompanied by an estimated two hundred supporters against a single government employee, spread quickly through Nye County and beyond. Soon, reporters began calling, then the news networks. Carver quickly became the leader of a movement, albeit one shadowed by armed extremists.

Like Hage, Carver was raised in a ranching family with deep western roots. Like other cattle drovers during the Gold Rush era, in the 1850s the Carvers herded hundreds of steers from Salt Lake City to Placerville, California, to feed hungry gold miners. The Carver clan eventually settled in the Big Smoky Valley, once home to a promising mining boomtown named Jefferson, with abundant feed and water. In later years, the county's largest town would be named Pahrump, a Paiute word meaning "water rock," after the artesian springs that made the area a popular place for cattle grazing and desert farming. At the time of Carver's one-man insurrection, only eighty cows grazed his land.

And like Hage, Carver bristled at rangeland reform measures promoted by a Democratic president. This time, it was Bill Clinton and his Secretary of the Interior, Bruce Babbitt, who imagined that ranchers and environmentalists might find common ground and compromise as they had in fast-growing Colorado. Among many changes, Babbitt's Rangeland Reform '94 called for a substantial increase in grazing fees and a rewrite of some water-rights rules. Babbit's program was part of a broader slate of initiatives pressed in

Congress, including a failed attempt to reform the General Mining Act of 1872. Miners and ranchers used federal land differently, but they found consensus when it came to anyone making substantive changes to the pat hands they'd been dealt.

With Republicans reading from a familiar campaign script that some called "The War on the West," Clinton and Babbitt found themselves in a quandary to which Carter and Andrus could have related: push too hard for reform in the West, and even members of your own party will call you out. Clinton, forever penciling out the political calculus, eventually scrapped some of the most meaningful elements of the reform proposal.

Carver was quickly propelled into the national spotlight. Like Hage before him and Cliven Bundy who followed, Carver was a staunch conservative who conflated his narrow reading of the U.S. Constitution and his Christian beliefs to affirm his defiance of federal law. His herd couldn't match Hage's, but Carver was even more adept at rounding up supporters and publicity. Some of those supporters were armed and prone to violence—actions he reminded skeptics that he condoned. Some of the publicity came from national outlets, including the popular CBS *48 Hours* news magazine, the *New York Times*, and the *Los Angeles Times*. Carver's contention that microchips were hidden in hundred-dollar bills, along with his fundamentalist Christian philosophy and white-supremacist and anti-Semitic rhetoric, complicated his major television appearance. Christian Identity, with which he identified, "rose to a position of commanding influence on the racist right in the 1980s." The Anti-Defamation League calls it a "religious ideology popular in extreme right-wing circles.... Its virulent racist and anti-Semitic beliefs are usually accompanied by extreme anti-government sentiments. Despite its small size, Christian Identity influences virtually all white supremacist and extreme anti-government movements."

Carver accepted an invitation to be a featured speaker at the Christian Identity–sponsored 1994 "Jubilee," despite his understanding the group's basic tenets. Although he denounced white supremacy prior to the event, he also suggested that the federal government perhaps fomented the race-issue controversy. Carver was irritated by the group's racist talk, preferring to be called a leader of the wise-use movement and county rights. "The weapon I have in my pocket is the Constitution of the United States," he said in 1995. "That does not cause bloodshed."

His rhetoric aside, Carver was challenged to distance himself from violence-prone supporters after one was suspected of planting a pipe bomb that exploded outside the Forest Service's Carson City, Nevada, district office on March 30. On August 4, a second bomb went off, this time under forest ranger Guy Pence's van, which was parked in front of his family home with his wife and children inside.

Like most Forest Service and BLM employees, Pence made a poor villain. His previous tenure in Tonopah had been peaceful, and even some of the ranchers found good things to say about him. But during a time of increasingly heated land-rights rhetoric in the West and debate in Congress over changes to grazing regulations, he became an easy target for criticism, harassment, and worse. At the time, a piece of legislation sponsored by Republican Congressman James Hansen of Utah and backed by the livestock industry would have made enforcement of grazing laws more difficult for the BLM and Forest Service rangers, who were regularly accused of overstepping their authority.

Although meaningful efforts to change grazing legislation in Congress were doomed to break down, the Department of Justice under U.S. Attorney General Janet Reno took action against Nye County by filing a lawsuit that challenged its ordinance denying federal control of public land within the county. Meanwhile, Carver took to the road through the West and Midwest, speaking out on returning control of federal lands to the state and county levels and on the wise-use movement, which critics defined as self-appointed wise men making private use of public property.

Carver claimed to be elated that the government had made its move. "We've worked very hard to get to this point and can't wait to get into court," he told a reporter. Meanwhile, a group of Nevada legislators headed by state senate Democrats Dina Titus and Joe Neal barely derailed an attempt to rewrite Nevada's state constitution to no longer recognize federal control over public land.

Carver's followers painted his actions and promotion of what he called the "Nevada Plan for Public Land" in heroic terms. In less than two years, nearly seventy counties across the West had passed similarly unconstitutional laws taking control of everything from BLM land to entire national forests. However, even elected state officials who empathized with the ranchers, miners, loggers, and other offended parties expressed concern about the cost of maintaining such a large piece of the country. While the Justice Department made ready to sue Nye County, Republicans in Congress floated a bill that would have turned over 270 million acres under BLM control to the states if governors approved. As in the Reagan era, the rebellion's new iteration was more about painting a political narrative that led to privatizing public land than about actually privatizing it. In Nevada, Governor Bob Miller questioned the fiscal sobriety of such a transfer, explaining that it would cost the state $73 million to manage the land but would generate only $39 million in revenue.

Carver barnstormed across Washington State through small towns and farming communities where he found his fiery rhetoric appealed to some frustrated locals. His populist bluster at times went far afield to include the Second Amendment and motherhood, but he inevitably returned to his pitch for Christianity, the Constitution, and "county supremacy" before groups such as the Snohomish County Property Rights Alliance and the Freedom Forum. Outside Nevada, Carver appeared to feel even more uninhibited about his mission. "We're in a Civil War," he said. "You cannot compromise with the federal government."

In Wisconsin and Minnesota as a guest of the "Win Back the Midwest" land-rights group, Carver denied that he was the leader of a "war." "There is going to be no bloodshed," he said, but he would rein in "federal bureaucrats who think they're above God and above the law. We have to weed them out."

Others also had their say. Following the Pence bombing, normally mild-mannered Nevada United States Senators Harry Reid and Richard Bryan called out what they saw as Sagebrush ruffians and their elected supporters from the floor of the Senate. Those behind the Pence attack were "cowards," Reid said. Bryan warned that "the incendiary rhetoric espoused by those in the county supremacy movement has created an atmosphere that promotes extremism."

Their criticism of Carver only made him a bigger man in the eyes of many of his fellow ranchers. While everyone offering comment in the press appeared to renounce violence against Pence and others, threats to federal workers continued. Although Pence himself expressed fear for his family, sadness over the seemingly unending mess, and anger at the intimidation attempts that might have killed those dearest to him, he remained undaunted. "My work is to take care of the valuable natural resources that belong to all Americans," he said.

Agents from the FBI and ATF continued to investigate the Pence Forest Service bombings. Although an analysis determined that the bombs were similar in style and material, no arrests were made. Pence was relocated to Idaho out of concern for the safety of himself and his family. The harassment of BLM and Forest Service employees continued, and some filed their own lawsuits. The new county ordinances made it nearly impossible for them to work in the field amid an increasingly hostile environment.

The Department of Justice dropped the anvil on Carver's crusade with a lawsuit in March 1995. When Carver finally got his day in federal court before U.S. District Judge Lloyd George, the sun began to set on Sagebrush Rebellion II. George, a devout Mormon and U.S. Air Force veteran, had little patience with the county ordinance claim, ruling it illegal. It turned out that despite the efforts of Carver and his lawyer, former Reagan administration Assistant Attorney General Roger Marzulla, the United States still had the right to own and manage federal lands for all the people.

Although it was what Carver didn't want to hear, Judge George ruled the obvious, that the federal government "owns and has the power and authority to manage and administer the unappropriated public lands and National Forest System lands" within Nye County. The judge gave the rancher a brief history tutorial, reminding him that the Treaty of Guadalupe Hidalgo remained valid, and that President Abraham Lincoln had indeed intended that Nevada would cede its public land to the federal government as a condition of statehood.

Justice Department attorneys had seen such legal stunts before. They compared the theory of Carver and his lawyers to the lawsuits filed in the 1960s by counties in southern states in an effort to avoid complying with federal civil rights laws.

Carver retreated from his confident position and called the dispute nothing more than a private trespass case. One problem: he'd used county-owned equipment for his public display of rebellion. George was unimpressed. But just as Carver's attorneys had wanted to test the judicial process, so too did the Justice Department. For the county-supremacy crusaders and their wealthy behind-the-scenes backers, it was a tactical error. They had underestimated the mettle of the judge. Those who didn't respect—or even recognize—the rule of federal law remained unmoved by Judge George's rebuke of the arguments of Carver and the sagebrush rebels.

For her part, Attorney General Reno struck a conciliatory note now that the rule of law had prevailed: "Now it's time to come together and address our differences." Mike Dombeck, director of the BLM, expressed relief that the issue had been settled in the "proper forum" and talked of rebuilding relationships. "It is time to find common ground," he said generously, perhaps not fully appreciating how naïve he sounded.

Carver's reboot of the Sagebrush Rebellion, urged on from behind the scenes by the wise-use philosophers in the mining and timber industries, had collapsed under the weight of federal law. Beaten in court, he remained undefeated before the media.

"We made our point," Carver said. "We got what we wanted.... And now, they are listening to us." He sang a similar tune with the passing months, even though the federal government still controlled 87 percent of Nevada and 93 percent of Nye County. "We can't complain now, with federal agencies working with us.... Five years ago, the feds wouldn't even talk to us."

The song changed the next year when the controversy-courting cowboy received the bill for the damage he'd done with the county bulldozer: $82,855 for carving into the road in Jefferson Canyon, which was an old stagecoach route that was being studied for its archeological value. To little surprise, he vowed not to pay it.

Carver was just fifty-eight when he died on January 9, 2003, in Nye County. His views of the federal enemy had softened in recent years, at least publicly. His widely published obituary reminded one and all that the rancher from Nevada had used a bulldozer to lead a land rebellion and made the cover of *Time* magazine.

Although a ballot initiative calling for the return of federal public lands in Nevada to state control passed with 56 percent of the vote in the November 1996 election—to the delight of crestfallen rebels—the initiative remained a symbolic gesture, a tale more compelling over a campfire than in Congress.

The impact of the Bunkerville standoff rippled through the ranching community and appeared to embolden others at odds with the BLM—even some who took pride in the fact that they'd always gotten along with the government men. In Northern Nevada, longtime Battle Mountain ranching families were forced to remove their herds from the 365,000-acre Argenta allotment and sprawling North Buffalo and Copper Canyon allotments due to drought conditions. They bristled at the decision, which forced them to dramatically reduce herd sizes and feed their animals expensive alfalfa while the range grasses made their slow recovery. Without a speedy resolution in sight, ranchers Dan and Eddyann Filippini and Pete Tomera and his family said they were forced to take action against BLM Battle Mountain District director Doug Furtado. The ranchers were shadowing Bundy's boot tracks without declaring all-out war, even as their attorney publicly questioned whether there actually was a drought emergency on the Battle Mountain allotments.

When their litigation and Honk to Impeach Furtado signs posted outside BLM headquarters failed, the ranchers staged a twenty-one-day, three-thousand-mile protest ride on horseback from just outside San Francisco to Washington, DC. Dubbed the "Grass March Cowboy Express," eight family ranchers, along with lawyer and former Elko County commissioner A. Gant Gerber, drew attention to their plight and leveled more criticism at Furtado, who deadpanned to a reporter, "This is not an easy job that we have here, and I accept it." The transcontinental protest was shrouded after Gerber suffered a severe concussion when his horse tripped in Kansas. He completed the ride to Washington, but later died from the injury.

By 2015, the Filippinis took action of their own, returning their herd to the land. Instead of facing arrest for trespassing and the impoundment of their animals, a strange thing happened. The BLM levied a fine, but compromised and allowed the cattle to graze as long as the ranchers agreed they'd committed willful trespass and paid an enhanced grazing fee. The agreement also called for the dismissal of further litigation in the case.

To their local newspaper and other boosters of the ranching class, the Filippinis came away looking like selfless heroes. A closer look revealed that they'd padded their bets by applying for six-figure relief from the U.S. Department of Agriculture's Livestock Forage Disaster Program. Journalists with the Center for Investigative Reporting's Reveal Project documented evidence showing the same families that were doing all the shouting had received a combined $2.2 million in federal drought-disaster relief. For a drought that supposedly didn't exist, relief from it appeared to pay very well.

For environmentalists, the victory was another sign of the BLM caving in to public pressure and failing in its mission to protect the public lands. At Idaho's Western Watersheds Project, director Ken Cole jabbed, "The ranchers generate public sympathy for their custom and culture, all the while despoiling land, wildlife, and water and disregarding the laws that govern the heavily subsidized grazing permits they feel so entitled to."

The ire of the environmentalists was aimed largely at Doug Furtado, who had also drawn intense criticism from the cattlemen. In 2019, Furtado would be the subject of a scathing federal whistleblower complaint filed by BLM environmental specialist Daniel Patterson for allegedly abusing his authority by fast-tracking mining permits and allowing other abuses within his jurisdiction.

The Filippinis weren't as caustically constitutional as Bundy, but they were just as fed up with an agency they saw as more interested in driving them out of business than helping them survive hard times. On Facebook they'd post, "Badger Ranch makes a stand!" Later, while still talking about their lack of trust in the government managers, Eddyann Filippini allowed that the family had begun running its herd differently after meeting with range-management specialists.

A BLM press release tried to accentuate the positive and down-play the simmering controversy:

> Grazing on upland areas met the agreement's sustainability goals of leaving a sufficient amount of grass for the plants to recover by the next grazing season. On the allotment's riparian areas, however, grazing did not meet the prescribed utilization levels set in the Settlement Agreement, which if repeated chronically could adversely affect plant vigor and riparian function.

In short, the Filippinis had gambled and won. As Nevada journalist Thomas Mitchell observed, "Sometimes you just have to call their bluff."

Author and photographer Jeanne Sharp Howerton was raised on the Blue Eagle Ranch in the long shadow of Blue Eagle Mountain, part of the Grant Range in Railroad Valley in Nye County outside Tonopah. Her family had ranched in the region since the late 1890s and held on until 2016. They weren't driven out by BLM bureaucrats, but by time.

In fact, she remembers her father for the most part getting along "quite well" with most of the BLM rangers assigned to the area. Her father's diaries betrayed no animosity toward the government men he knew, although they were generally viewed negatively by many of the arid-country ranchers, who didn't like to be told where to graze their cattle or when to turn them out on the range. Many ranchers perceived new BLM rangers as college kids who wanted to put into practice what they'd read in books without a greater understanding or empathy for those who'd spent generations on the land.

"I remember we had to follow the rules, and some ranchers didn't like being told what to do," Howerton recalled.

> Around there the worst three words you could say in the English language were B-L-M. The reputation was dreadful, really bad. But the longer they stayed, and the BLM did seem to let their people stay longer in one area, the better they got along, and you got to be kind of friendly with them. Some would come out and have dinner with us. They tended to listen more to what the ranchers were doing.

Much of the county was battered from overgrazing in the early part of the twentieth century when the United Cattle & Packing Company ran the largest operation in the state under the ownership of Orville Knighton "O.K." Reed. Born in Unionville, Nevada, in 1873, Reed built Nevada's largest ranch on land not meant for hard grazing and heavy hooves. When the land collapsed, so did his fortunes. He lost thousands of cattle to mismanagement and drought and died in 1941 in Tonopah.

The Howerton family, meanwhile, ran a small and responsible outfit. In an interview, Howerton alluded to the United Cattle story as a reminder not only of the rough-and-tumble history of the region but of the importance of not exploiting the range. "The restrictions sometimes don't make sense to the ranchers, and they don't like being told what to do," she said. "But I do think you have to have rules. You have to have management. You have to have oversight."

When her family sold off most of the remainder of the Blue Eagle in 2016, it wasn't due to pressure from the government but from another reality on the arid range: "It's just plain hard living out there. You're on dirt roads, seventy-five miles to any kind of town or services. The kids don't want to manage it. And when you really get old, you can't do it."

Each January since 1985, ranchers, buckaroos, city folk, and the just plain curious have gathered at Elko for a week of rhyme, music, and storytelling at the National Cowboy Poetry Gathering. This town of twenty thousand, set in the heart of Nevada's cattle country, not only knows how to throw a helluva hurrah, but the event also provides examples of a diverse cowboy culture that transcends politics and redefines the definition of what it means to practice conservative values on the range.

During a break between shows at the Pioneer Saloon, longtime poetry-gathering official David Stanley talked about the nature of some conservatives he'd met and interviewed in his career as an academic folklorist and author. It wasn't a matter of politics. Nevada has a long tradition of libertarianism, and Elko County is predominantly Republican in party registration.

Stanley called many of the ranchers he'd met "conservatives in the best sense of the word. This is not knee-jerk conservatism, this is not Tea Party or Rush Limbaugh or anything like that. It's based on experience and an ideal, and it's deeply embedded in the idea of conservation: conserving natural resources, conserving land, conserving timber, conserving in most cases wild animals—with the possible exception of wolves. Ranchers today are in it for the long haul. They want to pass along their land, their allotments, their stock and their traditions to their children and their grandchildren."

With pressure from the government and big business interests, the family ranch is being squeezed into the history books. Stanley continued:

> Even though beef prices seem high today, the cost of everything from feed and fertilizer to power equipment—everything is against the small-scale family rancher or farmer. Everything is slanted toward large-scale operations. And that makes it very difficult to maintain those traditions, because agri-business doesn't give a hoot about these ideals.
>
> It's very difficult because of many issues: tax rates, financing, the cost of land, the pressure of condo and resort developments, ski resorts and ranchettes, and sheer population

pressure. The politics is a very practical one. I think we should be cautious about generalizing too much because I know plenty of cowboys who are anti-war pacifist liberals, and I know plenty of cowboys who are extremely patriotic, military veteran conservatives. But what they do have in common, I think, is being told what to do—and their antipathy to that. It doesn't matter whether the Tea Party or the Democratic Party or the Republican Party is trying to organize people in lock step, they're going to resist that with every bone in their body.

Howerton echoed a similar view:

Ranchers face the same pressures as farmers, it's become corporate farming and ranching. It feels like the ranchers have been getting pushed out their whole life. It's very hard to make a living only from ranching. My mom taught school. My sister ran a mail route and started a trucking company, worked for oil drillers moving water and cleaning up spills. Virtually every ranch family I knew had to have a little source of outside income. If you tried to do it just with the ranch, you barely survived.

In a partnership that outsiders might have thought impossible, some cattlemen have even linked arms with conservation trust foundations to preserve the land's unique and delicate qualities while also preserving the ranching way of life.

Increasingly in modern Nevada, not all ranchers are born on the range. Some, like Madeleine Pickens, want nothing to do with cattle at all. The wealthy widow of Texas energy magnate T. Boone Pickens is a longtime thoroughbred owner and horse-breeder whose interest in protecting the state's wild horse population led to purchasing the 14,000-acre Spruce Ranch in the Goshute Valley and the Warm Springs Ranch adjacent to the BLM's half-million-acre Spruce Mountain Grazing Allotment. With the federal government's wild horse adoption and management program foundering only a few decades after the 1971 Wild and Free-Roaming Horses and Burros Act, since 2010 she's reportedly poured $25 million into the creation of the Mustang Monument Wild Horse Eco-Resort. Designed to be an upscale dude ranch for wild horse lovers, it has met with a decidedly mixed reaction from Northern Nevada cattle ranchers, who see it as a land grab, and the BLM and Elko County officials, who were suspected of being tough on her. We could put it differently—these bureaucracies have cut no slack for the wealthy horsewoman.

As of 2019, Pickens's foundation had changed its name, and her mustang ranch continued to have trouble getting out of the gate.

Not far from Pickens's enormous spread, Michael Stankovic and his wife, Susan Mitchell, are also ranchers without a herd. In 1993, the couple purchased the 160-acre Lone Pine Ranch, located approximately twenty-five miles south of Wells in the rugged Humboldt Mountains. They've had a few cows and horses, but have chased more children and grandchildren on the spread than steers and mustangs. The backcountry, managed by the BLM and U.S. Forest Service, is home to herds of deer and elk, and Stankovic is an avid hunter. And the natural beauty is hard to beat.

"I don't tell people I'm a rancher," Stankovic said, laughing. "I say 'I own a ranch.'"

He also has a different view of the much-maligned BLM. When wildland fires threatened the family ranch, Stankovic watched BLM and U.S. Forest Service crews, aided by state prison units and Hot Shot rapid-response teams, arrive and work around the clock for days at a time on behalf of the ranchers in the region. Wildland fires burned nearly 870,000 acres of public lands in Elko County from 1999 to 2001 alone.

In an interview, Stankovic recalled a 2001 blaze: "It was moving through tall grass and heavy sage. The BLM was very responsive to the ranchers. They had air support coming in there and dropping fire retardant. I have had a very positive experience with BLM. And I think other ranchers have, too. I've had two major fires right on my property line. I think everyone who experienced that would have to praise BLM and their ability to gather resources and put their lives on the line battling any wildfire in Nevada because of the changing climate conditions. I really laud them for that."

As for the endless disputes over public grazing, Stankovich said,

I'm okay with cows going in and grazing and eating off the grass that's otherwise kindling for fire. I think that's a positive thing. I also know that the purpose of the BLM is not to subsidize ranchers. It's public domain, and there are a lot of other people that drive the back roads and use the country that are not ranchers. They're nature enthusiasts, hunters, mining people and all this other stuff.

It's a pretty thin slice of ham that doesn't have two sides.

CHAPTER 5

The Senator from Searchlight

If Cliven Bundy's family and supporters were asked to name the man most responsible for attempting to drive the rancher from his land, their reply would likely be unanimous: Nevada's powerful U.S. Senator Harry Reid. For followers of *Fox News*, Rush Limbaugh, and incendiary internet sites such as *InfoWars*, Reid's name had become a brand unto itself. Whether counterpunching in the minority or driving the narrative as majority leader, Reid was the Democrat that Tea Party Republicans and Donald Trump supporters loved to hate.

Reid wasn't Nevada's first high-ranking Senate Democrat, just the first to stand up to the once supremely powerful cattle industry.

John Sparks, Nevada's previous powerful Democratic senator, rose from the saddle to the heights of political power as Nevada governor after winning election in 1902 and being reelected four years later. He replaced Reinhold Sadler, who was also a stockman. Born in 1843 in Mississippi, Sparks began cowboying as a teenager after his parents moved to Texas. He later served as an Indian-fighting Texas Ranger. Driving large herds west, first to Wyoming and then Nevada, Sparks picked up the nickname "Honest John." He became a cattle baron in Nevada in partnerships with John Tinnin and Jasper Harrell, and at one time he controlled more than 5 percent of Nevada land. He managed to survive occasional drought and the devastating freeze of the winter of 1889, losing more than thirty thousand head, but by 1901 he had sold his share of the Sparks-Harrell cattle company to his partner.

Sparks ruled the range at a time when cattlemen were commonly known to hire gunslingers to intimidate and occasionally murder rival ranchers, squatters, and especially the sheepmen whose flocks competed with cattle for forage. That sometimes meant hiring gun thugs such as Jackson "Diamondfield Jack" Davis, not in the name of patriotism but of profit. Working on behalf of the Sparks-Harrell cattle company, Davis was linked to the wounding of one sheep-herder and the shooting deaths of two others near the Nevada-Idaho border. Sentenced to death by hanging in 1897 in Idaho, his sentence was commuted to life in prison in 1901. A year later, Davis was pardoned by Idaho Governor Frank W. Hunt. He immediately moved south to Nevada, where his ally Sparks was just taking office in Carson City. Diamondfield Jack didn't die at the end of a rope, in a gunfight, or even from falling off a horse. He survived the cattle and sheep wars, only to be struck and killed by a Las Vegas taxi in 1949.

Just after the turn of the twentieth century, Mississippi-born Francis Newlands boosted the state's farming and ranching interests with the crafting of the Newlands Reclamation Act of 1902, which created the Bureau of Reclamation and laid the foundation for the construction of a federal system of dams and water systems that proved essential to the development of the arid West. Newlands's legacy would be marred by his virulently white-supremacist views and support for the repeal of the Fifteenth Amendment, which gave black American men the right to vote.

As Harry Reid's power in the Senate grew, he'd sometimes be compared to a Nevada political titan of a previous generation, Pat McCarran. Although both were native sons who created their own highly efficient political machines, the two couldn't have been more different—especially on the subject of ranching's place in Nevada.

Born in Reno in 1876, McCarran often recalled his youth spent in the saddle driving cattle along the Truckee River outside his home-town. He would prove far more adept at rounding up political strays as the leader of a Democratic Party political patronage operation that dominated the state from the late 1930s until the moment in 1954 when he suffered a fatal stroke during a campaign speech in Hawthorne. McCarran was highly successful at bringing federal pro-grams and jobs to the state, including dramatic improvements to Nevada, although he was known outside Nevada as an anti–New Deal Democrat and isolationist who had a fondness for Spanish fascist dictator Francisco Franco. McCarran was a skilled pork-barrel politician who brought federal programs and dollars back to Nevada towns buffeted by the state's frequent boom-and-bust cycles and in dire need of consistent economic assistance. By the time of his death, the senator was credited with important contributions to the development of the nation's airport system. He was best known as a crude, red-baiting, thinly veiled anti-Semite, a power-hungry man whose anti-immigrant bigotry under the guise of anti-Communism had gotten the better of him.

However, McCarran was a fierce defender of the interests of Nevada stockmen—an important constituency even as the state became increasingly urbanized—in their tumultuous relationship with federal public-land policy and the Taylor Grazing Act. The act, which had set up a permit-and-fee process through the Grazing Service, gave preference "to those within or near a district who are landowners engaged in the livestock business." Despite the built-in advantage, ranchers in the West litigated, first in Nevada courts, then more broadly, with McCarran battering Grazing Service officials over five years of bruising Senate hearings.

McCarran eventually managed to gut the Grazing Service's budget. It was then merged with the General Land Office to create the BLM. "And to add insult to injury," one western land historian observed, "for a brief period during this time the salaries of many BLM field personnel were paid by the stock-growers from the portion of federal grazing fees returned to the states.... When viewed against this background, it is not surprising that many critics dismissed the Sagebrush Rebellion as merely the latest in a long series of attempts by exploiters to 'rip off' public property."

In defending ranching barons at all costs, Newlands and McCarran were carrying on a dubious tradition in the state, one that only further promoted the myth of the noble cowboy.

When the first cattle herds reached the West following the arrival of Coronado in the 1540s, the Mexican vaquero wasn't a legendary figure but a laborer-on-horseback who worked hard for little pay and less respect. The myth of the noble cowboy grew far faster than his pay and benefits. Channeling Nevada social reformer Anne Martin's groundbreaking work of the 1920s, historian Wilbur Shepperson joined a growing chorus of academics in the latter half of the twentieth century who pierced the folklore and reached a grittier reality. Observing that the myth had "refused to die," he wrote that the caricature had become an archetype. "The ordinary working cowhand was neither a myth nor a legend; he was a long-enduring, often drifting, generally exploited mortal. And within recent memory he has tended to succumb to either cirrhosis of the liver or agribusiness."

Anne Martin noted that in the state's cow-punching prime, half of Nevada's male population—approximately twenty thousand people—lived essentially in the field "outside the home environment" and "aimlessly wandering the streets," "corrupted by gambling, whiskey and prostitution." She blamed the livestock industry for a degree of worker exploitation that played out not on a silver screen but in an abnormally large population of "homeless workers" who too often wound up housed in the state prison and local jails during economic downturns. "In a sad and negative way," Shepperson reflected, "Nevada was paying the price for its ruthless cattle industry with its legions of displaced cowboys."

The creation of the BLM did nothing to change that. Ranchers bristled at the BLM from the start, despite the obvious damaging effects of overgrazing and the inability or unwillingness of stock associations to self-regulate. In years of good rainfall, ranchers expanded their herds and overgrazed the land. In dry years or drought, the cattle starved and the depleted soil blew away. With its intention to "stop injury to the public grazing lands," the grazing act was a fine idea on paper. In reality, the same stockmen it was intended to monitor often enforced it. And this cozy relationship continued after the Grazing Service was folded into the BLM.

Future Forest Service chief Lyle Watts, who worked aggressively to create a system of rules that allowed for the scientific and orderly development of the national forests, catalogued and chronicled the environmental damage and its cause in *The Western Range Revisited*:

The lack of constructive national land policy designed to fit the semi-arid and mountain grazing lands of the West has been a major factor in the depletion of our once great range forage resource. The belief in universal private ownership of land, the application of such a region to land laws designed to fit humid conditions, the failure to classify lands according to their highest use, and interpretation and administration of the statutes all played a definite part. The adverse effects of our past land policy on the ownership pattern of range lands and its influence on forage depletion are matters for national concern.

Few in Congress beyond the act's namesake, Colorado U.S. Representative Edward Taylor, paid much attention. Ranching barons held politicians in thrall. The insightful and scientifically important document "failed to precipitate either additional oversight of the managing agencies or further legislation to address 'the western range problem,'" according to historian Debra Donahue. Overgrazing continued. "Range conditions failed to improve, where they did not actually worsen."

In essays for *Harper's* and other magazines, Bernard DeVoto pierced the façade of the noble rancher. For every iconoclastic Bundy type, there were range barons, corporate titans, bankers, and timber kings who played the Taylor Grazing Act to best advantage, locking up thousands of square miles for pennies per cow. The Bundys of the range amounted to little more than shills and showmen for the ranching, mining, and logging industries. The damage caused by overgrazing turned parts of the West into a dustbowl, and brought cheatgrass and other invasive weeds that not only spread like wildfire but also helped to fuel it. As DeVoto wrote:

> So, at the very moment when the West is blueprinting an economy which must be based on sustained, permanent use of its natural resources, it is also conducting an assault on those resources with the simple objective of liquidating them. The dissociation of intelligence could go no farther, but there it is—and there is the West yesterday, today, and

forever. It is the Western mind stripped to the basic split. The West was its own worst enemy. The West committing suicide.

Although McCarran was loud in his support for Nevada ranchers, he also knew that handing over the state's vast tracts of federal land to the ranchers would be a mistake. He tempered his politics with pragmatism: in a sparsely populated state, it was better to lease the grazing land for pennies from the federal government than to take responsibility for its management.

Harry Reid's unlikely rise to the heights of political power was even more compelling than those of his powerful predecessors. The tale of the poor boy who became the most powerful man in Nevada political history begins in Searchlight, a played-out desert mining town cut from a dreary patch of greasewood fifty-eight miles south of Las Vegas.

In keeping with its bleak prospects and notorious past, even Searchlight's name is of dubious origin. Was it titled after a brand of wooden matches, or the searchlights used to lure drivers off the highway and into its many brothels? Most likely, it derived from an offhand remark delivered in 1897 by G. F. Colton when he first discovered pay dirt there. "There is gold here, all right, but it would take a searchlight to find gold there," Colton supposedly said.

His find rapidly turned the greasewood-littered smudge of a mining camp into a noisy gold-fevered boomtown. Searchlight was soon a tent city littered with jackass prospectors chasing the scent of riches on the parched desert breeze. By 1907, it sported its own narrow-gauge railroad and telephone exchange, and, as part of Lincoln County, it had become the most populated burgh in Southern Nevada, with forty-four mines and five thousand residents.

Like those wooden matches, Searchlight's fortunes burned hot— and quickly. The gold played out, the railroad washed out, and most of the town busted out. By the Roaring Twenties, Searchlight was known more for its illicit booze and willing women than its gold ore. By 1939, the year Harry Mason Reid was born the son of hard-drinking parents in a two-room, cold-water shack made of old railroad ties, those whorehouse bosses were the town's most successful businessmen.

Although protective of his humble hometown, Reid would reflect dryly in his history of the place: "At the beginning of the century Searchlight had had a vast commercial horizon before it.... But before the end of the first decade, gold waned, and the economic view became more bleak."

"When I was a boy, it was barely hanging on," he'd later recall in a memoir. "And we knew none of the luxuries that those who came before us had enjoyed on the same spot. Searchlight never became a ghost town, but it sure tried."

In an odd nod to his future fortunes in public office, the poor boy, who would become Searchlight's most famous son and rise to the heights of power as majority leader of the U.S. Senate, was gifted by circumstance with every politician's dream: a verifiable "log cabin" story. For if Searchlight's own origins were unclear, Reid's beginnings one day would be heralded by ally and enemy alike. He was raised in a wooden shack with an outhouse in the back, thirteen brothels within walking distance—and not a church for forty miles. (At least one pundit would crack that the latter fact prepared him for a long career in Congress.)

With a hard-rock miner father and a mother who did laundry at the brothels, Reid preferred to credit town-founder Colton rather than the other possible sources for the namesake "The Camp That Didn't Fail," the subtitle of his affectionate history of the place he called home, *Searchlight*. The fact remained that Searchlight shone brightest at night, when its signs for clubs such as the El Rey and Crystal Club offered the promise of cheap liquor and women of easy virtue. But no matter its true namesake, Searchlight was no place for children. Fair-skinned and rail-slim, Reid grew up with three brothers who ducked their father's alcohol-fueled rages.

But the recalcitrant elder Harry Reid, by his backbreaking work with a pick and shovel, offered his sons an important lesson of appreciating the value of the outwardly desolate land where they scratched out a living. While some had made a fortune clawing beneath the surface for gold and valuable minerals, given enough time—and in the right hands—the land itself would hold great value. It was a lesson young Harry took to heart and used throughout his life. He learned to see what most others missed.

Young Harry, nicknamed "Pinky" because of the easy way the desert sun burned his fair skin, attended first through eighth grades in Searchlight's two-room schoolhouse. Then, faced with the bleakest of options and opportunities, he hitchhiked forty-five miles to Henderson, a post–World War II industrial town thirteen miles south of Las Vegas, to attend Basic High School. It was there he met a barrel-chested Korean War hero and government teacher named Mike O'Callaghan, the man who would become his lifelong mentor. Barely slowed by a battle injury that took his left leg at the knee, O'Callaghan taught Reid to box in the ring and to pursue an education and goals that would take him not only to college and law school, but into politics at a time when he didn't appear old enough to shave. In high school Reid also met his future wife, Landra Gould, with whom he would father four sons and a daughter.

During his college days in Utah, where he paid more attention to classes and continued to box, Reid marked another life-defining moment: his conversion to the Church of Jesus Christ of Latter-day Saints.

Reid's early career as a lawyer, Henderson city attorney, and member of the state assembly were marked by the unquenchable thirst to rise through the ranks and prove himself, a drive well known to poor boys and sons of alcoholics. By 1970, he was advised by political bosses to put on twenty pounds, "so I'd look older," he told a reporter. When Reid decided to take a shot at the lieutenant governor's seat, he allied himself with O'Callaghan's quest for governor, with both running as underdogs for statewide office. The Irish Catholic O'Callaghan, who had rapidly climbed his way through federal and state government jobs and Nevada's Democratic Party, would win the first of two terms as governor, thanks in substantial part to Reid's balancing influence as a Mormon in steadfast step with his mentor.

Less than two years into his term, the thirty-two-old Reid learned that his tough old man had committed suicide. After commiserating with a few close friends, he took the news in the understated manner that would characterize the rest of his political career. He buried the emotion as deep as any Searchlight shaft, and went back to work.

Reid's four years as lieutenant governor were marked by his unflinching loyalty to the pugnacious O'Callaghan, whose administration could be characterized as pragmatically progressive. "Governor Mike," as he was fondly known, attended Catholic Mass each morning and loved to travel Nevada to meet the miners, ranchers, and farmers whose ways of life were increasingly marginalized in a state gaining a national reputation for its breakneck growth and its powerful and controversial casino industry.

Reid's appetite for political advancement at times caused him to make unforced errors. In 1974, he left the security of the popular O'Callaghan's side to run against former Republican Governor Paul Laxalt for the U.S. Senate seat vacated by Democrat Alan Bible. Reid experienced the first defeat of his career, losing by just 611 votes.

Instead of taking time to regain his bearings, against friends' advice Reid jumped back into the ring in the 1975 race for Las Vegas mayor against a likable neophyte named Bill Briare. As Reid would later recall in his memoir, "My friends begged me not to. But my pride got in the way. Well, my pride and I got beaten again, and this time it wasn't very close. . . . I woke the day after the mayoral election a thirty-five-year-old has-been. I assumed that I was finished with political office."

The free-swinging Reid had whiffed his way to the edge of oblivion. It was then that O'Callaghan, still governor and ever the mentor, made Reid an offer he couldn't refuse: the chairmanship of the Nevada Gaming Commission. He served with distinction and much controversy, at one point even being suspected of corruption and mob connections after a government wiretap captured a connected casino insider calling him "Mr. Cleanface" and saying he had "a Clean Face in my pocket." Although he'd eventually rise above the alleged mob associations, Reid's political enemies stoked suspicions for years to come.

The tar of past defeats and controversies didn't prevent Reid from easily winning a seat in the House in 1982. His two terms in the House were distinguished by his first major effort at affecting Nevada federal public lands, in 1986, with the political transformation of the Lehman Caves National Monument into the Great Basin National Park. It was a plan more than six decades in the making.

It is fitting that Absalom Lehman, the man credited with discovering the limestone caves that would honor his name, was a hard-luck miner who was pursuing cattle ranching when he came across his big find. Mining and ranching had been part of the area for generations, eventually displacing the Fremont Indians and other native tribes who had hunted, gathered, and sometimes farmed there. Had the state been possessed of different leadership and environmental sensibility, the popular caves located in the Snake Range of White Pine County near Wheeler Peak might have been given national park status as early as two years after President Warren G. Harding declared it a national monument in 1922. Instead, mining and cattle- and sheep-ranching interests ensured that access to the area would be open for tungsten and other mineral extraction as well as animal grazing. In keeping with the state's odd working relationship with the federal government, although the U.S. Forest Service officially administered the caves, its scarce presence enabled well-connected private operators such as Clarence Rhodes—former chauffeur to Nevada Governor James G. Scrugham—to profit from ticket sales into the natural wonders.

A national park proposal forwarded by Scrugham and U.S. Senator Key Pittman was introduced in Congress but never reached a public hearing, thanks to the clout of the Nevada Livestock Association and other ranching interests who claimed hardship. Grazing was prohibited in national parks, a regulation that would remain a sticking point whenever subsequent efforts were made to increase protections for the ruggedly majestic area that contained not only the natural beauty of Wheeler Peak but culturally valuable Native American artifacts.

That stubborn self-interest began to soften in the mid-1950s, when business-minded citizens of Ely acknowledged the economic benefits of what would later become known as eco-tourism. Although located far off the beaten path, the Lehman Caves had still managed to become a popular tourist destination for families from across America. And tourism was proving far more predictable than the price of minerals and beef.

The rediscovery of the Wheeler Ice Field and glacier by conservationist and writer Weldon F. Heald led to the 1956 publication of an enthusiastic article in the *Sierra Club Bulletin* titled "The Proposed Great Basin Range National Park." With a circulation that reached a small but informed environmentalist community, the *Bulletin* launched a broad-based campaign to see the area gain national park status. The effort was derailed once again, this time by Agriculture Secretary True D. Morris and Assistant Secretary of the Interior Roger Ernst, who argued that the area should be left open for multiple use, which included grazing and mineral extraction.

Supporters made another attempt in 1959, with Nevada Governor Grant Sawyer leading the charge and the state's congressional delegation placing enabling language bills in both houses. But the political ground began to shift almost immediately under the feet of backers. Influenced by ranching, mining, and agricultural interests, a majority of Ely residents who responded to a survey on the subject rejected the idea. Despite the best efforts of Sawyer and conservation groups, who stressed the park's economic potential to attract tourists, the proposal was stopped in its tracks and never reached a vote.

A two-term governor, Sawyer was born in Twin Falls, Idaho, to osteopathic physicians. He was no rancher, but he grew to appreciate the tradition and political clout of Nevada's stockmen while serving as district attorney in Elko County. The career of the staunch Democrat, considered a leader on civil rights during his tenure in Carson City, gives insight into the politics of the public-land debate. Like so many, he considered himself a conservationist at heart, but in rural counties he campaigned in a cowboy hat and showed a sore spot when it came to federal control of so much of the state.

Late in his life, in an oral history Sawyer reflected on the West's public land "wars" with the federal government and pointed to the "peculiar condition" of Nevada's and eight other states' founding and the conditions of their admission, acknowledging that "the Union retained ownership and control of the public lands." He also reminded an interviewer that other states didn't suffer the same circumstance. "I almost have an obsession about this inequitable treatment," he said.

Unlike Congressman Walter Baring and others who amounted to little more than lobbyists for mining and ranching, Sawyer saw the wisdom of U.S. Senator Alan Bible's attempt to balance industry with conservation and to promote the creation of Nevada's first national park through his role on the Interior Committee. He disagreed with Stewart Udall's call to increase grazing fees, but Sawyer didn't join in the ranchers' braying because he admired and respected the Interior secretary.

"After becoming governor I got exercised over the fact that one hundred and ten thousand square miles of Nevada really wasn't under my control at all, and I made my concern known at the federal level," he said. He added:

> Quickly the message came back that this was not our land, it was theirs. Well, what are they going to do with it? Whatever they do has to have our consent, and if they develop any land, they have to buy it from us. It seemed absurd to me that although Nevada had grown and was able to control its own destiny and to develop its own infrastructures, its centers of population were still surrounded by millions of acres of empty land that the state did not own.

Sawyer's answer was to craft a resolution and submit it to the Western Conference of Governors for distribution to Congress, lamenting the fact that at the time 87 percent of the state was under federal control. As governor, Sawyer saw the passage of the 1960 Multiple Use-Sustained Yield Act as commonsense progress on the issue.

Although he understood the potentially disastrous consequences of a wholesale transfer of such a large amount of land, and the responsibility that went with it, Sawyer remained a happy warrior on the edge of the rural rebellion: "Let us go! You are treating us like serfs out here. You gave us a bit of land to start with, but you still have over 80 percent of the total, and we've outgrown the little that we got. We're civilized and we need to develop. The federally-controlled public lands in Nevada should be put on the public market!"

Although never a rancher, Sawyer's fondness for wearing white Stetsons and the imagery that went with it made the hats standard attire on his trips outside the state and on a trade mission in Europe.

When it came to benefiting from cowboy imagery, perhaps no Nevada politician was more successful than Republican Robert List, whose family came from California's agriculturally rich San Joaquin Valley and purchased ranches in Elko, Washoe Valley, and Lovelock. Educated in the law, List was Carson City district attorney and a Paul Laxalt loyalist. But when he decided to run for state attorney general in 1974, "with branding iron in hand," he grabbed his hat and saddle and barnstormed around Nevada, riding in every small-town parade in a campaign against heavily favored three-term incumbent Harvey Dickerson. "I was allergic to horses, all kinds of hay," he told an interviewer. "But I was interested in politics at a very young age."

Cutting commercials with celebrity Nevada gentleman rancher Art Linkletter, List knocked Dickerson out of the saddle and four years later mounted a successful race for governor. Linkletter was one of a long line of entertainers and investors who owned Northern Nevada ranches for the wrangling and the tax write-offs, with Bing Crosby, Joel McCrea, and Dean Witter among them.

List's rise came at a time when the cattlemen's long-standing clout at the Nevada legislature was eroding, as the population and Assembly and Senate reapportionment shifted toward the population centers of Clark and Washoe counties. "Sagebrush Rebellion" founding-father legislators Dean Rhoads, a Republican, and Norman Glaser, a Democrat, were among the few remaining lawmakers with ties to working ranches. It's no coincidence that the Sagebrush Rebellion and Jarbidge Shovel Brigade grew while ranchers were losing ground in other political arenas. In the new century, ranchers were well represented in the legislature by Eureka cattleman Pete Goicoechea, who brought a moderate conservatism to Carson City and an understanding of the state's political power shift.

At heart, members of Nevada's congressional delegation weren't so different from most politicians. Once elected, they wanted to stay that way. In general, the best way to do that was to work hard for constituents—especially those from the industries that held

Nevada's interests, and much of its political clout, in the palms of their hands. Following the McCarran era, Senators Alan Bible and Howard Cannon were staunch supporters of the state's mining and ranching concerns. They picked up where the racist Newlands and red-baiting McCarran had left off, promoting everything from zinc and copper exploration to new water-reclamation projects throughout the state. Bible was a pragmatist when it came to everything from international trade partnerships to public-land use. "His goals were simple and parochial: he was interested in what was best for his constituents," Bible's biographer wrote. "Bible believed that his constituents would judge him by what he accomplished for them. That meant support for mining, livestock raising, and water development." But Bible was far more than a mouthpiece. In fact, he was far ahead of the industries, especially mining, in understanding that changing times called for a less-rapacious image.

Bible started his Senate career as a conservationist in the decades before politicians felt safe talking about "environmentalism." Like Teddy Roosevelt and Gifford Pinchot, he extolled the virtues of balancing natural resources with economic development. Considered one of the "invisible leaders" of the Conservation Congress of 1963–64, Bible had a front-row seat during the creation of the Wilderness Act, Land and Water Conservation Act, and many national parks and recreation areas.

He considered the failure of the creation of the Great Basin National Park among his most stinging setbacks in Congress. "He labored long on behalf of the park, but in the end a combination of mining and livestock interests led by their spokesman Walter Baring, defeated him," historian Gary E. Elliott observed. "It is ironic that Nevada was the only state without a national park when Bible left office, despite his contribution in creating parks throughout the country."

Whatever his defeats, Bible was Nevada's first conservationist in Washington, and he cut a trail that Reid used to secure the state's first national park.

A compromise that would reduce the size of the proposed national park from 147,000 acres to 125,000 acres also failed, in part due to a new mineral discovery in the immediate area. Even when revised legislation managed to pass the Senate, it foundered in the House. Further changes and compromises were also fruitless. Even the destruction in 1966 of a nearly five-thousand-year-old bristle-cone pine, considered the oldest living tree on earth, failed to soften opposition to the creation of a new national park.

It wasn't enlightenment but economic necessity and the waning political strength of ranching that changed the odds in favor of the creation of the Great Basin National Park. White Pine's largest employer, the massive Kennecott Copper Mine, had ceased operations. Left without work, hundreds of families moved on. Businesses closed in Ely, the county's largest town.

While locals may have been suspicious of Harry Reid and federal control, enough saw the economic potential to be gained from throngs of national park visitors. As one astute observer noted, "As Reid and others steadily pressed his case, an infestation of park rangers and a plague of tourists began to look like a business plan."

The stage was set for the final campaign to establish Great Basin National Park in 1985, with Reid in the middle of the action. Legislation that gave federal wilderness status to several areas in Nevada included one called the South Snake Wilderness Area—a geographic template for the national park.

The area's new status didn't sit well with ranching families who had been running cattle in the Snakes for decades and passing their grazing rights down through the generations. At times, their suspicion of the federal government bordered on paranoia. In an interview years afterward, Reid would reflect, "I didn't know the intensity that people had. It was like it was some kind of a plot, you know, like putting fluoride in water."

Allowing grazing to continue "in perpetuity," in direct conflict with the philosophy of the National Park Service, was one grand compromise of the national park's creation. Another was its size. Although Nevada ranchers held a declining influence, they still found friends in Republican Senators Paul Laxalt and Chic Hecht, whose knee-jerk insistence on trimming the park's scale from the already trimmed 129,000 acres favored by Reid to just 44,000 acres threatened to turn the national park into a national laughingstock. Great Basin's eventual size would be 77,180 acres.

Reid was outnumbered but not outmaneuvered as both bills passed in their respective houses. With those responsible for drawing prospective boundaries far apart, Bruce Vento stepped in to forge a compromise. A Minnesota Democrat and former public schoolteacher, Vento ranks as one of the most compassionate and progressive members in the history of the House, forging a career from 1977 to 2000 that focused on protecting the environment; increasing affordable housing; and helping the poor, homeless, and immigrant populations. By the time a compromise was reached, Reid and his formidable opposition could boast of a park that stretched 77,180 acres. With a signature from President Ronald Reagan, Great Basin National Park was born.

With Laxalt gone from the Senate in 1987 and replaced by Reid, and Hecht ousted in 1989 by Democrat and former Nevada Governor Richard Bryan, Reid returned to doing what he did so well in a place where the loudest roosters often have the least to crow about: grinding behind the scenes to ensure that Great Basin National Park became known more for its beauty than its bovine residents in what was sometimes disparaged as the least-visited national park in America.

To a great degree, two-term Nevada governor and U.S. Senator Bryan enhanced the legacy started by Bible. Although not as much in the news as Reid, Bryan was a key opponent of the Department of Energy (DOE) plan to bring high-level nuclear waste to Nevada with the proposed Yucca Mountain Project. In the Senate, conservation-themed legislation was among his greatest accomplishments as the primary sponsor of an act to amend the National Forest and Public Lands of Nevada Enhancement Act, and a measure to authorize the Forest Service to transfer land at Lake Tahoe for use as the site of a public school. All told, public lands and natural resources, energy, and environmental protection would comprise nearly half the legislation in which Bryan was involved.

It took nearly a decade, but with help from Great Basin superintendents Al Hendricks and Becky Mills and private funding

assistance from the Conservation Fund, Reid managed to craft yet
another compromise to help ensure that the park would be cow-
free, cutting a deal with local ranchers that compensated them for
their grazing rights and freed up other areas for their animals to
feed. His arrangement was celebrated by conservationists as "good
for the park, good for the ranchers and certainly good for the land
and visitors who come to Great Basin."

By the end, it wasn't a controversial call for ranchers, one of
whom would note, "It became obvious that it was no longer a possibility to graze on the park with the conflicts between people and
cattle and the attitude of the park service. We were willing sellers.
This is the best solution."

Such conciliatory rhetoric would prove hard to come by in ensuing years, which often found Nevada ranchers facing increasing
pressure to conform to federal public-lands policy. But the Great
Basin cattle compromise was considered a win-win and an even bigger political victory for Reid.

It also had the effect of placing him in a different light in the wake
of media fallout from federal organized-crime trials that dredged
up the mob's unflattering nickname for Nevada's former state gaming commission chairman. As one clever journalist put it, "With the
formation of the Great Basin National Park in 1986, as Harry Reid
ascended from the House to the Senate, 'Mr. Cleanface' became
'Sierra Harry.'"

Perhaps appreciating that there were far more votes to be had
from park visitors than Herefords in the wake of the grazing coup,
Reid offered, "Now instead of having to share the scenery with grazing cattle, hikers and campers will have thousands of acres to enjoy
undisturbed."

By the end of the century, the Great Basin's cows were home on
another range, and Harry Reid and others in the delegation were
involved in greater federal public-lands challenges. Although the
creation of Great Basin National Park was a major accomplishment,
the Wilderness Protection Act of 1989 was remarkable in its own
right. It was the state's first such bill focused on U.S. Forest Service
land, carving out thirteen wild areas stretching over 733,480 acres

of pristine territory. Among the locales were Mount Charleston in the Spring Mountains outside Las Vegas, Mount Rose near Lake Tahoe, Table Mountain in Nye County's Monitor Range, and the Ruby Mountains of Elko County. The Ruby Mountain Wilderness, with its year-round snowfields, includes ten peaks of more than 11,000 feet in elevation, glacier-carved high country, and Lamoille Canyon, known as Nevada's Yellowstone. With mountain goats, big-horn sheep, and one of the largest mule deer herds in the West, it shimmers like a jewel in arid Nevada.

Safeguards meant to appease ranchers and rural residents wary of any move by the federal government included grandfathering in livestock grazing, protecting water rights, addressing road-closure concerns, and allowing flyovers by military aircraft that for decades had used Nevada's wide-open air space for training exercises.

Reid had several energetic allies in the conservation community, including the Friends of Nevada Wilderness. Among the Friends' founders was Lois Sagel, an environmentalist well known for her advocacy for Nevada wildlands. During the long push for the Wil-derness Protection Act, Sagel reported receiving multiple death threats from those who opposed the legislation. The Friends helped to raise awareness of the importance of adding pristine lands in the state to the U.S. Forest Service's Wilderness Preservation System. In Sagel's group and others, Reid found steadfast and loyal troops. (The Friends of Nevada Wilderness also worked to help create the Spring Mountains National Recreation Area in 1993.)

The importance of the new Wilderness Act wasn't lost on the environmental community, which had seen many areas lost to min-ing development and poor management since the Wilderness Act of 1964 and the designation of the Jarbidge Wilderness in north-ern Elko County for protection. By the early twenty-first century, Nevada could boast of sixty-eight wilderness areas encompassing more than 6.5 million acres.

However popular the new designation was to environmentalists and outdoors lovers, it was attacked as a sign of federal overreach by those allied with Elko County's powerful ranching and mining interests. It was in the Rubies, after ranchers lost a legal fight over access to a dirt road into the wilderness that crossed a creek that provided habitat for the endangered bull trout, that the original Sagebrush Rebellion was sparked. It's no wonder, then, that it took more than a quarter century for the new Wilderness Bill to emerge. As Nevada environmentalist and prehistoric archaeologist Greg Seymour observed, "In the early 1980s, local and national wilderness advocates began to build an interest in some remote areas of Nevada. Interest was so great that a tour was provided for certain pro-wilderness legislators out of Washington. A helicopter ride over the region convinced them of the merit of these efforts."

The greatest victory of Reid's emerging congressional career came with a price. He had made lasting political enemies in rural Nevada. "The day I voted for that bill was the day I lost the rural vote," Reid said.

Few of Reid's innumerable actions affecting land, water, and environmental policy illustrate his masterful dexterity at balancing diverse interests—including his family's own—as his shepherding of the Clark County Conservation of Public Lands and Natural Resources Act of 2002 through the process. His Senate career was on the rise as Nevada's senior U.S. senator, minority whip, and leading Democrat when he sponsored and introduced the breakthrough bill that had the effect of transferring thousands of acres of federal public land in Southern Nevada into private hands for development while safeguarding more environmentally sensitive areas.

Although much thought had gone into the bill, and many stakeholder interests were consulted and heard, the bill's hearing lasted only a few minutes and was dominated by Reid's sweeping assessment that it had bipartisan approval. New Nevada Republican Senator John Ensign was an enthusiastic supporter. With that, Reid said, the act was "important to Southern Nevada and [a] priority for the Nevada delegation," as well as the nation as a whole. It sought "to establish wilderness areas, promote conservation, improve public land and provide for high quality development."

Reid took his colleagues on a long rhetorical hike through histori-cal terrain in Nevada and its overwhelming amount of land under federal management and ownership. The bill in discussion was a collection of what had been determined to be Southern Nevada's most important and pressing federal public-land issues.

As Reid explained:

> The sheer number of public lands bill requests Senator Ensign and I receive is daunting. If we introduced separate legislation to address each legitimate issue that constituents bring to our attention, we would create an awkward patch-work of new federal laws. The Clark County Conservation PLAN provides a comprehensive vision and framework for conservation and development in Southern Nevada that bal-ances competing interests.

The bill was discussed on October 17, 2002, then moved through the process by unanimous consent at Reid's request and was signed by President George W. Bush in November. As the *Los Angeles Times* later reported, the soft-spoken senator offered up a dense piece of legislation that meant little to nonresidents of the Silver State and caused not a ripple of controversy when he moved it through the process: "The name alone made the eyes glaze over." But what later drew the attention of many was the newspaper's 2003 exposé linking Reid's family members as lobbyists who received hundreds of thousands of dollars in corporate largesse in connection with the bill.

Although advertised by the senator as a way to protect the envi-ronment while opening the doors to further development in boom-ing Southern Nevada, "What Reid did not explain was that the bill promised a cavalcade of benefits to real estate developers, corpora-tions and institutions that were paying hundreds of thousands of dollars in lobbying fees to his sons and son-in-law's firms, lobbyists reports show."

A lobbying scandal could potentially ruin a political career that was reaching new heights of power, and as the vice-chairman and former chairman of the Senate Ethics Committee, Reid couldn't claim ignorance of the rules. It was the kind of moment that had sent many other careers in Washington off the rails.

An analysis of four years of records by the *Los Angeles Times* showed that law firms, corporations, trade organizations, local governments, and other special interests had paid two million dollars to law firms associated with Reid's attorney sons Rory, Leif, Josh, and Key. It was also true that the law firm in question, Lionel Sawyer & Collins, had been a political powerhouse in Nevada long before their association with it. In all, at least five clients of "Reid family lobbyists" profited from the legislation.

Married to Reid's daughter, Lana, son-in-law Steven Barringer was a partner in a Washington lobbying firm that was paid $300,000 by the Howard Hughes Corporation to secure 998 acres of real estate for the further development of its handsome Summerlin planned community in Southern Nevada. In a process often marked by bruising political maneuvering and sharp legal elbows, the federal public-land release for the Hughes Corporation was a proverbial layup.

Using its own appraiser, Hughes valued the land at less than $25,000 per acre—a fraction of what nearby real estate was going for. The result was a huge financial boon for the company at a time the Las Vegas population was booming. Only a national recession would slow home sales and the broadening of the corporation's brand in the community.

In life, Hughes's influence on Southern Nevada land was enormous but rarely chronicled in the press. In death, his corporate namesake turned his voracious appetite for acquisition into one of the largest planned communities in America.

The Hughes Corporation initiated a BLM land exchange back in 1988, swapping five thousand acres of land acquired near Red Rock Canyon for three thousand acres of real estate "more suitable for development," as its environmentally themed website page enthused, which would allow it to expand its sweeping Summerlin project on the northwest end of the valley. "The exchange was facilitated by The Nature Conservancy and it created a crucial buffer zone that protects Red Rock Canyon and serves as a gateway into the National Conservation Area." Much of that gateway, as it was called, rested in an enormous alluvial floodplain unsuitable for home building.

After the turn of the new century, the Hughes Corporation crafted a second BLM exchange that helped transform a thousand acres of high ground near Summerlin's western border into a county trails park, which was added to the conservation area.

To reporters from one of the nation's largest newspapers, Reid carefully downplayed the appearance of conflict. "Lots of people have children, wives and stuff that work back here," he deflected. "It is not as if a lot of cash is changing hands." And the fact was, the story of the Reids was a common one in Washington, a place that, like Las Vegas, runs largely on alliances and associations.

Had more Nevadans read the revelations published in the *Los Angeles Times*, the damage might have been greater for Reid and might have been more painful for the legions of Nevadans who supported him. Reid's staff was far more assertive in questioning the veracity of the reporting in interviews with Nevada's largest newspapers, the *Las Vegas Review-Journal* and the *Reno Gazette-Journal*.

The reporting acknowledged that Reid was far from alone when it came to members of Congress being lobbied by family members. More than two dozen others were in similar circumstances, including then-Minority Leader Tom Daschle, the South Dakota Democrat whose lobbyist wife Linda's many clients poured $14 million into her Washington consulting firm.

Although troubling, especially for those not accustomed to the coziness of Washington politics, the potential conflicts of interest were bipartisan. Addressing the Daschle family affair, a top Republican admitted, "Putting aside the jokes about politicians being in bed with special interests, in all seriousness it's not a big practical problem."

Reid's knack for balancing environmental, business, and personal interests would become a trademark throughout the rest of his career. In the new century, it would be unwise to stand in the way of progress in Las Vegas or of Harry Reid at any time.

Although the 1998 passage of the Southern Nevada Public Lands Management Act appeared to be a good-faith effort to end problematic and often ethically shoddy federal-private land exchanges and replace them with the competitive auction process that, at least in theory, held a grater benefit for residents and taxpayers, the 2002 bill included a notable exception. Reid acknowledged it during the hearing.

He said,

> at the time the law was enacted, Congress did contemplate that a limited number of ongoing land exchanges should be completed because of their benefit to the public. The Red Rock Canyon–Howard Hughes exchange is one such exchange. This land exchange has been contemplated for a number of years and enjoys unusually broad support ranging from the County to the environmental community. The time when this exchange should have reached completion through the administrative process has long since passed and a legislative resolution is now in order.

Those who might grouse that the Hughes Corporation was receiving special treatment would have a hard time arguing against such a pragmatic public defense. The 2002 act appeared to enjoy sweeping support from Nevada environmentalists, who had long sought official federal wilderness designation for dozens of pristine sites across the state under BLM control. A look at the details revealed considerable compromise with other stakeholders, including mining and ranching interests. Reid defended the bill's balanced approach:

> Those of us who wrote this bill hold different views regarding wilderness. But in developing the wilderness component of this bill, Senator Ensign, Congressman [Jim] Gibbons and I made good faith compromises that protect all interested parties as we designated 18 wilderness [areas] totaling about 450,000 acres and released 220,000 acres from wilderness

study area status. We believe that this solid compromise represents a critical step toward addressing the outstanding wilderness issues in the state of Nevada.

Another way of looking at the bill was as a modification of the 1998 Southern Nevada Public Lands Management Act. Although this act carved out wilderness designation in some areas of the state and not others, it also made available another 23,000 acres in the Las Vegas area for auction and development. For this, homebuilders also embraced the bill touted by environmentalists.

The act further designated a swath of dry lakebed off Interstate 15 between Jean and Primm, just south of the Las Vegas Valley, as the site of a new international airport. Reid called it the Ivanpah Airport, but he declined to reminisce about its location, less than an hour's drive from his humble beginnings in Searchlight. The man who saw value where others saw only wasteland was once again proven correct.

As if to illustrate his ability to juggle issues of importance to a diverse constituency, Reid also announced the bill's designation of an area not far from Henderson, the industrial town where he'd attended high school, as safe from urban encroachment. Called Sloan Canyon, it was festooned with Indian petroglyphs and was "in desperate need of protection because it is within a short walk of the Las Vegas Valley," Reid said. "The Clark County Conservation PLAN designates the Sloan petroglyphs and the area that comprises most of its watershed as the North McCullough Mountains Wilderness." Combined, the 32,000-acre open space in the future would be known as the Sloan Canyon Conservation Area.

In the Christmas sack of legislation was land designated for a Metropolitan Police Department shooting and training range and as urban real estate for "affordable housing." With his power increasing in the Senate and even members of the other party willing to allow the time-honored political tradition of a colleague to bring home the bacon to his constituents, Reid's efforts again paid dividends. Those same efforts met with more skepticism the following year.

Reid's dedication to Great Basin National Park burnished his reputation in the conservation community as a quietly effective official on the side of the environment. While some people weren't sold on his pragmatic approach in 1998, it was hard to argue with results. Concerns of environmentalists became more impassioned as Reid worked to push through the Nevada Public Lands Management Act of 1999.

While acknowledging his status as a "good friend of the environment," the astute editorial board of the *Reno Gazette-Journal* noted the "numerous concerns among environmentalists" of Reid's sprawling lands bill. Environmentalists were confounded with some of the developer-friendly designs of the act. "He thinks environmentalists don't fully understand the bill," the newspaper observed during the public vetting of the 1999 legislation. "They say if people who have spent 20–30 years on public land issues don't understand it, the bill needs clarification.... From the response so far, it seems that a lot of debate is needed—hopefully in workshops in Nevada, among other things."

As with the creation of Great Basin National Park, there were conflicting interests to balance—or at least to placate—who were easily offended and quick to take up arms, politically speaking, in defense of their positions. During this time, Reid found an unlikely partner in conservative Republican House member Jim Gibbons, a Sparks-born former U.S. Air Force fighter pilot who was also an attorney, hydrologist, geologist, and ally of the state's ranching community. Gibbons would eventually serve one term as governor.

But in the late 1990s, Gibbons served as Reid's friendly sparring partner as the state's congressional delegation, which included former House member John Ensign in the GOP-dominated Senate following the retirement of the bill's early sponsor and shepherd, Richard Bryan. Reid received the lion's share of the media attention and public credit for its success. One name almost never mentioned among the bill's earliest supporters was that of former Democratic Congressman James Bilbray, whose office sought a way to assemble small BLM parcels for public auction and invited the bill's diverse stakeholders to the table. Riding the "Republican Revolution" wave, Ensign defeated Bilbray in 1994, but the bill remained alive, thanks in part to Bryan's efforts.

The bill had valid intentions: to improve planned urban growth in Northern Nevada, in part by freeing federal lands for development in rural areas and raising funds to purchase environmentally sensitive lands. A wide swath of Northern Nevada would be affected by the bill, and stakeholders ranging from environmentalists to mining and ranching interests weighed in with suspicion. Was the plan really an end-run to grab water, further reduce cattle-grazing range, and restrict mineral exploration?

While Reid assured skeptics that any disposal of land was subject to previously existing rights and leases, environmentalists expressed concern that changes could cut off public access to some areas. Representatives of the mining and ranching industries, perhaps remembering the shifting Great Basin National Park deal, didn't trust Reid's motives.

Environmentalists were especially suspicious, noting that nearly all the federal land in question was already under grazing allotment and asking, "Thus, virtually no land could be sold, so what's the point of the bill?"

Reid's pragmatism, and the fact that he remained close to the mining industry throughout his career, made him a subject of suspicion in environmental circles. Through the first decade of his career in Congress, he wasn't much of a conservationist at all. In 1984 he cast a vote against cutting synthetic fossil fuel subsidies and water projects that impacted wildlife. This son of a miner was always a soft touch for mining, even when it became obvious that the industry was a major environmental polluter that, thanks to the long-term impact of the General Mining Act of 1872, paid little in taxes and had been protected by generations of members of Congress.

Votes that pleased the mining industry look particularly egregious with the passage of time. Reid helped block legislation that would have improved the public's right to know details about mining's toxic pollution, waste disposal, and large-scale mountaintop mineral extraction. From 1997 to 1999, Reid repeatedly helped block substantive mining reforms and important legislation addressing "clean coal" technology.

In what became a predictable rhetorical dustup whenever the subject of changing the 1872 mining law was broached, Arkansas Senator Dale Bumpers could be counted on to portray the industry in terms that would have made Gilded Age robber barons blush. The law, he said, was "a license to steal and a colossal scam. To paraphrase the old song, they get the gold and we get the shaft." In a later exchange, Bumpers protested that his colleagues were owned by the mining industry: "They [the mining companies] own enough people in the United States Congress; they know they don't have to pay a royalty and never will."

Reid, ever the industry's pit bull, reportedly clenched his fist and snarled, "Thinking that people here are voting because somebody owns them—I consider that an insult. I consider it an insult and I think that should be stricken from the record. Nobody owns me, and I've been insulted."

By 2005, those who studied Reid's votes on conservation issues saw a measurable shift by the senator on several fronts. With some exceptions, most of them votes associated with legislation attempting to increase mining regulation, Reid became a reliable environmental vote at a time when he was approaching the pinnacle of power in the Senate.

While others grew gray in Washington, Reid became greener with age, according to the National Environmental Scorecard kept by the League of Conservation Voters. In his brief tenure in the House and early years in the Senate, Reid cast a number of votes on the side of what environmentalists considered dirty-energy bills and legislation that weakened clean-water laws. Later, he would become the Senate's biggest booster of renewable energy during President Barack Obama's eight years in office, and few remembered the votes he had cast more than a decade earlier against clean-energy initiatives.

Only those critics who noticed Reid's near-obsession with pro-tecting mining had much to grouse about. Calling Reid "one of the mining industry's most reliable allies in Congress," a 2009 article in the progressive *Mother Jones* jabbed, "Reid has been instrumen-tal in blocking efforts to reform the archaic General Mining Law of 1872," which enabled extractors to pull $408 billion worth of gold and other hard-rock minerals from public lands and leave behind an environmental mess costing more than $30 billion to clean up. "But Reid, who owns a handful of defunct gold mines and whose sons and son-in-law have ties to mining companies, has vigorously fought off efforts to make the industry pay its way."

Mining's spell on Congress is no secret. The 1872 act cast the industry as "the highest and best" use of the West's vast federal pub-lic lands. Whether the miners were jackass prospectors from Search-light or massive open-pit gold operations headquartered in Canada, with nominal claims and leases they could extract minerals without paying Uncle Sam more than a pittance. While the fossil-fuel indus-try—oil, gas, and coal—operating on federal land had to pay royalties of up to 17 percent, hard-rock minerals have always been treated differently—and few in Congress have dared to challenge tradition. In a particularly egregious example, Barrick Gold of Toronto once paid less than $10,000 for nearly 2,000 acres of Nevada land that experts estimated held $10 billion in gold beneath the surface. Call-ing it "the last great boondoggle in the West," a policy adviser for environmental watchdog Earthworks estimates that the 1872 law has saved mining companies from paying more than $100 billion in royalties. "It's a legacy of the 19th century that doesn't make any sense in the 21st century."

But it made perfect political sense for Reid. Being Big Gold's best friend in Nevada might not have won him a majority of the votes in conservative Elko County—an area he never carried during his long career—but it did dissuade deep-pocketed mining corporations from betting against him.

Ever the pragmatist, in an interview after his retirement Reid offered a balanced perspective of his undeniably integral role in the state's environmental and mining issues. But his efforts at balance didn't prevent him from collecting formidable critics, the Pew Charitable Trusts among several.

Founded by Pennsylvania oil-industry executive Joseph N. Pew Jr. and his siblings, the Pew Charitable Trusts were created in 1948 with a focus on addressing societal needs at home and abroad. Early in the new century, the Pew Campaign for Responsible Mining began assessing the long-term impacts of mining, especially in the West, and the deleterious effects of Congress's failure to address the shortcomings of the 1872 Mining Law. The result was a research-based effort to educate the public and policymakers in stakeholder states and in Washington. Calling it "a law that has been out of step for decades," in the waning days of the George W. Bush administration the Pew campaign found new friends in Congress, including West Virginia House Democrat Nick Rahall, who sponsored a sweeping reform bill that, to the surprise of many, passed by a vote of 244–166. Rahall, representative from a coal-rich state not protected by the mining law, was pleased by the momentum, but he remained a realist. "This is a pirate story with the public lands profiteers robbing the American people blind. The robbery of American gold and silver must stop," he announced before later adding, "The industry has beaten back attempts to update the mining law for decades."

Politics aside, the argument for reform was overwhelming. Although the mining industry complained that in the modern era extraction operations were enormously costly and the profit margins often scant, in Nevada the industry enjoyed such a plethora of operations deductions that it annually paid only a tiny fraction of those profits. In the case of gold-mining mega-producer Newmont, it paid no taxes on millions of profits, thanks to the generous deductions on the books. Although Barrick's Carlin Trend operation generated nearly $80 million in gold profits that year, it paid just $1.1 million after adjusted write-downs. One operator based outside the United States withdrew a billion dollars each year in gold from federal public lands without paying a penalty in royalties.

The 1872 law was created in part to spur development in the West. Signed by President Ulysses S. Grant, the law remained unchanged for 135 years, long after the West was won, and it had proven to be a government protection act for gold and other minerals. While the oil, gas, and coal industries paid extraction royalties from approximately 8 percent up to 16 percent, gold's comparatively free ride federally had an annual cost to taxpayers estimated at $100 million.

Gold mining also enjoyed priority status on federal public lands. For a nominal fee, claims worth millions were scooped up by the score and maintained in perpetuity with annual on-site assessments that could be written off as a loss. According to Pew's findings: "The law allows claimholders to buy public land for $5 an acre or less, and to use it for anything from condominiums to casinos." With criticism growing, Congress placed a temporary hold on the land grab.

In Nevada, mining was an important employer—especially in the gold-rich northern counties, where a majority of the industry's eleven thousand workers were employed at high-paying jobs. With its "Mining: It Works for Nevada" mantra, the Nevada Mining Association in 2014 reported an average salary in the industry of $91,300, compared to $44,720 for the state's other workforce.

Long-term gold-mining corporations also racked up multibillion-dollar cleanup bills, according to the EPA. In the previous decade, taxpayers had doled out $2 billion cleaning up after the mining industry. A 2004 EPA inspector general's report listed 156 hard-rock mining sites that would need to be remediated, at a cost ranging from $7 billion to $24 billion. A BLM survey charted 12,204 abandoned mines, but environmentalists, citing other historic mining areas, countered that more than 500,000 abandoned mines needed remediation at a cost that could climb as high as $72 billion.

When it came to pay something for environmental cleanup, both sides would eventually find room to send at least some money back to the states. The Nevada Mining Association, the industry's representative in the state, argued that its corporate practices included setting aside funds for "complete reclamation and remediation of exploration and mining sites." But when it came to its toxic pollution of water systems below ground and on the surface, gold mining was considered a largely unchecked bad actor.

Some of the West's most cherished and environmentally sensitive lands—including the Grand Canyon—were threatened by marginally restricted mining operations that enjoyed protections provided by the 1872 mining law. And, Pew warned, commercial exploration for gold and uranium on public lands was rising dramatically.

Not that Reid's views or loyalties were ever in doubt. Although he'd made many friends in the environmental community and with progressive green political interests—and he liked to remind them of the pine tree symbolism on his campaign signs—he remained solidly in the camp of big mining. National press coverage often mentioned his Searchlight upbringing and miner father. Now that he was the Senate majority leader, as Pew's Jane Danowitz acknowledged, "All roads to reform go through Nevada. There's no reason why through his leadership a reasonable reform package couldn't be put into place."

As he had done so often throughout his career, Reid had thought several steps ahead of his opponents as he sought to protect the mining industry. So it should have come as little surprise that, despite the ominous House vote, he'd already had a sit-down with Democratic Party presidential hopeful Barack Obama to explain the industry's regulatory dilemma.

During an August 2007 teleconference with Nevada reporters, the future president announced, "What is clear to me is that the legislation that has been proposed places a significant burden on the mining industry and could have a significant impact on jobs. Given the difficulties that the industry is already having in maintaining its operations, I think it is important for us not to move with royalty payments that are so significantly higher than they were previously."

When Congress recessed for the summer in 2008, the push for mining reform was being buried under weightier issues in a presidential campaign season. Majority Leader Reid also appeared ready to move on, telling an interviewer, "I don't see it this year.... We need mining law reform. It's important that we do that. The mining companies want it. It's appropriate that we should do it as soon as possible."

But substantive change, the kind Reid could have encouraged, never came.

After retiring from the Senate, he reflected on his style and substance when it came to defending the Nevada mining industry. "You have to look at what's best for the state," Reid said. "Politicians need to understand that. I got a lot of hell for supporting mining in Elko County. I didn't do it for the votes—they didn't vote for me up there—but I'm just a mining adherent."

When it comes to understanding the ecological, economic, political, and cultural complexities that Reid and other Nevada elected officials navigated in recent decades, few rival the intrigue surrounding the care and control of Lahontan Valley's 80,000-acre Stillwater National Wildlife Refuge outside Fallon, approximately sixty miles east of Reno. The Stillwater wetlands had long attracted wildlife and travelers but became increasingly distressed as the area's population grew. Between conservationists, the Sierra Pacific Power Company, ranchers, farmers, Native Americans, business owners, and the military, there didn't appear to be much common ground. And it showed.

"One of the real difficult things that we had to do was to get people to sit down and talk," Reid told an interviewer. "People literally would not sit down at the same desk. That is, you couldn't get the Indians to talk to the farmers. You couldn't get the farmers to talk to the conservationists. You couldn't get the people from Sierra Pacific Power [Company] to sit down with any of them. It was really a very difficult problem…the negotiations we had were as difficult to put together as the Middle East negotiations."

Reid gradually learned that, although Fallon and Churchill County were well known for agriculture in arid Nevada, "the vast majority of ranching that takes place in Churchill County is done on a part-time basis." Admittedly ignorant of all the history and political in-fighting that had taken place for decades, with so much at stake Reid brought together allies to learn about the issues and forge compromises.

At first he had few takers. Eventually, even staunch conservative Nevada Congresswoman Barbara Vucanovich came on board the increasingly broad-based plan to share Stillwater's resources in the name of preserving and protecting them: "When she realized this was an important piece of legislation for the people of Reno and Sparks, and that it would be helpful to the people of Churchill County in due time, she supported this," Reid recalled. Then came another turning point. When respected U.S. Senator Daniel Inouye, chairman of the Indian Affairs Committee, began participating in the process, the region's Native Americans were shown increasing respect and a place at the table.

Although grievances were aired, Reid's was a table where decisions eventually had to be made. He mused, perhaps jokingly, to an interviewer, "One of the good qualities I have, I tend to forget people who mess around with me."

Reid overcame critics in Congress, the Air Force, the Department of the Interior, and elsewhere to reach a compromise that gave each stakeholder something to take away from the table. One thing that helped move the process forward through the Senate was the lack of communication and comity between key federal agencies, including the Department of Fish and Wildlife, Bureau of Reclamation, and Bureau of Indian Affairs. The unimpressive and ill-informed hearing testimony of Department of the Interior Assistant Secretary John Sayre only further damaged the government's argument. Interior official William Bettenberg was a prickly critic, but he saw that the argument was lost. Musing about the federal government's bureaucratic set, Reid reflected, "Part of their problem was, you see, in government, if it's never been done before, don't do it. That's the rule of a bureaucrat. And here we did everything that hadn't been done before, and some of these bureaucrats, it was hard for them to handle that. But after they got on board, things have moved along quite well."

Illustrative of the collective victory and of his own recurring political challenges in Nevada's conservative rural communities, Reid boasted,

> Now, this is really landmark legislation. Pretty good for some-body that didn't know what they were talking about when

they said something should be done when it happened. And even the people in Fallon have accepted it. I mean, it's like some people never—say this as nice as I can—some people never give up.... So I think we've come a long way. We've negotiated a settlement, that calls for implementation, but that's taking place almost on schedule.

Reid's realistic approach to political power, balancing conservation and development interests with his own, was again a proven key to his success. In a business where the love rarely lasts and animosities can run miles deep, there's an art to incumbency. Reid endorsed and shepherded environmental and water-conservation causes when possible and embraced big mining and development when necessary.

Around the Southern Nevada Water Authority (SNWA) offices, it's known as "The Groundwater Development Project." This is an innocuous title for a long-range plan to pump and pipe groundwater from four valleys in central and eastern Nevada some two hundred miles to endlessly thirsty Southern Nevada at a construction cost estimated as high as $15 billion. Distilled to its essence: "The Groundwater Development Project will reduce Southern Nevada's reliance on Colorado River water and provide flexibility to respond to drought conditions on the river system." After acquiring land and water rights from the region's ranches, some of which had been worked for more than a century, the groundwater would be drawn from the Spring, Cave, Dry Lake, and Delamar valleys of rural and conservative White Pine County and sent through a buried pipeline.

This plan was only one part of the SNWA's long-term water-resource vision, but one that put the agency at odds with some rural ranchers and a cross-section of the conservation community. The issue also tested the political power of Harry Reid.

The ubiquitous Reid wasn't named as the project's author, but he was part of the planning from the start. He played an integral role in not only creating the Great Basin National Park and negotiating the removal of cattle herds from within its boundaries, but in passing enabling language that made possible the groundwater-pumping proposal and the lengthy right-of-way essential for the construction of the pipeline.

Reid wasn't alone. Beyond the central players, another individual played an integral role in water and land issues in the West for four decades but has managed to remain in the background while elected officials and water czars receive accolades in the press. If Reid was the unnamed on-the-record influencer of the SNWA groundwater project agenda, lobbyist Marcus Faust ranked as its political choreographer in chief. If Reid was a behind-the-scenes driver of the plan, Faust was a veritable ghost in the machine—often felt, seldom seen.

The ironically named Faust was known among clients for his vast knowledge, top political contacts, and calming influence as he mapped out long-term land and water strategies that crossed county, state, and federal jurisdictions. Born in Salt Lake City, he attended Cottonwood High School and Brigham Young University. Although his deep roots are in the West, his business flourishes in Washington, DC.

He may have come by that gentle hand from his father, James Esdras Faust, who, in addition to being an attorney and politician, was Second Counselor to the First Presidency of the Church of Jesus Christ of Latter-day Saints. Born in 1920 in Delta, Utah, he served in World War II, graduated from the University of Utah Law School, was elected to the Utah State House of Representatives, and was appointed by President John F. Kennedy to the Lawyers Committee for Civil Rights.

But it was in his religious life that he shone most. The First Presidency is the highest presiding body in the LDS faith. He previously served four years as an Assistant to the Twelve, the second-highest ranking body. He served for three decades as an LDS Church apostle and was a general authority of the Church for thirty-five years, until his death in 2007.

In a sermon to the LDS General Assembly titled "What's In It for Me?" James Faust observed that it was the pursuit of short-term gain that often came at the expense of long-term fulfillment, as illustrated by his tale of an associate whose impatience for profit revealed his true character. "The relationship between the two was never quite the same after that," the elder Faust held forth. "Our self-serving friend did not prosper, as his selfishness soon eclipsed his considerable gifts, talents, and qualities. Unfortunately, one of the curses of the world today is encapsulated in this selfish response, 'What's in it for me?'" It was a question that would make even the most pious congregant stop and think, but one that was asked as a matter of course in the political world.

"I learned from him the meaning of loyalty," Marcus Faust once reflected. "My father would make two haircut appointments, one soon after the other. The first appointment was with my grandfather's barber, a buddy from World War I who was so old he was losing his eyesight and the steadiness in his hands. The second appointment was with another barber who would even out the work.... Father has a soft touch and can deal with sensitive situations without leaving hurt feelings. He can walk on wet concrete without leaving any footprints."

If it weren't for the Senate Office of Public Records and the minutes of local and state government water meetings, Marcus Faust might have an even less traceable imprint. But Faust gradually caught the eye of environmental reporters and Las Vegas journalists who covered Clark County government and the SNWA, which for nearly two decades had chosen him as its favored water-issue lobbyist. To some, he became known as "an oddly Sidney Greenstreet–like figure among Washington lobbyists, whose influence is pervasive in Western water."

By 2009, Clark County Commissioner Steve Sisolak had recognized the well-paid ubiquity of Faust and other top lobbyists, more than one of whom had close ties to Reid. Although baffled by the numerous consultant, lobbyist, and public-relations contracts tied to the county, Sisolak, a Democrat who would be elected governor of Nevada in 2018, tried to take care not to antagonize the most powerful Democrat in the state. But Faust's name was impossible to miss. Paid $150,000 in 2009 by the SNWA, a contract he'd then held for seventeen years, he also held deals with the Water Reclamation

District, Department of Aviation, Las Vegas Valley Water District, and Regional Transportation Commission.

Still, it was Faust's other clients, including the enormous Coyote Springs Investment residential development project operated by Reid's close ally Harvey Whittemore, that for Sisolak held clear potential for conflict. "You mean to tell me we can't find other people here, or in Washington, who might be able to do the same job?" Sisolak asked.

The SNWA's General Manager Pat Mulroy, who considered Reid a major influence in her professional life, countered that lobbyists of Faust's expertise were expensive but saved time and money in the long run, despite any inherent conflicts. "You can't find a qualified lobbyist who doesn't have a conflict...it's how you manage those conflicts," she told a reporter. A Water Reclamation District official noted, "It's valuable to have someone in DC assisting, there's a value in terms of return of dollars to having someone do that."

In keeping with Faust's long-term approach to all things, six years later he found himself on the receiving end of a glowing profile in the same newspaper that had previously singed him: "The native Westerner specializes in understanding the minutia of law, a valuable skill set in Washington," the profile enthused. "Faust prefers to remain behind the scenes, but his fingerprints are on landmark legislation that created the Southern Nevada Public Lands Management Act, a national monument at Tule Springs and a payments-in-lieu-of-taxes program for rural Nevada counties with federal land."

As late as 2014, Faust was still a solo practitioner specializing "almost exclusively" in representing local and county governments, water districts, and regional utilities companies in the West. For his part, Faust takes pride in giving his clients their money's worth, which in 2013 amounted to approximately two million dollars in lobbying fees, according to the Senate Office of Public Records. In a 2014 survey covering the previous five years, Faust represented 77 percent of his firm's clients from four states with something in common: large-scale federal public-lands challenges and water-conservation projects. Some of his Nevada and Utah clients included the Las Vegas Valley Water District, Southern Nevada Water Authority, Clark

County Water Reclamation District, Colorado River Commission of Nevada, Great Basin Water District, Central Utah Water Conservation District, and the City of St. George, Utah. He was also listed as a lobbyist for the Water Resource Network, a nonprofit research foundation whose subscribers include water utilities and companies. On the foundation's website, Southern Nevada water officials are some of its most enthusiastic supporters.

And why not? Faust is known for providing the equivalent of concierge service for bureaucrats and elected officials, from drafting bills to providing tips on giving testimony. He's intimately familiar with elected officials at the state and federal levels, and that has long included a relationship with Harry Reid.

With clients paying Faust up to $50,000 per quarter for his insight and lobbying expertise, his philosophy appears simple: "There are other business models out there among lobbyists trying to maximize revenue on each individual account, but the clients we have are long-term relationships. They are getting value for their dollar, particularly as many are public entities who have to justify their expenditures."

Described as "a large, slightly palsied and professionally discreet man" by one reporter and as a "genius" by a client, Faust has remained in the background while Nevada's land and water issues have played out in Congress and the press. Observed one reporter, reminding readers that it was Faust who was responsible for the strategy and draft of the Southern Nevada Public Management Land Act, "If you want water, or land, or to keep conservation development-friendly in the West, you become his client."

Nearly four decades after starting his lobbying career in 1981, Faust has become known as a tried-and-true friend of water districts and local and regional governments, especially those in Southern Nevada, and his lobbying income has reflected that trust. Groups that retained Faust spent $1.98 million in 2016 for the privilege. Among those, according to Senate records, were opensecrets.org and the Center for Responsive Politics, the Nevada electricity utility NV Energy ($200,000), and the SNWA ($120,000).

Opposition to the SNWA's "water grab," as conservationists called it, attracted diverse groups with seemingly little in common into a broad-based coalition of environmentalists and cattle ranchers. Reid was politically radioactive in White Pine County and remained far off-stage. But, to borrow a phrase from Mark Twain, in the new century water issues ran uphill to the Senator from Searchlight.

With the water-pipeline issue came a schism, however brief, from some of Reid's most reliable allies in the progressive and environmental communities. When it came to providing water for booming Southern Nevada at the expense of rural counties, Reid quickly morphed from environmentalist defender to pro-growth booster.

Reid's mentor, "Governor Mike" O'Callaghan, was adamant about the lack of fairness inherent in the SNWA's formidable push to approve a multibillion-dollar groundwater-pumping plan that would tap aquifers in rural northeastern Nevada counties. As executive editor of the *Las Vegas Sun*, a title Reid recalled helping to secure for his close friend, O'Callaghan weighed in regularly and sometimes daily about a broad range of issues, from the local minor-league baseball team to the State of Israel. While some might have disagreed with him, few were left confused about where he stood on issues. In a February 27, 2004, column, O'Callaghan made it clear that he stood at a great distance from the Senator from Searchlight when it came to the rural pumping and pipeline proposal being forwarded by Pat Mulroy and the SNWA. He immediately called out Mulroy's minions and warned of the dangers of large-scale groundwater pumping in the arid region:

> The severe drought has Las Vegas builders and other water users and suppliers wanting to reach into northern counties to replace dwindling supplies. This isn't a new idea but has, until now, been put on the back burner. Big bucks and the drought have dragged it out of hiding again. Of course, it hasn't been very well hidden in recent years as a private company designed to sell water and a legislative lobbyist have joined the Southern Nevada Water Authority in buying and selling water.

After all but declaring that power players were putting in the fix for the project, whose cost estimates would rise from $1.5 billion to

$15 billion in just a few years as forces on either side litigated the issue, O'Callaghan reminded readers of the area's history of over-pumping. "We must remember this lesson before deciding to build a pipeline and water collection system that costs billions of dollars and reaches all the way into White Pine County," the popular former governor wrote a week before he suffered a fatal heart attack while attending a Catholic Mass.

Like Harry Reid, Bob Fulkerson is proud of his Nevada heritage. In fact, he can trace his family's roots in the state back five generations. Fulkerson fell in love with the outdoors as a boy growing up in Reno, and in time, he saw Nevada's beautiful places endangered by development and mining interests. His concern for the environment and opposition to the proposed nuclear-waste dump site at Yucca Mountain led to his participation in the mid-1980s with Citizens Alert, a progressive organization founded in 1975 by Susan Orr and Katherine Hale and inspired by their friend, legendary Nevada social-justice activist Maya Miller.

By the mid-1970s, Miller's name was already part of Reid's personal political history. Where Reid was a consummate political pragmatist, Miller was an unabashed ecologist and humanitarian. Perhaps they were destined to clash, as they did in 1974 when Miller challenged Reid in the Democratic primary for the United States Senate seat vacated by the retiring Alan Bible. A far-left Democrat whose name was placed on President Richard Nixon's infamous "Enemies List," ostensibly for her outspoken opposition to the Vietnam War, Miller fought for the rights of Nevada's women and children, welfare mothers, and Native American tribes. She was no match for the safe and savvy Reid, but the juxtaposition of the two disparate personalities was telling.

As Miller's daughter, documentarian Kit Miller, observed in the Nevada Women's History Project, "Maya wasn't a real politician. She was an outside agitator fighting the powers that be. She ran for the senate because she felt the cause was right." Miller won 38 percent of the vote and weakened Reid in a year of reliable support for Democrats. Reid went on to lose by 611 votes in the general election to former Nevada Governor Paul Laxalt.

After a decade with Citizen Alert, in 1994 Fulkerson and Maya Miller worked to establish the Progressive Leadership Alliance of Nevada (PLAN), a nonpartisan nonprofit organization of diverse activists dedicated to protecting the environment and improving the human condition in the state. PLAN members weighed in on issues ranging from antipoverty proposals to civil rights and social justice advocacy. One particular area of longtime concern for Fulkerson has been defense of Nevada's environment.

While Fulkerson agreed that no Nevada leader had played a greater role in shaping environmental issues than Reid, he said, "It's a complicated legacy, the scales being tipped depending on how much emphasis you want to put on the various issues."

Although as young elected officials in the mid-1970s Reid and his colleague Richard Bryan had liked the idea of storing nuclear waste in Nevada when it was first raised, later, as U.S. senators, they eventually became the plan's greatest critics in Congress. As Reid reached senior leadership positions, Fulkerson observed, "Yucca Mountain was stopped solely because of Harry Reid's power, strength and commitment to keeping it out of the state."

In Northern Nevada in the late 1980s, Reid stepped in to stop a developer from sending water from Honey Lake north of Reno to a proposed large-scale housing project. And it was young House member Reid who used his budding federal clout to contain the expansion of military installations in the state. Fulkerson credited Reid with halting a 1988 Nevada National Guard proposal to create an operations facility in Hawthorne that would have included a 300,000-acre tank-training range stretching across miles of BLM land in central Nevada, from the edge of Walker Lake to the fringes of the 79,600-acre Gabbs Valley Range Wilderness Study Area. This controversial project was literally stopped in its tracks.

Reid's time in the House was brief, just four years, but his emphasis on public-lands issues and the environment was obvious from the outset. He took a swing at amending the Engle Act of 1958, which set rules for the withdrawal of federal public lands for military purposes. On September 12, 1985, he introduced the Nevada Wilderness Act of 1986, which sought to define and set aside pristine public lands in the state for federal protective status. Weeks later, he carried a bill calling for a transfer of property to benefit the booming town of Mesquite in Southern Nevada, near the Utah state line. He picked up a co-sponsor in Nevada's Republican House member, Barbara Vucanovich, for the National Forest and Public Lands of Nevada Enhancement Act of 1986. Months later, he returned again to fight for his wilderness bill in the House, and he continued the fight when he crossed over into the Senate. Although many of his efforts weren't signed into law, Reid had established himself as an authority on Nevada public lands.

At times during an interview, Fulkerson described Reid's efforts in almost heroic terms when Reid came up with a way to save a scenic gateway to Lake Tahoe from a ski resort and condominium development, a place where the environmentalist had "snowshoed, hiked, and gone cross-country skiing. Reid and Richard Bryan were able to get the funding to buy all that out, not only to buy it out but to then declare that whole area wilderness. Every time I go up there, I think about it. We almost lost it."

Environmentalists and outdoor enthusiasts across the state tell similar stories. Ranchers complained and occasionally attracted the attention of conservative political contributors—one of whom sarcastically had "Anybody Butt Harry Reid" and "Will Rogers Never Met Harry Reid" signs made and staked through rural central Nevada. But Reid's efforts were popular in urban Clark County in the south and in the Reno-Tahoe area of Washoe County in the north.

Reid's record on water, however, was far more complicated. Along with his response to the attempted water diversion at Honey Lake and other substantive successes throughout the state, he also enjoyed big successes dealing with water-quality issues on the Truckee River and Pyramid Lake. But Reid's decision—to endorse and outline the transfer of groundwater from ranching communities in White Pine County by pipeline to feed burgeoning Southern Nevada's unslakable thirst—would test the limits of his alliance with Fulkerson and fellow conservationists.

Buying up ranches along the Snake Range would be mostly a matter of cutting checks. Ranchers in the region had used snow-fed aquifers for more than a century to water their cattle and grow alfalfa, but outside competition and increasing restrictions by the BLM had reduced their margins and turned them into symbols of a fading way of life. That seemed just fine to Reid, who saw many of them not only as all but freeloading on federal public lands, but as controlling water that could be put to more productive use in Southern Nevada's burgeoning suburbs and along its world-renowned casino tourism corridors. The Senator from Searchlight left no doubt where he stood on the issue in an interview when he repeated a favorite phrase, "I'd rather flush toilets on the Strip than water alfalfa in Northern Nevada."

Reid and Mike O'Callaghan found themselves on opposite ends of the argument in one of the few strong differences of opinion the two would ever express publicly. In a surprisingly pointed letter to Reid on July 12, 2004, a coalition of conservationists and progressive activists calling themselves the Nevada Ad Hoc Water Network— many of whom had often sung Reid's praises—looked askance at what they considered the bold power move of the water exportation effort, which surfaced under the innocuous title of the Lincoln County Conservation, Recreation, and Development Act of 2004. If some of those environmentalists had been forgiving of Reid's multi-faceted approach to public lands and water issues, they made their views clear in the letter. They were concerned about "the serious ramifications this legislation has on rural and urban Nevadans and eastern Nevada ecosystems and as models for future legislation and for future generations of Nevadans."

Then they attempted to hit Reid where it was bound to hurt. They invoked the name of his mentor and best friend O'Callaghan, who had died just a few weeks earlier:

Former Governor Mike O'Callaghan editorialized about the proposed exportation project (attached) with a warning, "don't rush to destroy." The Lincoln County Conservation, Recreation, and Development Act of 2004 (bills) appears to circumvent federal policies and national laws related to environmental protection and management of public lands,

therefore undermining environmental and economic protections for rural and urban counties and Indian tribes. The
bills provide tacit Congressional approval of the first steps in
turning eastern Nevada into another Owens Valley with the
potential for severe environmental and socio-economic harm.

The group focused on what it called the "premature and unnec-
essary" inclusion of language approving the proposed pipeline's
right-of-way without taking into account "existing administrative
procedures.... These federal laws and procedures provide for full
and open public participation in these critical decisions on public
lands and waters."

To the Nevada Ad Hoc Water Network and its allies, the Nevada
congressional delegation appeared to be fast-tracking the legislation by waiving the pertinent parts of the federal land-policy act
and the National Environmental Policy Act (NEPA). Then they wondered whether all the talk of drought, however severe, was being
used conveniently to call for emergency action: "We share Former
Governor O'Callaghan's concerns about...destroying the natural
environment in neighboring counties to satisfy the added development of an ever-expanding man-made environment of Las Vegas,"
they wrote.

Pushing through legislation meant that sending groundwater to
a booming Las Vegas Valley, which then was home to 1.7 million
residents and attracted millions of annual tourists, at the expense
of Lincoln County (population 3,700) and White Pine (population
8,100) might have made political sense, but it failed the fairness
test as applied by O'Callaghan. The letter referred to a *Las Vegas Sun*
column that O'Callaghan penned in 1990 that read in part, "There's
nothing wrong with seeking additional water from surrounding
areas. But this should be done judiciously and in cooperation with
the residents of those rural areas."

From the lack of an environmental-impact statement to the failure to assess the "serious impacts of ground water pumping" in the
arid region, the conservationists continued their assault on Reid.
They pointed to the fact that the bill called for a hydrology study

only in White Pine County, excluding other Nevada counties and adjacent counties in Utah.

They also criticized Reid for including provisions in the bill that had "no public benefits" but appeared to boost the interests of his close political ally and fundraiser, Nevada attorney and lobbyist Harvey Whittemore, whose Coyote Springs development in Lincoln County was fast running into cost issues.

The groundwater pumping would also prevent large sections of the rural counties from ever having their own development booms. The group sought time to meet with Reid's staff, to conduct field hearings "so that all Nevadans will have an opportunity to testify on the merits or problems with the proposed legislation."

Their strong complaints were duly noted, but the right-of-way bill steamrolled through the process without delay. Although a national recession and challenges to the plan that wound up before the Nevada Supreme Court would slow the plan's momentum, it continued to be considered one viable option by the SNWA in its fifty-year plan to provide water for one of the nation's fastest-growing communities.

And then the giant stumbled. In March 2020, a district judge in White Pine County rejected the SNWA pipeline plan, calling its pumping applications invalid and its mitigation strategy vague and lacking supporting evidence. Conservationists and ranchers cheered. After spending millions, the water authority then announced it was shelving the project.

Not all of Reid's friends fared well under the pressure of public scrutiny. Nevada power lobbyist and developer Harvey Whittemore, a loyal and longtime supporter and the beneficiary of the senator's guiding hand in parlaying a federal land exchange for big profit, fell hard in 2013 when he was convicted of violating federal campaign-contribution laws. Whittemore was caught using his family and friends to make illegal campaign contributions to Reid. Slapped with a two-year sentence for committing what a judge called "an incredibly criminal, intentional act," Whittemore served twenty-one months.

After his release, Whittemore joined the land and energy consulting firm Abbey, Stubbs & Ford, LLC, which boasts of its experience in providing technical services, oversight, and advice to municipalities, utilities, landowners, nonprofits, and major real-estate developers on issues involving federal, state, and local government agencies. Whittemore's corporate biography included his educational and career accomplishments and heralded his association with the firm "after an impressive and successful career in providing land use planning, development and other critical services to a wide variety of private companies." It neglected to mention his vacation at government expense for playing the bagman on behalf the Senator from Searchlight, or the protracted litigation and civil-fraud allegations he'd been buried under in association with the collapse of the Coyote Springs project.

Years in the making, the Coyote Springs story began as a small part of the behemoth MX Missile project and appeared to end when the rail-based rocket system was scrapped. Bechtel—the company that helped build Hoover Dam in the 1930s and had longstanding ties to Nevada—"expected to receive the DOD contract to build the system's massive infrastructure, as well as provide the necessary enriched uranium for the warheads," according to a history of the company. The plan lived for fifteen years past the fall of the Soviet Union and the Cold War, eventually being cancelled by President George H. W. Bush in September 1991.

Coyote Springs reached Whittemore's hands through a circuitous route.

Sponsored by Nevada Republicans Chic Hecht in the Senate and Barbara Vucanovich in the House, an act authorized the Secretary of the Interior to convey 28,800 acres of BLM land in the public domain located in Coyote Springs Valley in rural Clark and Lincoln counties for exchange and lease to the Aerojet-General Corporation of Ohio, along with another 10,040 acres located in Mineral County. As part of the exchange, Aerojet agreed to hand over approximately 4,650 acres located in the Everglades in Dade County, Florida, and deemed environmentally sensitive by the U.S. Fish and Wildlife Service. Prior to the exchange, Aerojet's Florida land had no restrictions and was the proposed site of a rocket-manufacturing and testing facility, which was never built. One condition provided in the federal bill was the requirement that any land exchange "would be on the basis of equal value, as determined by land appraisals using Bureau of Land Management procedures." Aerojet's control of the Nevada land for the purpose of developing a site for the MX Missile project included 50,000 acre-feet of groundwater. This small outfit, which at the end of World War II employed scientists from Germany's V-2 rocket program would be heralded by *Time* magazine in 1958 as "the General Motors of U.S. Rocketry" for its large-scale production and 34,000 employees company-wide. Aerojet helped put astronauts into space and would later play an important role in fueling the Space Shuttle program. But its MX Missile mission was destined to founder and fail.

The Nevada Coyote Springs Valley land didn't remain in Aerojet's possession. It was sold in 1996 to Harrich Investments, LLC, with Whittemore as its listing officer. Two years later, it was sold to Coyote Springs Investment Group, which Whittemore also controlled, for a reported $23 million, as part of a master-planned development that he envisioned would one day include ten championship golf courses, sweeping commercial development, casinos, and 150,000 homes. It all may have sounded too good to be true, but in those days, before his conviction, no one doubted Whittemore's contacts or his ability to get things done, from Carson City to the halls of Congress.

By the time Whittemore got his hands on the MX site, it was empty and almost forgotten—except by those who appreciated its enormous scale and precious 50,000 acre-feet of water. Shortly after completing the purchase of the land, with no limits on its use, Whittemore was contacted by Pat Mulroy of SNWA with a proposal to purchase a small portion of his water rights for $25 million. In little time, Whittemore had turned a $2-million profit and had effectively received the land free of charge, courtesy of Southern Nevada's water users.

Over time, those who once bought Whittemore's vision of a new city growing in the desert fifty miles outside Las Vegas began to wonder whether he could deliver. Although a Jack Nicklaus–inspired golf course was to appear like a verdant island in a sea of greasewood and Joshua trees, those who watched the site noticed that the few employees at work there spent most of their time operating Caterpillar bulldozers and moving dirt. Reporters would later note that Coyote Springs had a golf course, but not a single house and only one full-time resident, a mutt named Mitch.

The Coyote Springs website once enthused, "Perhaps the most important aspect of any community is not where it stands, but where it is headed." It turns out that Coyote Springs was headed down the long road to bankruptcy and scandal, despite handouts and hand-ups from some of the most powerful players in Nevada politics and public policy.

In fact, no homes would be built under Whittemore's stewardship. Investors lost millions and sued Whittemore as the dream of development faded rapidly and was made more complicated by one of the worst economic recessions in decades.

"In Nevada, the name to know is Reid." A *Los Angeles Times* headline writer perhaps inadvertently offered this line redolent with greater meaning, but that's also what made the right-wing conspiracy-mongers' wildest speculations about the mysterious hand of Harry Reid's influence on the region surrounding the Bundy Ranch so laughable. Their attempts to link Reid to everything from crooked Chinese solar projects to top-secret uranium mines were breathless. But in reality, there was no need to exaggerate Reid's influence on federal public-land, water, and environmental issues in Nevada. The smoke of distant scandals real and perceived aside, his influence was preeminent, his brand on policy undisputed.

Which brings us back to Searchlight, home of Harry Reid Elementary School and a populace that expresses a mixture of great pride and mumbled disgruntlement about its favorite son. What's undisputed is Reid's impact on the area as a driving force for renewable energy in the West. A short distance from Searchlight, lakes of solar panels shimmer in the light of Eldorado Valley, but plans for rows of hundreds of towering wind turbines west of town stalled for environmental reasons. The conservation group Basin and Range Watch criticized the proposed project, asserting that it would be "surrounded by important lands and holds unique biodiversity and cultural landscapes."

As of 2018, another wind-farm developer with ties to a Swedish wind-energy company had offered a new proposal. By then, Reid, who left the Senate the previous year, was well into retirement after moving with his wife, Landra, from Searchlight to Henderson, a Las Vegas suburb, to be closer to his family. Despite battling cancer, he remained active. Upon Reid's retirement in 2017, Utah billionaire and Republican diplomat Jon Huntsman Sr. donated a million dollars for the creation of the Harry Reid Endowed Chair for the History of the Intermountain West at the University of Nevada, Las Vegas (UNLV). Huntsman, part of the upper echelon of the LDS Church, was a descendant of Mormon pioneers who crossed the mountains with Brigham Young on wagon trains in the 1840s. On the way to building Huntsman Corporation into an $8-billion multinational, he served in the Nixon administration and was appointed ambassador to Russia by President Donald Trump. "Senator Reid is a dear friend and a great, honorable man," Huntsman said upon presenting the endowment. "He has been very instrumental throughout his life, particularly during his time in the U.S. Senate, even though we are on opposite sides of the aisle."

That same year, Reid was named the first Distinguished Fellow in Law and Policy at UNLV's Boyd School of Law. In 2018, Reid was named co-chair with former Speaker of the House John Boehner of the MGM Resorts International Public Policy Institute, a program housed in UNLV's Greenspun College of Urban Affairs. Reflecting on his career, Reid counted his efforts to protect Nevada's environment while serving the interests of a rapidly growing state as his greatest political achievements. Of the 80,000-page archive he donated to UNR for research, half of the documents are related to Nevada's land, water, and environmental issues.

For some environmentalists, Reid was something of a Mormon John Muir, a fearless defender of Nevada's wild spaces and a man who had an uncanny sense of balancing interests. For ranchers feeling frustrated by his political skill and bushwhacked by the pragmatic policies he pushed through Congress that pushed their way of life close to a Nevada sunset, Reid was a sleight-of-hand artist, a double-dealing Keyser Söze—that fictional master criminal who always flummoxes authorities and slips the noose. In the classic juxtaposition of Reid's long political career, his efforts to protect the land would earn him two national awards from the Sierra Club and the Stewart Udall Conservation Award for his work to protect public lands, yet he was also celebrated with a lifetime-achievement award from the Nevada Mining Association and given a place of honor in the American Gaming Hall of Fame—two industries known for their lack of environmental sensibilities. In the end, he finished his long career with an 82-percent lifetime score on environmental issues.

"When I was elected to Congress, we had a few puny acres of wilderness [designated] in Jarbidge," Reid said. "Nothing else. Now we've got more than five million acres. And I did that. I don't mean I did that alone. I introduced the bill and others had to support me to make it become law. And that was a tough deal. We have national monuments.... I think one thing we can protect in Nevada is our outdoors. There's still more that can be done. But we've set aside five million acres. That's pretty good."

CHAPTER 6

When the Cows Come Home...to Roost

Months after the splash of headlines and national television news broadcasts faded like desert starlight on Cliven Bundy and his militia followers, they remained topics of keen interest to those standing on either side of the metaphorical fence in a politically polarized nation. As ever, curiosity mixed with concern.

For their part, the Bundys had their suspicions about an FBI investigation confirmed in a May 2014 news broadcast from Las Vegas television station KLAS-TV. They had grown accustomed to reporters' questions. Stung by his own impolitic racial views and further chastened by the awful violence wrought by his former followers, the cop killers Jerad and Amanda Miller, Cliven had grown more skeptical of the journalists whose questions he had once entertained with such authority. The Bundys also didn't appear overly concerned with the increasingly paranoid rhetoric of their supporters, who spoke in terms of the government preparing for a "civil war" against the citizenry that would result in "mass graves" and camps run by the Federal Emergency Management Administration (FEMA).

When right-wing radio host Michael Savage assured his listeners that the Obama administration was planning to kill whites like Bundy to "stimulate insurrection in this country in order to declare martial law," he wasn't just promoting his latest book. He was striking a note that appealed to his predominantly older white audience. "The entire government is geared up to fight a war against white people," he said, wondering aloud whether the Obama administration was the "most racist" in the history of the Republic. Alex Jones, whose inaccurate and incendiary *InfoWars* reports prior to the standoff had inspired action from the militia, used a similar prediction of civil war after the Malheur occupation.

Bundy's intention may have been only to preserve his ranching lifestyle, but his story had become a canvas on which America's warring political tribes painted their own fears and beliefs. He'd become a cause célèbre to conspiracy theorists who usually occupied their time theorizing about "chemtrails" and black helicopters.

Perhaps emboldened by the Nevada standoff, two men menaced BLM rangers at gunpoint during an altercation in Utah. Thereafter, BLM rangers were instructed to travel in pairs. Some expressed concern that their uniforms alone would make them targets of public harassment, or worse. While the militia-tracking SPLC noted increased activity from sovereign-citizen and other antigovernment organizations, the BLM was sometimes criticized for taking a posture deemed too militarized and authoritarian. Even if the government land managers weren't on the run, they were certainly circling the wagons.

Back home in Arizona, Idaho, Montana, and elsewhere, Bundy's militia friends were still flush with the intoxicant of their victory. Their Facebook and YouTube posts made it clear that they relished victory and were hungry for more adventures in the name of their definition of liberty.

Parker and his pals in the Idaho Three Percent militia and Oath Keepers kept busy in April 2015 defending the Sugar Pine Mine from perceived BLM overreach. Located near the Rogue River in the forested mountains of southeastern Oregon's Josephine County, the gold mine and its outbuildings had fallen into noncompliance. When BLM officers attempted to serve Sugar Pine co-owner Rick Barclay with a letter of notification, he responded by calling for help from the Oath Keepers. Parker and Idaho Three Percenters president Brandon Curtiss converged on the mining camp, along with a collection of others who identified themselves as militia associates. One was Todd Engel, still buzzing from his Bunkerville participation. Social media again lit up with talk of a standoff fueled by the supposed unconstitutional behavior and questionable jurisdictional authority of the BLM. It was clear that the Bundy Ranch–fueled vigilantes weren't finished drinking their own bathwater.

Barclay would later admit that the land dispute had "taken on a life of its own" as it dragged on for six weeks with the Oath Keepers in camp, and he wound up spending much of his time trying to reduce tensions that arose after the government officials began being menaced over the phone. Barkley implored his overanxious allies, "We don't need any more volunteers, we're not under attack, this is not the Bundy Ranch. Please stop calling the BLM and threatening their personnel."

Although the situation was no Bunkerville standoff, an increasingly anxious Barclay noticed that much of the circus-like atmosphere "is mostly a spectacle caused by social media and 'keyboard commandos' whooping it up. A lot of the stuff going around on social media is absolute bullshit."

Parker and Curtiss eventually left the Sugar Pine, but not before posing for a victory photo with Barclay in which all three men gave the camera a defiant middle finger.

In the world of the right-wing Patriot militia, social media provided a cyber-battlefield on which tough talk and outright threats to safety flew like sniper fire. As federal public-lands managers, the BLM provided a soft target for the soldiers of misfortune. Self-styled "Rogue Infidel" Jon Ritzheimer raised his public profile in May simply by chanting epithets about Islam outside a Phoenix mosque. His internet posts drew more than two hundred like-minded haters. Not blessed with the gift of understatement, Ritzheimer compared himself to one of the Founding Fathers and seemed to believe that if he ran for office against American war hero U.S. Senator John McCain he might come away the winner. Some considered him dangerously deluded, but he also drew applause under the Arizona sun. A few months later, the former Malheur occupant kept busy selling Fuck Islam bumper stickers online and raising support for his favorite presidential candidate, Donald Trump.

By the time the Western Governors' Association met in Nevada in the summer of 2015, Interior secretary Sally Jewell all but guaranteed that Cliven Bundy would pay for his grazing transgressions. "We will continue to pursue that," she said somewhat cryptically.

Although it had refrained from telegraphing its every move on social media, the FBI had been quietly pursuing an investigation. Bureau special agents Sharon Gavin, Michael Abercrombie, and Joel Willis, who was an eyewitness in Toquop Wash and would produce a chilling FBI legal document that spelled out the dangers presented by the militia guns that day, were leading the probe.

Other agents were also deeply involved in the investigation, including an undercover team representing itself as Longbow Productions—a film crew headquartered in Nashville, Tennessee, that claimed to be researching a documentary on the standoff. Longbow's "Charles Johnson," the agent's undercover identity, first made contact with Bundy in the spring of 2014 about the filming of *America Reloaded*, as the fictional documentary was titled. Anticipating trouble from the armed standoff, the family was initially suspicious of the project. Ammon Bundy expressed concern about the company's lack of an internet footprint and its spartan website. Eventually, his skepticism softened somewhat. Longbow's cameras began a long series of interviews with many of the standoff's principal players. The faux documentarians returned time and again to questions about the organization and strategy behind the standoff, and whether the Bundys had anticipated bloodshed.

In footage that later became part of the court record and eventually appeared in a dramatic *Frontline* special, Cliven Bundy's sons allowed Johnson and his crew into the family home but were obviously never entirely comfortable with them. They certainly weren't answering any questions that might incriminate themselves in a larger conspiracy. Ammon denied that he had ever anticipated a violent end to the standoff. Ryan Bundy was even more suspicious, at one point cracking, "I want to know if this is an interview or an interrogation."

Several militia associates who were interviewed, Parker and Drexler among them, chose their words carefully. Parker told Johnson how he'd knelt on the northbound bridge and prayed for a peaceful ending to the standoff. The braggart Burleson, however, couldn't help talking tough. After drinking a couple of the beers the crew offered, the Arizona man stared into the camera and said he'd traveled to the standoff "to put some BLM agent six feet under." He chided others who brought arms to the standoff but weren't "brave enough for a fight," which almost certainly would have resulted in casualties in a crowd that included hundreds of unarmed adults and children. Burleson's bravado would later be complicated by the revelation of his status, since 2012, as an occasional FBI informant, a development that only fueled defense contentions that the undercover operation practiced more entrapment than investigative technique.

Burleson's defense attorney Terrence Jackson would complain that the FBI's documentary cover was marred by the offer of alcohol to a man with a documented drinking problem. But if the agents had gone looking for "incriminating admissions," they had found their unstable militia poster boy in Burleson. He didn't need much priming to start talking about shooting government employees.

The Patriot-supporting *Redoubt News* made much of Burleson's brief FBI association, and a jury would eventually learn of the connection. It was ever more clear that the Bundy family story had inspired militia members across the country. Ammon's attorney Dan Hill would reflect that the undercover film crew, while producing paltry results, had succeeded in harming journalism with its impersonation of investigative technique. The Reporters Committee for Freedom of the Press later argued just that point as its own lawyers sought facts associated with Longbow's fiction.

Whatever evidentiary benefits the undercover operation produced, less controversial investigative fact-gathering produced far greater results. In a matter of months, agents would collect and collate twelve thousand social-media messages, hundreds of hours of digital video and audio from BLM body cameras, government vehicle dash cameras, citizen cell recordings, and other sources at the scene of the standoff. In all, there would be 1.4 terabytes of discoverable evidence—enough hard-drive space to store approximately 410,000 pictures.

The 2016 occupation of the federal headquarters at the Malheur Wildlife Refuge in Oregon was widely ridiculed as little more than a stunt, but it also presented brothers Ammon and Ryan Bundy in a light that could only help their defense in the Bunkerville case. Ammon's expression of faith and defiance defined him not only as the leader at Malheur, but as someone increasingly positioning himself as a political activist—albeit one who didn't mind having armed militia associates back his play. Brother Ryan spoke increasingly in religious brushstrokes, blending his constitutional views and his fundamentalist LDS beliefs.

When they were taken into custody following the Finicum shooting and later charged with criminal conspiracy in the forty-one-day occupation, the brothers argued that their actions in Oregon were within their rights under the First and Second Amendments. Although they would eventually beat the charges associated with the Malheur occupation, the Bundy brothers would remain in detention.

After flying to Portland to support his incarcerated sons, Cliven Bundy joined them behind bars. Since he hadn't taken part in the Malheur action, his arrest was seen as a sign that the federal government was getting close to moving its investigation of the Bunkerville standoff to the next level. Alarm ricocheted through militia circles. One pro-Patriot columnist would observe that some of those who had traveled to Bundy's side "may now find themselves rounded up."

His instincts were correct. On Wednesday, February 17, 2016, a federal grand jury in Nevada indicted Bundy, sons Ryan and Ammon, militia leader Ryan Payne, and radio broadcaster Peter Santilli on sixteen charges, which included conspiracy to impede a federal officer, assault with a deadly weapon, assault on a federal officer, extortion, obstruction of justice, and five counts of criminal forfeiture totaling at least $3 million. If convicted, the defendants faced twenty-year sentences on the assault and extortion charges alone.

In an unintentionally ironic statement, U.S. Attorney Daniel Bogden of the District of Nevada concluded that "the rule of law has now been reaffirmed with these charges," in a case stemming from more than two decades of utter disregard for the rule of law by a defendant who didn't even recognize the jurisdiction of the federal government. If the rule of law had indeed been reaffirmed, the cavalry was a long time coming.

It finally appeared that Bundy's rhetorical sleight of hand was coming back to haunt him. "They have my house surrounded," he had written. "The federal government is stealing my property.... The [BLM] are armed with assault rifles...they have snipers. I haven't called no militia, but, hey, that looks like where we are...there is a strong army out here...somebody is going to have to back off...we the people will put our boots down and walk over these people.... They are up against a man who will do whatever it takes."

The indictment may have sent "a resounding message to those who wish to participate in violent acts that our resolve to pursue them and enforce the law remains unwavering," as Las Vegas FBI special agent in charge Laura Bucheit put it, but the prosecution's plan wouldn't be complete without indicting the militia associates who had waved and pointed their weapons at federal officers.

The prosecution didn't have to wait long. The culmination of a nearly two-year investigation into the Bunkerville standoff came on March 2, 2016, when a federal grand jury handed up a sixty-three-page superseding indictment of Bundy, four of his sons, and fourteen other men in connection with what the government alleged was a "massive armed assault against federal law enforcement officers."

The FBI's legal brief by agent Joel Willis gave insight into the government's view of the dangers it faced on April 12, 2014: "The 200 Followers in the wash included a significant number brandishing or raising their assault rifles in front of the officers. Some of these gunmen took tactically superior positions on the high ground, while others moved in and out of the crowd, masking their movements behind other unarmed Followers. The most immediate threat to the officers came from the bridges where gunmen took sniper positions behind concrete barriers, their assault rifles aimed directly at the officers below."

Although he wrote in the Bureau's legalese, Willis conveyed a clear message—he didn't like the odds of ending the showdown without bloodshed:

> Outnumbered by more than 4:1, unwilling to risk harm to children and other unarmed bystanders who had accompanied the Followers, and wishing to avoid the firefight that was sure to follow if they engaged the snipers on the bridge who posed such an obvious threat to their lives, the officers had no choice and were forced to leave and abandon the cattle to Bundy and his co-conspirators, who promptly released and returned the cattle to Bundy.

With nineteen defendants, dozens of charges, hundreds of potential witnesses, and millions of words and images as possible investigative leads, the case would prove a far greater roundup than anything that took place in Toquop Wash. Although many of the published photographs of the militiamen captured them heavily armed, with some in the act of aiming at federal officers, the simple fact that no shots were fired complicated the case's jury appeal. With a steady stream of claims by Bundy family members that they were under duress and in physical danger from armed shock troops and "snipers" on the hillside, without the proper strategy the government might appear to be as heavy-handed as the rancher had advertised.

Prosecutors in the indictment divided the defendants into three categories—leaders and organizers, mid-level leaders, and gunmen—in an effort to focus the charges and distill the facts of the case. The government depicted Bundy as a rancher who was as capable of revising the facts in his favor as of rounding up strays. Bundy's emphasis on the imminent danger the BLM security force represented, greatly magnified on the internet by Santilli and Payne, was a pivotal part of the government's case.

The indictment: "On or about April 7, 2014, Payne used the internet and other facilities in interstate commerce to recruit gunmen and others to travel to the Bundy Ranch for the unlawful purpose of interfering with impoundment operations, stating falsely, among other things, that the Bundy Ranch was surrounded by BLM snipers, that the Bundy family was isolated, and that the BLM wanted Bundy dead." Payne made his dramatic assessment, by his own admission, before he'd looked with any depth into the public facts of the impoundment issue. Only a considerable shift in perception, it seemed, could move such an argument in Bundy's favor, based on the law and the facts.

Outside the courtrooms in Oregon and Nevada, facts didn't appear to matter to some who followed developments in the cases with a kind of visceral zeal. Within days after the Oregon arrests, the Deschutes County Sheriff's Office logged more than eighty threats against law-enforcement officers and government employees. Perhaps the most chilling was the anonymous message sent to Oregon Governor Kate Brown's office: "We're going to shoot to kill."

Increased lawlessness and threats of violence on public lands also inspired environmental and progressive organizations to action. Unlike their militia counterparts, they took up pens instead of arms, compiling reports and writing letters seeking action from Congress and the Department of the Interior. Given that 2016 was the centennial of the American National Park System and of the creation of the Malheur National Wildlife Refuge, the chance for demonstrable change might have seemed ideal.

In its call for congressional scrutiny of what it described as "violent extremism" on federal public land, the Center for American Progress submitted its investigation into the increasing number of armed actions meant to intimidate government employees. Among several requests, the group asked Representative Raúl Grijalva, the ranking member of the House Committee on Natural Resources, to press for an examination of the financing of the antigovernment groups in order "to guarantee that they are in compliance with federal laws"—the laws these groups disregarded so easily in the name of exercising their constitutional rights.

"It is also vitally important that elected officials send a clear signal that lawlessness on public lands cannot and will not be tolerated," the CAP's public-lands specialist Matt Lee-Ashley implored, acknowledging that the growing use of antigovernment rhetoric by some politicians promised to increase tensions and the potential for violence.

Political observers debated whether the rising tensions in the West were a reflection of, or being stoked by, the greater political division widening in a presidential election year as wealthy reality TV host, real-estate pitchman, and bankrupted casino-owner Donald Trump bested a pack of experienced challengers and emerged as the Republican Party nominee. Trump exploited fears and fomented racial tensions with his nativist rhetoric in a country still rising out of an economic recession and was credited by his supporters for "telling it like it is" under his slogan "Make America Great Again."

A genius at marketing and self-promotion, Trump knew an opportunity when he saw one, and the Bundy land issue made ideal political fodder. Prior to the indictment, Trump called the Oregon takeover problematic, that "you don't have a government anymore" if people take over federal property, but he added that the cause was "constitutionally just."

Prior to Bundy's baffling remarks about "the negro," Trump again lauded the rancher's character. "I like him, I like his spirit, his spunk…I respect him," Trump told *Fox News* commentator Sean Hannity. It was also clear that Trump liked the style of Bundy's militia supporters and others so fond of their Second Amendment rights.

As the presidential campaign wore on and it appeared that former Secretary of State Hillary Clinton would win, Trump alluded to an armed response without mentioning the Bundy standoff, publicly offering, "Although the Second Amendment people, maybe there is, I don't know." Some observers wrote off Trump's tough talk and allusions to violence as part of his bravado, but he also appeared to be tapping into a level of anger generally unappreciated by the mainstream press. When Trump loyalist and Milwaukee Sheriff David A. Clark referred to "pitchforks and torches time," and former Illinois Republican Congressman Joe Walsh said he was "grabbing my musket" should Clinton prevail, they didn't appear to be kidding. In the wake of the standoffs, flouting federal authority and the rule of law had become an acceptable stance on the American right.

Bundy found fast friends inside the halls of Congress as well. Some of them faded following his racial comments, but none retracted their statements of support. Among the more cogent was Kentucky Republican Senator Rand Paul, who related to Bundy's libertarian constitutional views. Paul went to the effort of actually meeting the rancher in 2015 and later recalled their discussion on federal land issues, states' rights, and education policy.

Like Paul, Texas Republican Senator Ted Cruz mounted an unsuccessful run for the White House, but he took time to offer support for the Nevada rancher. He managed to blame President Obama in the process for the "unfortunate and tragic" path the federal government had taken. He was part of a chorus of conservatives calling for the transfer of federal public lands to the states, where major Republican Party donors such as David and Charles Koch and many others were poised to capitalize on the anticipated and unprecedented boon to extractive industries. Cruz was eager to please his allies, the American Lands Council and Federalism in Action, by echoing their "Free the Lands" mantra, which evidence suggests was a driving force behind the "anti-government ideology, and land seizure activists and militants." Cruz enthused, "If I am elected president, we have never had a president who is as vigorously committed to transferring as much federal public land as humanly possible back to the states and back to the people."

Perhaps Cliven Bundy's most unbridled supporter among 2016's Republican presidential hopefuls was Dr. Ben Carson. He too appeared to appreciate the powerful imagery being beamed to masses of Americans who were feeling picked on by their government. "It always starts like this, and freedom isn't free—and there may come a time when people actually have to stand up against the government," Carson said, referring to the Bundy standoff. "I hope that doesn't happen."

Other conservatives were only too happy to tip metaphorical cowboy hats to the Bunkerville rancher. "I'm not here to jump in to the middle of whether Cliven Bundy ought to pay the state or pay anybody for the chance for his cows to eat some grass," said former Arkansas governor and evangelical Christian influencer Mike Huckabee, leaping in with both feet. "There is something wrong when a government believes that some blades of grass that a cow is eating is so... egregious affront to the government of the United States that we would literally put a gun in a citizen's face and threaten to shoot him over it."

Huckabee had his facts wrong, but his audience cheered.

As attorneys jockeyed through the withering pretrial process and daily protesters waved at passersby on the sidewalk outside the courthouse, the defendant- and evidence-laden case took on a lumbering elephantine rhythm that revealed its strengths, but also raised troubling questions about the thought process behind the prosecution. The little-reported detention hearing of Bundy son David H. Bundy was a good example. Bundy, sometimes called Davey by his family, had suffered scrapes in an altercation with the BLM during the impoundment, when it was alleged that he attempted to capture the faces of government personnel with the camera of his cell phone. He was accused of being one of the "leaders and organizers of the conspiracy" that helped recruit the gunmen and other followers to the standoff.

There is no cash bail in federal pretrial detention procedure; a defendant is released unless deemed a flight risk or a danger to the community. Could David Bundy qualify on either account?

He hadn't worked at the Bundy Ranch in years. Like many of the other boys, David had grown up and moved away, making a family and place of his own in Delta, Utah. A successful contractor, he was married with six children. He was a licensed pilot with a bachelor's degree in aviation administration, a volunteer in his predominantly LDS community, and a regular at church. Back in Delta, the Millard County sheriff thought enough of David Bundy to offer to take custody of him before trial, which was nearly eight months away.

During the detention hearing in U.S. Magistrate Cam Ferenbach's courtroom, David Bundy's attorney Cal Potter III argued that his client didn't approve of the family's stance, was unarmed, and had come to help keep the peace. He didn't recruit any militia or invite anyone to follow him to Bunkerville. Contrary to some press reports, his lawyer contended, David Bundy had been arrested for photographing federal officers, not for attempting to physically block the impoundment convoy.

There was a catch: the county sheriff didn't have jurisdiction, and for all his piety David Bundy didn't recognize the federal government's jurisdiction in the pending case, calling it a powerless "foreign entity," as he'd called the BLM's presence in Oregon, instead of the law of the land. As such, how could anyone believe he'd follow a court order? And in the indictment, David was labeled a leader of a heavily armed action against the government. "He's a danger to the community," Ferenbach said. "Specifically, to BLM employees."

The magistrate clearly appreciated the nuance that Assistant U.S. Attorney Nadia Ahmed was attempting to convey when she spoke of the influence the Bundys held over their followers. It wasn't certain, even at that early stage in the proceedings, that a jury would take the scenario as seriously as the government did.

For the first of several times during the grueling roll-up to trial, Bundy's family members, who often prayed before a hearing or even minor proceeding, chided the judge aloud inside the courtroom. One barked, "They [federal authorities] have to sleep at night. I hope they can." Another called the judge a liar and raised the smoke of conspiracy because Ferenbach had read from a prepared text.

David Bundy returned to the federal detention facility in Pahrump, sixty miles from Las Vegas. He'd spend nearly two years there.

Determining how to take a case with nineteen defendants, thousands of pieces of evidence, and high public interest to trial would challenge U.S. District Judge Gloria Navarro. Defense attorneys sought separate trials, which would not only enable lawyers to humanize their clients but would have the effect of separating the accused armed militiamen from the rest of the defendants. With a dozen of the defendants seeking separate trials to avoid confusion and "guilt by association," oddball standoff instigator Santilli received the most entertaining defense from his attorney, Chris Rasmussen, who conjured up a First Amendment defense and called his client "a new breed of journalist that offers an alternate news channel to the public."

Steven Myhre and his team of prosecutors sought a single trial, citing efficiency and economy and the importance of a jury seeing "the entire picture of an alleged crime." It was also true that the courtroom impact of the government's case threatened to be substantially diminished if the alleged leaders of the conspiracy weren't seated next to those who had carried arms and pointed weapons during the standoff. The judge eventually decided to cut the case into three sections that followed the prosecution's theory of culpability: leaders, gunmen, and others.

Not all the action took place in the courtroom. Fallout from the Nevada and Oregon actions continued to reverberate through militia circles. One case involved Patriots Defense Force militia leader William Keebler, who had driven to Bunkerville in 2014 from his home in Stockton, Utah, and later had traveled to Burns during the Malheur takeover. Keebler was also a close associate of LaVoy Finicum, whose memory was often invoked outside the Las Vegas courthouse.

With so much attention focused on developments in the Bundy case, Keebler's arrest in June 2016 drew little notice. Not satisfied with protesting what he considered BLM overreach on the cattle-grazing issue, Keebler had allegedly schemed to bomb government property. An FBI undercover operation working inside the militia unit arrested him after he attempted to plant explosives at a BLM cabin in a remote part of Arizona near Mount Trumbull, deep in the heart of Bundy family country. A friend described Keebler as the glorified leader of a group of "grownup Boy Scouts" who just happened to dress in camouflage and carry semiautomatic rifles.

An FBI charging document alleged that Keebler had scouted the cabin with Finicum in the fall of 2015. The militia group had considered bombing a BLM office in Salt Lake City, but they reconsidered after their surveillance showed that it was located in a shopping center and not far from where the homeless congregated.

Cliven Bundy's worldview received an unprecedented level of endorsement when Republican Congressmen Rob Bishop and Jason Chaffetz of Utah sponsored legislation to remove federal law-enforcement authority from public lands and hand it to local police and sheriffs—an unofficial celebration of the bullying tactics of the militia. However, this act, though lauded in sparsely populated rural areas, would have a devastating economic impact on many counties, a factor not much discussed by Bishop and Chaffetz as they courted the political zeitgeist in the conservative West.

Bristling in the minority, Representatives Raúl Grijalva of Arizona and Bennie Thompson of Mississippi hit back, opining, "These homegrown militias threaten our public lands, the American people who want to enjoy them and the public servants who manage them." Grijalva and Thompson saw through the B-movie-western façade of the ranchers who just "want their land back" to a "much darker" reality. Grijalva was the ranking Democrat on the Natural Resources Committee, with Thompson holding similar status on the Committee on Homeland Security. The darkness only began with the right's deep-seated hatred for Barack Obama, America's first black president, they wrote, pointing out that some of those who participated in the Oregon and Nevada standoffs had actually called for the killing of BLM and Forest Service officials:

> In the guise of giving land "back," these lawmakers—and the extremists who now use this campaign as a rallying cry—have undermined the very idea of public lands as a shared and cherished resource.... [It] is high time we acknowledged that our nation's own home-grown terrorists also threaten public safety.

While warring political tribes traded rhetoric in Washington, DC, the Malheur case ground steadily through the federal system in Portland. A week after Independence Day, Blaine Cooper cut a plea deal to a single conspiracy count and let it be known that he was also settling accounts in the Las Vegas case. He even admitted that inviting militia members to come armed to Oregon "could be intimidating." His defense attorney, Krista Shipsey, said Cooper hoped the Bundys would respect his decision. Cooper would make his deal official in August, along with Gerald DeLemus, the New Hampshire Tea Party soldier and Republican Party stalwart who had been late to the standoff but stayed long enough to implicate himself in federal conspiracy and extortion charges.

Over the objections of attorneys for the defense and the media scrambling to cover the case, U.S. Magistrate Judge Peggy Leen ruled that a "credible risk" of the intimidation or influence of witnesses existed if she approved a defense and media request to unseal a voluminous portion of discovery materials in the case. Citing prosecutors' nearly two dozen examples of attempts at intimidation by the Bundys and their associates, the order alluded to a previous federal ruling prior to the 1997 trial of Oklahoma City bomber Timothy McVeigh. Whether the defense was presenting the Bundys as heroes or villains, defending them was becoming more difficult.

Combined with the defense's loss in its discovery request, speculation grew that more guilty pleas were coming. Out on Las Vegas Boulevard, Bundy supporters took some of their frustration out on Judge Navarro with hand-painted signs accusing her of bias and reminding passersby of the plight of the defendants.

It was clear that the real-estate-pitchman-turned-Republican-Party standard-bearer didn't really know what to think about the Bundys. Although Trump had generally embraced their cause, in a moment of candor in January he'd admitted that he didn't know much about their plight or the history of federal public lands in the West. That, however, didn't prevent him from expressing an opinion—several, in fact, in the ensuing months as his views evolved. When it came to transferring control of federal land to local hands, in a matter of months Trump went from "because I want to keep the lands great, and you don't know what the state is going to do" and "It's not a subject I know anything about," to preferring "a shared governance structure" that echoed the GOP platform and the talking points of the most outspoken members of Congress.

In a move that presaged his future status as Secretary of the Interior in the Trump administration, Montana Congressman Ryan Zinke resigned from his state's delegation to the Republican National Convention. The strapping former Navy SEAL became an outspoken critic of state ownership, instead espousing the need for state and local management but federal ownership—much to the approval of his future boss in the White House. A proponent of increasing access to environmentally sensitive public lands for extractive industries,

Zinke would resign from his cabinet position after a single year amid a travel-expense billing scandal.

The country was increasingly focused on the 2016 presidential election, but in mid-September the Bundys were again in the national headlines with the start of the Malheur trial. The case wasn't complex, but after seventeen years on the federal bench U.S. District Judge Anna Brown knew trouble when she saw it. Brown, a Clinton appointee, managed to remain patient as Ryan Bundy filed oddball proper-person motions—in one of which he described himself as an idiot. He got into a scuffle with a detention officer after refusing to be taken to have a bullet removed from his arm, and he was overheard discussing a jail escape. Co-defendant Shawna Cox, who had sued the government for a satanic $666 billion, was admonished to keep the craziness under control.

By the time of the Oregon trial, Cox was best known for having kept her cell phone recorder playing during the law-enforcement stop that ended with the fatal shooting of LaVoy Finicum. On the witness stand in her own defense, she testified about the fear she had felt, despite the fact that when ordered to surrender, she refused. Co-defendant Ryan Payne had exited the vehicle without further incident. Cox could be heard on her own widely circulated recording telling a death-obsessed Finicum to "gun it, gun it." He did, and Oregon State Police shot a few minutes later after Finicum reached for a pistol under his coat.

Cox was more experienced at antigovernment action than many of the armed militiamen at Malheur, having logged a record of protest reaching back to at least 2009. She had planned an ATV ride through the Grand Staircase–Escalante National Monument's Paria Canyon in defiance of a BLM trail closure. Later, she reemerged in the public eye as a Kanab, Utah-based Tea Party activist and publicly declared the federal government "evil." As a member of the Bundy family's inner circle of supporters, she called herself Cliven's "personal secretary" and would write a self-published book about his legal travails, *Last Rancher Standing: The Cliven Bundy Story*. She prevailed in the Oregon case, then raised eyebrows with an unsuccessful countersuit claiming malicious prosecution and damages "from the works of the devil" in excess of $666 billion.

Her rambling, eight-page lawsuit was easy to laugh at, but it gave insight into the worldview of Cox and other antigovernment extremists and sovereign citizens. She wrote, "State and Federal employees organized together to attempt to murder me and they executed...Lavoy Finicum" in an effort to "terrorize the people of the United States of America so they could continue to socialize and communize the United States of America."

Cox had come to Oregon to assist the Hammonds and defend them from the officials "who have organized together to highjack and steal our Constitutional form of government from the people of the United States of America." Charges against Cox and the rabble-rouser Santilli were eventually dismissed.

For his part, Ammon Bundy attended his trial in blue detention scrubs. Given the option of wearing civilian clothing, Bundy, according to his attorney J. Morgan Philpot, believed the jail-issue outfit was a better reflection of his status as a political prisoner. In a scene already familiar outside the Las Vegas courthouse, numbers of flag- and sign-waving supporters now assembled each morning in a park across from the Mark O. Hatfield United States Courthouse on Third Avenue in downtown Portland. While the Las Vegas protests were serious to the point of being somber, the turnout in Portland was far more eclectic, with flag- and sign-wavers blending with occasional livestock sightings, colorful street characters, and at least one instance of cowboys racing on horseback.

"Welcome to another day of liberty and justice for all, Portlandia edition," journalist Rick Anderson wisecracked in the *Los Angeles Times*.

The trial was not without its lighthearted moments. When Ryan Bundy, representing himself, asked the judge to provide a jury verdict form with only the words "not guilty" inscribed, Brown replied, "And I'd like to be tall, thin, and blonde."

The merriment wasn't universal. As a Clinton appointee, Brown was immediately the subject of conspiracy theories in a presidential election year in which former Secretary of State Hillary Clinton was the Democratic Party nominee. Whenever Brown denied a motion, her motivation was immediately questioned on conservative and conspiracy-based websites and blogs. In the eyes of skeptics, she had morphed into a "Clinton loyalist."

Judge Brown appeared to express surprise when, after a six-week trial, the jury returned a sweeping "not guilty" verdict on the charge of conspiracy to impede federal officers by threat or intimidation. Ammon and Ryan Bundy and five other defendants had beaten the federal government's best effort with what one defense attorney assistant called a "common sense" approach. Militiaman Ryan Payne, who cut a deal before trial, immediately sought to withdraw his guilty plea as the government licked its wounds and Oregon U.S. Attorney Billy J. Williams and FBI Special Agent in Charge Greg Bretzing were reduced to expressing their "extreme disappointment" at the outcome.

When Ammon's defense attorney Marcus Munford's request to have his client released from custody was rebuffed by Judge Brown, the lawyer caused a scuffle that resulted in him being tackled by courtroom personnel. Bundy and his brother would be transferred to Southern Nevada, where their business at the federal court there was just beginning.

The Bundys would have to celebrate their Oregon victory behind bars at a privately run federal detention facility in Pahrump, an hour's drive outside Las Vegas in rural Nye County. The distance presented a challenge as the defendants prepared for trial. Whether they met in Pahrump or at a detention facility adjacent to Las Vegas in Henderson, the daily transfer and travel were time consuming and physically withering. The trial was still months away and would follow the courtroom showdown between the government and six alleged militia gunmen.

By early November, the incarcerated Bundys kept their eyes on the detention facility's three wall-mounted televisions. On the family website, they left little doubt about their favored candidate:

"Blow your 'Trumpence'! Family and Friends Blow your 'Trumpence'! Then get your Family and friends to blow their 'Trumpence'!...Praying for America." Cliven Bundy on his blog site noted ads "stating him saying slur language about women, I do not like that." But then he noted that television was filled with "nudeness, guns pointing at someone, domestic violence, youth involved with sexual or homosexual dialogs," and more. By downplaying Trump's admitted sexual battery and crude behavior, as conveyed on a recording that became known as the notorious "*Access Hollywood* tape," the rancher echoed the sentiments of millions of Americans who saw the tough-talking reality TV star as a viable alternative to the status quo inside the Republican Party.

If the surprise November election of Donald J. Trump to the presidency gave the Bundy family some solace, it didn't replace prayer in their daily routine. Nor did it slow the defense team's efforts.

Pundits were still ruminating over Trump's surprising victory when President Obama, with a nod to Senator Reid in late December 2016, signed a proclamation setting aside nearly 300,000 acres of remote and majestic desert in southeastern Nevada as the Gold Butte National Monument. It was a place Bundy Ranch cattle knew well, for they had been grazing on it illegally for two decades. Gold Butte's red sandstone, slot canyons, and vast empty desert provided habitat for a variety of plants and animals, including a herd of bighorn sheep. The land was considered sacred to the Moapa Band of Paiute Indians and included famously beautiful rock art, the work of some of Gold Butte's earliest inhabitants who had drawn on its sandstone cliffs twelve thousand years earlier.

In 2013, Reid had begun pushing for protection of Gold Butte through the usual Senate channels when he introduced legislation to have the region designated as a National Conservation Area. Nevada Democrat Dina Titus pressed the case in the House. "Republicans hate public lands," Reid said after being rebuffed.

He then reached out directly to President Barack Obama. In the tradition of other presidents, Obama agreed to use his executive powers to designate Gold Butte as a national monument under the Antiquities Act of 1906, which President Theodore Roosevelt had first used to protect the Devil's Tower butte in the Black Hills of northeastern Wyoming.

Bolstered by a report that designated Gold Butte as an "Area of Critical Concern" due to the ongoing damage being done through vandalism and environmental degradation, some of it related to overgrazing, Reid and Titus made the case for the monument in the press. Titus noted that the designation would be good for the business community as well as the environment, and that more than 70 percent of the public favored the protected status. They were aided in their argument by former Moapa Band of Paiute Indians Chairman William Anderson.

The new national-monument designation ensured a continuous habitat that connected Gold Butte with the 600,000-acre Grand Canyon Parashant National Monument, which stretched from the Great Basin through parts of the Mojave and Sonoran deserts, all the way to the Colorado Plateau. The designation was also meant to protect the environmentally sensitive habitat and preserve its Indian petroglyphs and rock art. However, it was immediately politicized as an attempt to lock up range land by the departing president and Reid, who was nearing the end of his three-decade tenure in the Senate. Some accused Reid of carving out Gold Butte as a way of further pushing the Bunkerville rancher out of business.

The new designation came just weeks before a new president with an entirely different sensibility about federal public lands took office and began tearing down programs and regulations Obama had built up over eight years. That included naming Montana Republican loyalist Ryan Zinke as Secretary of the Interior and immediately threatening to reduce the size of the Gold Butte National Monument and Utah's Bears Ears monument.

The new administration also stopped enforcing long-standing grazing policies on federal land that most ranchers understood and accepted without complaint. The rules had changed. This was a decision certain to please Trump's Bundy constituency within the

West's ranching community. The BLM employee who reported the policy change was fired.

Not only did BLM employees in the field face increased threats of violence and the impossible task of helping to manage more than 600 million acres of federal land, they also had to contend with being overruled at the highest levels of government. The change would do something favored by many ranchers: make the BLM even more reliant on local sheriffs for support. Historically, that meant more influence for the ranchers.

In the new year, the strain of detention and the threat of spending decades in prison continued to grind on the defendants. Near the end of January 2017, Ryan Bundy returned to federal court representing himself. This time, he was accompanied by his wife, Angela, and the couple's eight children in an attempt to win a pre-trial release before U.S. Magistrate Judge George Foley Jr. Moments before the start of the hearing, Bundy on bended knee led a group prayer in the hall outside the courtroom. Although not often seen in any jurisdiction, the prayer would be repeated with regularity in the months ahead and should probably come as no surprise to those who followed the family's emphasis on their devotion to the Church of Jesus Christ of Latter-day Saints, whose hierarchy officially distanced the religion from the Nevada and Oregon actions.

Inside Foley's courtroom, the Ryan Bundy branch of the family took up half a row of seats. Experiencing what was by his count his 370th day of incarceration with his trial still months away, the frenetic defendant appeared anxious to express himself, at one point saluting the court as if reporting for duty, then putting his hand over his heart. His prayer for freedom wouldn't be immediately answered in the affirmative, but the presence of his tow-headed blonde children would have softened an ogre's heart. After Bundy's odd self-swearing-in, he promised to tell the truth, acknowledged his family and faith, referenced the Bundy clan's 140-year connection to the land, and spoke of the Declaration of Independence, Founding Fathers, and several amendments of the Constitution before he was admonished by the judge to state his case for release.

This behavior had a purpose: if he made the mistake of allowing himself to be sworn in, he'd open himself to cross-examination by a team of skilled prosecutors.

When Judge Foley implored him not to bog down the proceedings, Bundy couldn't help himself. "My time has been very much bogged down for 370 days," he replied. "I'm not afraid of the truth. The truth will set me free."

Not that time. Bundy waded in deeper, referenced his knowledge of the law, his version of facts and events, and his state of mind during the days leading up to the standoff. He called the indictment wildly inaccurate, adding, "There was no threat to federal officers. I did not refuse to obey orders." He described the gathering as not organized but "a spontaneous public protest.... There was no conspiracy.... We had no intent to do anything illegal, and we did not.... I do not want to die. I have a good life."

For the first time publicly, Ryan Bundy, so full of his own opinions for so many months, at last appeared to appreciate that his life was on the line and his family's future hung in the balance. He glibly referenced the Gospel According to John, then argued that his opinions and statements were mischaracterized by the government and were "no more than political hyperbole." He would eventually be released before trial, but that day he bid a tearful goodbye to his family.

The six men accused of acting as gunmen on Bundy's behalf wouldn't be as fortunate. Eric Parker, Scott Drexler, Steven Stewart, Todd Engel, Gregory Burleson, and Ricky Lovelien were considered among the most dangerous defendants in the case as they sat in U.S. District Judge Gloria Navarro's courtroom during jury selection.

Just as the government at last appeared to have Bundy's Bunkerville posse rounded up, the trial began to unravel with the published details of a withering investigation that accused BLM special agent in charge Dan Love of misconduct and ethics violations in connection with preparations for the 2015 Burning Man festival in Northern Nevada's Black Rock Desert. Evidence was developed that showed Love abused his power to obtain benefits for himself and family members at Burning Man and betrayed his law-enforcement responsibilities when he attempted to intimidate BLM staff to remain silent about his unethical conduct. Although the Department of the Interior's Office of the Inspector General's report didn't mention Love's name, it was immediately clear that he was the focus of the inquiry.

Cliven Bundy's defense attorney, Bret Whipple, immediately set out to draft a motion to dismiss. While the final witness list in the Bundy case remained under seal, failing to call Love as a witness would have been a cause of great suspicion in a case in which he played such an important role at such a pivotal time. Utah Lieutenant Governor Spencer Cox, who had called for Love's firing in 2014 following the cattle impoundment standoff, only to be rebuffed, restated his position, telling the *Salt Lake Tribune*, "There comes a time when personalities get in the way of productivity."

Word of the devastating OIG report shed renewed light on Love's questionable role in a Native American antiquities theft investigation that resulted in a BLM and FBI 2009 raid on the home of Utah physician James Redd, who was one of four persons to commit suicide in association with the case. A lawsuit filed by Redd's widow against Love and another agent was dismissed, but not before a judge criticized the government's conduct in the investigation. Navarro declined to dismiss the case. She ordered prosecutors to produce the investigative report and allowed the defense to use the document for cross-examination and impeachment purposes, leaving Whipple and other members of the defense team talking with greater authority about government overreach. Ryan Norwood and Brenda Weksler of the Federal Public Defender's Office in Las Vegas noted that Love had been the subject of no fewer than eight anonymous complaints in the previous two years. By now, Love had become a millstone, and he threatened to take the whole case down with him.

If Navarro had been vilified by the Bundy family's followers, who suspected her of corrupt association and secretly taking her marching orders from Senator Reid and even from the president himself, the rumors had no impact on her professional approach to the increasingly testy legal proceedings. The revelation of the OIG report and its findings began to shift the light of scrutiny toward the government as it ground away in the trial of the gunmen.

Attorneys for the accused gunmen performed a balancing act as they studied dozens of potential jurors. Column after column of potential witnesses were flashed on a big screen inside the courtroom, and potential jurors who had relationships with possible witnesses were excused from service, as were those with strong views on the standoff, antigovernment sentiments, jobs in law enforcement, or direct links to the family or other defendants. Although tedious at times, the process was thorough and was kept moving along by Judge Navarro and her experienced staff.

The defendants had crossed state lines with high-powered weapons and had taken up military-style positions in support of the Bundys, whom none knew prior to April 2014. They weren't members of the family, or even of its inner circle, but they were attached to its general cause. Portraying the men as confidants might complicate their culpability, but describing them as ignorant might leave the impression that they were irresponsible yahoos intent on hunting federal officers. Indicted on ten counts, the men each faced up to a century in prison if convicted of all charges in what was scheduled to be the first of three trials. It was a Bundy trial without a Bundy in it.

"This isn't an undercard for Mr. Lovelien," defense attorney Shawn Perez told the Associated Press. "It is the main event."

Importantly for the Bundys, convictions of the six could spell big trouble for the rest. The indictment was laden with weapons-related charges, and the defendants were responsible for bringing the guns. Without them, the family's argument that the event was simply a heated exercise of First Amendment rights might hold sway. And in the wake of the prosecutorial breakdown in Oregon, anything was possible.

Drexler's attorney, Todd Leventhal, offered, "They're not the Bundys. But, realistically, this is a Bundy case. The outcome of this trial affects the other two."

Although on the family Facebook site the Bundys often embraced their supporters from out of state, and advocates on the sidewalk cheered them, thoughts and prayers were of little practical use in the crowded courtroom. The defense team did its best to warm up the six men to jurors by having them sit facing the jury box rather than staring ahead at Judge Navarro. Some noticed the youthful faces of Eric Parker and Steven Stewart in the front row, with Drexler and Engel in the center and the middle-aged militiamen Gregory Burleson and Ricky Lovelien in the back. Burleson, whose diabetes condition had resulted in blindness before the trial, was given an assistant, along with defense lawyer Terry Jackson. Engel, who represented himself, was appointed court veteran John George as a standby, although they rarely appeared to communicate. Engel's journey through the system would remind courtroom observers of the adage about the man who represents himself having a fool for a client.

Bundy family members were courtroom regulars, along with Ryan Payne's public defenders Brenda Weksler and Ryan Norwood, as was outspoken Nevada politician and gun-rights promoter Michele Fiore, until her name appeared on a lengthy list of potential witnesses. With no cameras allowed in the courtroom, interested parties from Utah, Idaho, and other western states traveled to watch the trial in person. Some took notes while sitting on the defense side of the gallery. Courthouse security was tight, with trial observers guided through one metal detector on the ground floor and another just outside the seventh-floor courtroom. Shirts and buttons carrying demonstrative statements were disallowed, and visitors in the courtroom were reminded more than once to keep their opinions of the proceedings and its players to themselves or face ejection and possible arrest. In her daily admonishment, Navarro reminded those present that the trial was not a "sporting event." No cheering or jeering was allowed, and to ensure that decorum was maintained, deputies from the U.S. Marshal's Office augmented the presence of courtroom security personnel.

Assistant U.S. Attorney Steven Myhre, who cut a tall and imposing figure in the courtroom in his gray hair and dark suit, led the prosecution team. Respected by colleagues in the prosecution and defense bars, Myhre was selected as Acting United States Attorney in 2006, after a shakeup in the leadership of the Las Vegas office. By 2016, Myhre had more than two decades of experience and a long list of convictions on cases ranging from fraud and internet piracy to price-gouging physicians and public corruption. Sovereign citizens and paranoid Patriot types lumped in Myhre with other federal "conspirators" whom they believed—without evidence—were working against Bundy at the behest of then–Senate Majority Leader Harry Reid—a flawed view mitigated by Myhre's successful prosecution of Nevada power lobbyist Harvey Whittemore for making $133,400 in illegal contributions in 2007 to Reid's 2010 reelection campaign.

Myhre also had experience dealing with federal public-lands disputes while representing the government in a dispute with Elko County, following the closure by the U.S. Forest Service of the South Canyon Road near Jarbidge. The Jarbidge Shovel Brigade case had been a test of wills and sovereignty in Nevada. Myhre had also been part of a prosecution team ridiculed by a federal judge for its "flagrant, willful and bad faith" misconduct in 2006 in a protracted criminal securities-fraud case that resulted in a mistrial.

Shortly after 9 a.m. on February 9, 2017, Myhre at last addressed jurors in an opening statement that included audio and video from some of the standoff's tensest moments. The fog of chaos depicted was palpable, as was the fear. The danger of the showdown turning violent was beyond doubt, but the prevailing concern was how it would all be perceived in the minds of jurors—as modern-day vigilantism on the prowl or as ineffectual bureaucracy on parade? As Myhre described the situation in his opening statement:

> They kept the pressure on by pointing and brandishing their long guns at the officers from the bridge and from the high ground. And it worked. They instilled fear in the officers and forced them to choose between using force to remove the obvious threats to their lives before them or backing down and leaving the post for the sake of the safety of everybody. And the officers chose to back away and give up the cattle. They chose safety over cattle. And in doing that, they saved lives on both sides of that gate including the lives of the six defendants.

Myhre was at his best as he tried to focus the jury's attention. Despite the enormity, technical complexity, and potential tedium of the evidence, he said:

It's a very simple case. This case is about these defendants on that bridge and on the high ground on April the 12th. The evidence will show that these law enforcement officers were there doing their jobs. They were where they were supposed to be when they were supposed to be there doing what they were supposed to be doing, what two court orders authorized them to do. The defendants interfered with them. They intimidated them. They threatened them. They forced them to leave their posts. They threatened. They intimidated. They interfered.

The evidence will show that this was no protest, or anything else. There was a similar purpose here, that their intent was to get the BLM to back down and get those cattle and that they would use force of violence [sic] to do it.

The evidence will show that Bundy did in fact do whatever it takes; that he got what he wanted, that he got it at the end of a rifle barrel; and that these defendants, these defendants, knowingly and willfully supplied that barrel. And we'll prove it.

When the defense had its say, Stewart's attorney, Richard Tanasi, struck back. "This case, folks, is about standing up for what you believe in. Nothing more and nothing less." Stewart had carried a long gun to the northbound bridge with his buddies Parker and Drexler, but where they were often depicted displaying various stages of sniper positioning, Stewart had only hustled their gear and offered them water. He was clearly a participant in the action, by law and the government's theory of the case, but more as a tagalong than a terrorist.

Under Tanasi's oratory, Stewart softened into a father of two, a loving boyfriend and uncle, a grocery-store butcher, an aspiring firefighter who "had a plan to protest."

And then the defense attorney couldn't help himself, laying on thick the constitutional virtues of his client. By the time he was finished, Stewart and the other defendants had morphed from intimidating militiamen to historic figures. Counsel threw everything at the jury but a fife and drum, and jurors could almost be forgiven for forgetting that the trial was about armed men using their weapons as muscle to intimidate federal employees following court orders.

History tells us about protesters from the Boston Tea Party, disgruntled Americans standing up to the British government; to today's political Tea Party born from Americans who were standing up against what they believe is a big government; countless brave women marched in the '20s, the 1920s, for the right to vote leading to the Nineteenth Amendment.

"Injustice anywhere," folks, "is a threat to justice everywhere," Martin Luther King, 1963, his letter from a Birmingham jail where he sat for protesting government discrimination. Protest is a sacred First Amendment right, ladies and gentlemen, that we all enjoy. That's what this case is about and that's what the evidence is going to show.

Then Tanasi cued the video of Cliven Bundy's sister, Margaret Houston, being taken down hard by a BLM ranger providing security for the impoundment. She appeared to have been trying to walk into the path of an oncoming cattle truck, but the image of a grandmother being thrown to the ground was no less jarring. Then there was the image of Ammon Bundy being Tasered as he physically tried to interrupt the roundup, and the scuffs that David Bundy took in his altercation with authorities—all of which had gone viral on the internet and YouTube. The final image was of Cliven Bundy with his head bowed near the government's ill-advised First Amendment Area sign, an image that also had flashed far and wide on social media.

Tanasi went even further, off-handedly comparing Stewart to Jesus Christ, "one of history's most popular martyrs." He then dialed back slightly: "I'm not going to tell you my client is Jesus Christ, folks. What I'm telling you, as the evidence will show, that my client is a man who will stand up for what he believes in; a peaceful man who will stand up for what he believes in. Nothing more, nothing less."

Acting as his own legal representative with an experienced but clearly bored John George seated next to him as court-appointed standby counsel, Engel gave the longest opening statement of the four defendants who chose to offer one. He admitted knowing nothing of Cliven Bundy's predicament or of ranching generally, and had never heard of the BLM. Where he lived in Emmet, Idaho, he said the U.S. Forest Service managed most of the federal public land. He also admitted being moved to action by the videos produced by Bundy and his family.

It was the images, the furor they created among his fellow gun-rights advocates, and encouragement from his militia-associated friends, that got him off the couch, despite recent back surgery, and in the truck with Parker, Drexler, and Stewart for the twelve-hour drive south to Bunkerville. "I had nothing to gain. There's no financial gain in this for me," he told jurors. "Cost me money. But I knew somehow I just had to go there."

He downplayed his armed presence at an increasingly agitated protest and shifted all responsibility to the BLM, which he recalled was "pointin' rifles at the protesters under the bridge." Engel neglected to admit that some of the protesters under the bridge were armed, and those atop it were aiming rifles downrange toward the rangers. Although his narrative meandered, Engel described some of the chaos and confusion that were present during the standoff's tensest moments.

Todd Leventhal, a former federal prosecutor who in private practice handled a wide variety of criminal cases, described his client, Orville Scott Drexler, age forty-five, as a father and grandfather and the son of an Idaho sheriff. Importantly for the purposes of the trial, Drexler had no criminal record or militia association outside his friendship with Parker and his arrival in Bunkerville.

His client, Leventhal said, was moved by the internet images, especially the one of Margaret Houston being tackled. "You see her legs actually kick in the air," Leventhal said. "These images haunted these people."

Leventhal also alluded to witness Michael Lynch, a freelance *Fox News* videographer on the scene at the standoff who inserted himself into the tense conversation at the gate. It was Lynch who told others in the crowd, "They're gonna shoot us."

Terrence Jackson, who represented Burleson, had perhaps the most difficult challenge. Following the standoff, his client had made incriminating statements about his views on authority and his violent intentions. So Jackson did what many similarly situated attorneys would have done—reminded jurors that the facts wouldn't support the government's conspiracy allegation, and that Burleson had learned whatever he knew about the rancher from social media: "they show that a few days before (April 12), as [i.e., like] some of the other defendants, he got knowledge of this from stuff that was posted on the internet by the Bundy family."

But Burleson had buried himself with damaging admissions. Even his comments gathered by the FBI's controversial "Longbow Productions" documentary team—remarks loosened with the help of a couple of beers freely accepted by a man with documented drinking-related arrests—were potentially devastating.

Then Jackson struck on something that resonated as true about Burleson. The internet fame he gained in the wake of the standoff was just about the most attention he'd ever received. As Jackson told the jury:

> One thing—after this happened, my client's picture was on the internet. I have a picture of my client holding his gun and that went viral. And, for one time in my client's life, for one time in his life, he was a celebrity. He had his picture on the internet and maybe half a million people saw it or maybe two million. I don't know how many people. But my client had his 15 minutes of fame when his picture was on the internet.

As attorney for Eric Parker, whom some of the press had labeled "the Bundy Sniper," linebacker-sized Jess Marchese cut a distinctive look in Navarro's courtroom in his colorful tailored suits and ties. He reserved his opening statement, as did defense lawyer Shawn Perez on behalf of Oklahoma resident Ricky Lovelien. Both defendants had undeniable connections to militia activity and the planning of the armed response on April 12.

Veteran officials from the Department of the Interior and the BLM outlined the history of the grazing issue and the Bundys' challenge of it, then FBI agents made a methodical presentation of sections of more than twelve thousand pages of Facebook posts and messages collected in a government search. It revealed defendants and others with ties to various militia groups communicating with members of the Bundy family and planning to bring their weapons to the increasingly tense scene of the April 12, 2014, standoff between the rancher, who owed $1 million in unpaid grazing fees, and BLM law enforcement charged with securing hundreds of cattle in a court-ordered roundup.

The testimony presented a different view of the defendants, whom their lawyers portrayed as patriotic citizens who came to Bundy's aid after viewing troubling internet video posts that were made in the days leading up to the standoff.

In reality, the only reinforcements the BLM and U.S. Park Service Police received came from Las Vegas Metro, the Nevada Highway Patrol, and the FBI. Most law-enforcement backup arrived in the wake of an intelligence report that noted dozens and even hundreds of militia members discussing converging on the Bundy Ranch.

One of the common misstatements about the impoundment is that it was already failing at the time of the standoff. In fact, according to government estimates, more than four hundred of Bundy's cattle had been gathered, with several weeks remaining in the roundup. But the government also found that Cliven's cattle, a Brahman-type breed, had been bred to survive in harsh environments. Their ancestors came from India and had highly developed sweat glands that help them thrive in the arid Mojave, according to Oklahoma State University's Department of Animal Science. Centuries of meager food supplies, insect pests, parasites, and diseases had made them remarkably resilient. They didn't take kindly to humans.

With all the video available, jurors received views of the standoff from every angle as the prosecution used the weight of its evidence to paint a picture of growing danger. From an altitude of twelve thousand feet, FBI Special Agent E.J. McEwen captured the standoff from a camera positioned inside a single-engine Cessna. Although difficult to see from the ground, the plane flew back and forth over the impoundment site for hours. The multiple views told part of the story that prosecutors hoped would be fleshed out by the officers on duty that day.

Emotional testimony from federal officers on the scene painted a picture of imminent danger, one reinforced by still images, video, and audio. After leaving the impoundment site in a hail of epithets, they had returned to Mesquite, where they were ordered to clear out of their hotel rooms. FBI intelligence indicated that militiamen were cruising the parking lot in an effort to hasten their departure, or worse.

But the challenge for even the best witness of recalling dramatic details of a traumatic day was simple: in the end, no shots were fired, no injuries sustained, only egos were bruised, the cattle were released, and everyone went home safely. It was a point that Marchese, Leventhal, and Tanasi returned to time and again. Perez appeared to make a point that resonated during one cross-examination when he reminded the government witness on the stand that members of the Love-led BLM team had at first refused to stand down when ordered. Reluctant to quit their assignment, perhaps also fearing to expose themselves to gunmen on the high ground, they dragged their feet long after learning the impoundment operation had been cancelled and the cattle would be let loose.

"Nothing would have happened," Perez said. "You wouldn't be having this trial because you wouldn't have these defendants here." Outside the courtroom, politicians continued to make hay out of the issue. Utah Congressman Jason Chaffetz continued his own roundup of the BLM in the wake of the scandalous Love OIG report. In a letter, he cited the "potential to not only taint your investigation, but to seriously undermine the trust in the BLM's law-enforcement office and thwart Congressional oversight of the bureau." The beleaguered BLM, forever at the political whipping post, was once again taking a beating.

While the fear and confusion that the federal law-enforcement officers felt was understandable, the chaos cut both ways. The testimony of U.S. Park Service police officer Tara McBride opened the door to doubt when, under cross-examination by Tanasi, she admitted that her colleagues were aware several hours before the standoff that the order to cease "all operations" had been given. The uniformed officers remained, she said, to provide security for the incident command post. "Despite that operations were over, despite your requests to fall back, your requests were being denied?" Tanasi asked.

Multiple government witnesses testified about learning of the decision at an April 11 briefing, where they also learned of a possible attack on the command post. The agent in charge, acting on law-enforcement intelligence reports, ordered them to take up a defensive position and remain on duty through the night. They used cell phones to speak to loved ones whom some feared they might not see again. Others testified that they prayed. One exasperated officer expressed his disbelief to the court that he'd had to dig a foxhole in his own country.

The challenge of the government's overabundance of evidence complicated the prosecution's dramatic portrayal of the facts. Although some officers were hunkered down in protected positions, others appeared to walk through the potential battle zone unprotected. Some failed to carry firearms.

Defense attorneys reminded the officers repeatedly that no shots were fired. But if image counted for anything with the jury, then Marchese had some work to do on Parker's behalf. The "Bundy Sniper" photo had been republished in newspapers around the world and had washed over every corner of the internet. With his rifle aimed and a long dagger strapped to his hip, Parker looked like a militia recruiter's dream. So the decision was made to put the confident young man on the witness stand, a calculated risk with an enormous downside, but one that held the possibility of humanizing and softening his image for the jury.

"I was not looking for a fight, but I was not going to be bullied into not exercising my First Amendment," Parker told the court, failing to acknowledge that if he hadn't pointed his weapon from a sniper position toward federal officers he wouldn't have found himself fighting for his freedom in a Nevada courtroom.

The goal of the prosecution had been to establish convincing evidence of a conspiracy, but the fact was that most of those on trial hadn't been at Camp Liberty long enough to unpack their duffels. Members of the defense spoke outside of court about the lack of evidence showing that the defendants were included in a greater plan to intimidate and extort the government on Bundy's behalf. The case was by no means secured when Navarro handed it to the jury on April 13, after two months of testimony, thirty-five prosecution witnesses, and four witnesses for the defense.

It was then that the government learned the first of several painful lessons. Although the lack of gunfire was a stroke of great fortune for those on the scene, the fact that no violence occurred appeared to weigh on the jury's ability to reach a unanimous verdict. The indictment had been accurate to call the alleged gunmen the "least culpable" of the defendants.

On April 24, jurors returned guilty verdicts on multiple counts for Burleson and Engel, both of whom had made damaging admissions after the standoff that left little doubt about their motivations and malicious intent. But the deliberating jurors shot holes in the government's theories of a criminal conspiracy. Lovelien and Stewart were nearly acquitted outright, with jurors hung ten to two in favor of their innocence. Jurors were evenly divided on the charges against Parker and Drexler, the men depicted on the northbound bridge with their rifles extended.

The case with so much evidence was falling apart. Although prosecutors argued that Lovelien should be retried, their proposal caught no traction with an increasingly frustrated Navarro as she declared a mistrial on the deadlocked counts. Lovelien and Stewart went free.

Burleson, who had admitted on camera that he'd traveled to the standoff to kill federal agents, was convicted of eight charges that included threatening and assaulting a federal officer. It was clear at sentencing that the blind fifty-three-year-old Arizonan had bragged and blustered his way into the penitentiary. The pathetic character who had told an FBI undercover agent, "I was hell bent on killing federal agents that had turned their back on we the people," at last displayed contrition as the weight of justice came crushing down. He told the judge he was ashamed of what he'd said, adding, "Looking back at them, it's like, 'wow, obviously I shouldn't drink.'" His epiphany had come too late. He received a sixty-eight-year sentence.

Jurors found Engel guilty of obstruction and interstate travel in aid of extortion. Navarro would sentence the man who had insisted on defending himself to fourteen years. Back in Idaho, Engel's family and friends set up an internet website and a funding account to support his appeal.

It was a substantial victory for the defense that set Myhre and his experienced prosecution team on their heels. Despite their best efforts, they hadn't come close to convicting four of the six defendants, who according to testimony had sent mortal fear through federal law-enforcement officers in 2014.

Although Cliven's defense attorney, Bret Whipple, would complain that his client's right to a speedy trial had been violated, and Navarro continued to take a beating with the defendants' many followers on social media and outside the federal courthouse, the lagging of the case mainly worked to the advantage of the defense. Much rested on the fact that Judge Navarro hadn't been open to the Bundy defense team's assertions that prosecutors weren't providing all available evidence during discovery. From the perspective of the prosecution, a conviction in the gunmen case might compel the rest of the defendants, even the most stubborn among them, to rethink their legal strategies in the face of the possibility of spending decades in prison.

The prosecution's prospects appeared to brighten after Navarro admonished defense counsel not to raise constitutional issues as affirmative defenses of their clients. Her pretrial ruling threatened real trouble for defendants. Navarro's strict instructions led to the rejection of five defense witnesses, and even the defendants themselves were forbidden from telling jurors their reasons for attending the rancher's protest. Although Drexler and Parker took the witness stand on their own behalf, the judge had Parker's testimony stricken from the record after he purposely refused to follow her rules.

But even with a streamlined twenty-day trial and help from veteran Assistant U.S. Attorney Daniel Schiess, Myhre's team found little traction with jurors. Since no shots had been fired, jurors were left to wonder about the seriousness of the threat, whatever ominous message the showdown sent about the lack of respect for the safety of federal employees tasked with carrying out a court-ordered cattle impoundment.

A strange thing happened on August 15 when it came time for the defense team to make its closing argument. After more than four weeks of trial, Marchese, Tanasi, Leventhal, and Perez stood silent before the jury.

Trial attorneys don't often pass up an opportunity to address the court. Prevented from applying several affirmative defenses that had helped deadlock a jury in the first trial, the four defense attorneys were compelled to battle a parade of government witnesses and a mountain of photographic, video, and social media images and messages without being granted the ability to counter with troubling images depicting alleged abuses of the Bundys by government officers. Defense counsel was prevented from arguing self-defense, the defense of others, and the government's constitutional abuses. Without the images of the Bundy family's edited videos that appeared to show them being brutalized by BLM rangers, the defendants were left looking like gun-wielding intimidators out to "put the fear of God" into federal officers while a mob of mostly unarmed protesters approached.

The defense attorneys' standing silent stoked their legal fairness narrative, laid the groundwork for a possible appeal, blocked Myhre's potentially devastating rebuttal, and fueled support from militia-friendly and right-wing webcasts. It also further tested Navarro's patience, which appeared increasingly strained in the waning days of testimony after repeated defense efforts to press issues forbidden by the court. In short, the defense lawyers were doing precisely what they were trained to do: represent their clients to the brink of contempt.

Parker, as his attorney put it in a hearing outside the jury's presence, was "ripped from the witness stand" for failing to follow the judge's clear and specific instructions. Leventhal's best efforts at preparing his client notwithstanding, Drexler's testimony didn't help him much when he was compelled to admit that he'd pointed a semiautomatic assault weapon in the direction of the BLM and NPS officers but supposedly wasn't aiming it, photographic evidence to the contrary. Tanasi's client, Stewart, was the closest thing to comic relief possible in an incident with so much potential for bloodshed—until he started bragging on the internet about his efforts. Perez, charged with defending the only acknowledged militia member among the accused, could take some comfort that no photographic evidence showed his client pointing his weapon. Although defense attorneys faced potential sanctions, Navarro cooled off enough to set them aside.

Their efforts paid off. If the first trial had been a disappointment to the prosecution, the retrial was devastating. When the jury returned its verdict on August 22, 2017, after four days of deliberation, it delivered the equivalent of a knockout blow by refusing to convict any of the defendants. Stewart and Lovelien were acquitted of all ten charges. Often appearing emotionally stricken during long days in the courtroom, Stewart shed tears of joy and relief.

Parker and Drexler were found not guilty on most of their charges, with the rest failing to receive unanimous votes. More than three dozen supporters in the crowded courtroom erupted in applause. Navarro ordered a return to decorum, but it was a moment of celebration that couldn't be contained.

Stewart and Lovelien were almost immediately released from custody. After declaring a mistrial on the undetermined charges still facing Parker and Drexler, the judge called for a hearing to determine possible conditions of their release.

Lamb, a bearded and gentlemanly budding citizen journalist who wore his biases on his sleeve in his increasingly popular daily Facebook videos, captured the moment when he told a reporter, "Random people off the streets, these jurors, they told the government again that we're not going to put up with tyranny." By the end of his time supporting the Bundys in Las Vegas, Lamb's one-man news broadcast would reach thousands of viewers.

The thorough rebuke of the FBI's investigative efforts, voluminous evidence in discovery, and the conspiracy-theory element of the case bode ill for the main event. If most of the gunmen were twice perceived by juries as mere protestors, would the rancher, two of his sons, and the military veteran Payne be likely to engender less sympathy from jurors? The government's hard ride for Cliven Bundy was fading by the day. "We the people," Carol Bundy said outside the courtroom, "are not guilty."

Parker's wife, Andrea, expressed joy at once again being able to hug her husband, and she spared little vitriol when discussing the government's case. Common sense suggested that Reuters photographer Jim Urquhart's picture of Parker prone on the northbound bridge, staring through his rifle sight downrange toward federal officers, was itself proof beyond reasonable doubt of the intimidating intent of the defendant. But that's not the way jurors saw it.

Released shortly thereafter, Parker and Drexler in October agreed to plea to a misdemeanor. Although they'd spent eighteen months in detention, they emerged victorious against substantial odds. Cliven Bundy's odds were improved by the breakdown of the gunmen prosecution, but he was still a long way from walking out of court a free man.

Although they were not always clear to a divided public, multiple factors were eroding the case by the day. The unethical behavior of BLM special agent in charge Dan Love, as illuminated in the Department of the Interior's Office of Inspector General's report, threw the government's judgment at the standoff into serious question. Although Navarro declined to grant a motion to dismiss in July, it gradually became more evident that the case was fracturing.

Then a withering eighteen-page memo written by a BLM investigator that called into question Love's behavior and motivation further weakened the case. Whipple filed a motion to dismiss, citing the government's repeated failure to turn over discovery in a timely manner. Navarro sent the jurors home for a week to allow the court enough time to sort through the allegations.

Myhre and his fellow prosecutors, unflappable for so long, showed their frustration as their efforts were called into question. Their mood darkened further when the allegations of former BLM official and self-described whistleblower Larry Wooten were made public. When Wooten testified before a federal grand jury—which eventually returned indictments in the Bunkerville affair—he claimed that he'd been removed from the investigation after he took his concerns to Daniel Bogden, then the U.S. Attorney for Nevada. In an email to the Department of Justice, Wooten described what he called "bad judgment, lack of discipline, incredible bias, unprofessionalism and misconduct," as well as ethically questionable and possibly illegal activity at the BLM's Office of Law Enforcement and Security—especially where it concerned the Bundy family. The lack of professionalism included displaying demeaning images of the Bundys and an "amateurish carnival atmosphere." Some officers, Wooten said, had bragged about battering David Bundy and forcing him to the ground so hard he had "little bits of gravel stuck to his face."

Wooten reiterated a defense contention—scoffed at by the prosecution—that officials had refused to act professionally during the discovery process by failing to turn over potentially exculpatory evidence. That accusation alone might be enough to compel Navarro to declare a mistrial.

It was also true that the job of an officer on federal public lands was difficult and increasingly dangerous. BLM rangers and contract researchers with the Great Basin Institute had reported gunshots in their vicinity during field outings in Gold Butte. *High Country News* regularly reported statistics kept by the Public Employees for Environmental Responsibility watchdog organization, which indicated that public land was no country for the timid. And when the BLM became more militarized, it drew criticism from ranchers for acting more like SWAT-team operatives than land managers.

The start of October usually marks the end of the heat season in Las Vegas, but the temperature reached ninety degrees on Sunday, October 1, 2017, before the partly cloudy day slipped into a scarlet sunset. It was a day that would end in infamy and change the psyche of the fun-loving tourism capital forever. Shortly after 10 p.m., a lone gunman equipped with a cache of two dozen weapons opened fire from a high window in a room at the Mandalay Bay Hotel and Casino, raining hundreds of bullets onto the crowded Route 91 Harvest Festival in a fenced pavilion just across Las Vegas Boulevard. In the largest mass shooting in American history, Steven Paddock killed fifty-eight people and wounded or injured more than eight hundred. His weapons of choice were assault rifles rigged to fire like fully automatic weapons.

The community reeled from the carnage and spent months in shock and mourning. Investigations by the FBI and Las Vegas Metropolitan Police did not conclusively prove the shooter's motive, but it was true that Paddock had resided for a time in Mesquite, just a few miles from Bunkerville, and had displayed the weapons worshiped so often by right-wing militias. Whether he was fueled by the same conspiracy theories and hate that motivated many of the militias would remain part of the dark mystery.

This mass killing put the Bundy standoff case in a different light for many reasons, not the least of which was the presence at the standoff of semiautomatic assault-style weapons carried by some of the defendants. Would starting the trial just days after the mass shooting, while all present agreed that the community was still in deep mourning, prejudice a jury? Could fair and impartial jurors even be found so soon after the smoke of gunfire had lifted?

Payne's attorneys, Weksler and Norwood, didn't think so. They immediately filed a motion asking Judge Navarro for a two-month delay in the trial. In their motion, the attorneys expressed concern that jurors might be prejudiced against defendants who believed passionately in the right to bear arms. They wrote, "The horror of this recent shooting is too recent, and the impact of this incident on the community is too severe, for a fair trial to commence next week."

With uniformed first responders being highly praised and Clark County Sheriff Joe Lombardo leading daily press updates, would jurors be able to give the defendants a fair trial? Lombardo had been in Toquop Wash during the standoff's most heated moments and had already testified in court.

Payne's lawyers wrote, "In time, the community's justified shock and outrage about this tragedy may subside enough to allow a fair trial," but their argument cut both ways. If they were correct, and their client couldn't be assured of an unbiased jury following a mass killing, would a two-month delay be enough? Would any amount of voir-dire probing be enough to establish certainty?

The defense lacked consensus on the issue. For his part, Whipple followed his client's wishes and wrote, "Bundy continues to demand a speedy trial, which has been denied for more than a year."

On Friday, October 6, Navarro granted a three-week delay in the start of the trial in an effort to avoid a tainted prospective jury pool. The delay may have frustrated Cliven Bundy, but it provided members of his defense team more time to explore their concerns that important discovery evidence hadn't been turned over by prosecutors. By the time Navarro reconvened the trial, those concerns had heightened.

During four days of jury selection, both sides raised a plethora of issues for dozens of prospective jurors, from opinions about law enforcement, guns, the Second Amendment, ranchers, wild horses, the federal government, the proposed Yucca Mountain nuclear-waste repository, the credibility of the internet, and even a long-rumored uranium-mine deal not far from the Bundy Ranch. The lawyers left little to chance and also made use of experienced jury consultants.

As jury selection ended, Navarro's courtroom was the scene of a juxtaposition that said as much about the political mood of the nation as it did about the charges before the court. Seated in the second row was Ryan Lenz, a senior investigative reporter with Alabama's SPLC, which for decades had tracked the activity of the Ku Klux Klan and other hate groups, white supremacists, and armed militias. To Lenz's right was firebrand conservative lawyer Larry Klayman, who had been consistently blocked by the judge from serving as part of Cliven Bundy's defense team but was suspected of sharing his insights behind the scenes. Klayman was a cofounder of

Freedom Watch and Judicial Watch and was known as a notoriously litigious lawyer who had hounded the Clintons and promulgated the "secret Muslim" lies about former president Barack Obama. In the SPLC's estimation, Klayman was a "professional gadfly notorious for suing everyone from Iran's Supreme Leader to his own mother."

He also was admired by Cliven Bundy. Arriving at Camp Liberty following the standoff, Klayman had been part of the Bundy inner circle almost from the start and was easily one of the trial's most interesting characters. With his shock of white hair and bird-of-prey focus, Klayman took notes and conferred with the Bundy family during breaks.

Although he was a Duke-educated former federal prosecutor, not a cowpuncher, outside the courtroom Klayman expressed an aw-shucks admiration for Bundy and raised suspicions that the rancher had been victimized by greater political influences. He also said he was promoting an inquiry into the Bundy investigation by Attorney General Jeff Sessions, Nevada Governor Brian Sandoval, and the state's Attorney General Adam Laxalt. Like President Trump's salty acolyte Roger Stone, Klayman couldn't resist the Bundy affair. "Bret [Whipple] can't handle this on his own," Klayman said. "It's a big case. He has the lead defendant. I'm not criticizing him. It's a big case."

As part of his effort to lead the defense, despite his own ethical entanglements, Klayman persuaded Bundy to file a motion with the U.S. Ninth Circuit Court of Appeals that would allow Klayman to represent Bundy at trial, in part because Whipple lacked vast federal criminal-trial experience. The court replied in its rejection, "The assertions made by Bundy about his counsel are demonstrably false. Either Klayman has failed to ascertain the facts by, for example, talking with Whipple or looking at Whipple's website, or he has deliberately misled the court. Neither option paints Klayman in a good light."

Nonetheless, Klayman remained close. Acknowledging that he'd met with the Bundy family perhaps two dozen times, Klayman said he expected to be back in front of Navarro "in the next few days" to press once again to join the defense.

Although he'd never make it to the defense table officially, Klayman remained a Bundy cheerleader: "I think this is the most important case I've been involved in. It's an example of how the small people can fight back against government tyranny.... If the Bundys get steamrolled, the rest of us can get steamrolled, too."

Claims of tyranny aside, Navarro managed to keep a courteous and disciplined courtroom. Despite all the criticism she was receiving on the sidewalk in front of the courthouse and on the internet, as the prosecution's case bogged down she granted the defense room to explore its missing-evidence theory. The Friday, November 3, testimony of former Nevada BLM assistant special agent Zachary Oper and former NPS chief ranger Mary Hinson would provide a dramatic turning point in the trial.

It started innocuously enough. Oper, who had moved on from the BLM to the U.S. Fish and Wildlife Service, recounted his role as assistant to embattled Special Agent in Charge Love. Oper was in charge of the complex planning of the impoundment operation and spent his workdays gathering data about the roundup from a trailer at the Incident Command Post. As tensions rose, by April 11 he said the emphasis had shifted from impoundment to ending the operation.

Under Norwood's direct examination, Oper acknowledged something the prosecutors had denied—that some paperwork was destroyed in the course of the day's business. "You know, as we printed the sheets, we'd collect them, shred them, and then they were retained electronically," Oper said. In a case with such a volume of evidence, this seemed little enough, although Oper later denied actually seeing the sheets shredded.

Then it was Hinson's turn. Retired for a year, she took the witness stand and calmly testified that she'd never seen any documents destroyed as part of her role as an NPS supervisor at the incident command trailer, which was shared with Special Agent in Charge Love and other officials. She hadn't seen documents destroyed, and she had spent some of her time at the communications trailer in the run-up to the standoff. Under Whipple's direct examination, Hinson was asked about the structure of her NPS team as it interacted with other agencies. She also acknowledged that tensions rose after an early-evening conference call updated the group that "there were dangerous individuals in the area."

She said:

> After the meeting we made a decision that we were going to secure the equipment, secure documents, and make sure that individual—nonessential individuals that were in the compound, either make sure they could get out safely or have a plan on how we would get them out in the event that there was a confrontation.

The decision included securing any documents that might contain the personal information of government employees working the impoundment. Under direct examination by Morgan Philpot, Hinson recalled seeing Love type notes into a laptop computer, which potentially could possess discoverable information. Was this a sign that the government was hiding something?

But some of her most compelling testimony was elicited by Ryan Bundy, representing himself, when he asked whether the FBI was also on hand at the incident command post.

"There were FBI agents at the command, but they weren't part of the unified command," Hinson said.

"Were you aware of a device, possibly a camera device, a listening device, perhaps, that was set up on the hill just northeast of the Bundy home?"

"Yes," she replied.

She recalled few other details, but that was enough to set the courtroom buzzing. Prosecutors had scoffed at the surveillance that family members said they'd seen and had downplayed their claims of being watched by snipers on the hillside. Now the judge and jury had heard that surveillance cameras had been set up and were transmitting images to a trailer at the command post. Hinson wasn't sure if the live feed was being recorded, but the damage was done.

Suddenly, Judge Navarro joined the examination, asking Hinson for particular details:

"So was it anybody's job to watch what's being displayed and take notes, if they saw something that needed to be shared?" the judge asked.

"That was being operated by the FBI," Hinson replied.

For the most part, she recalled, the surveillance showed cows, occasionally Camp Liberty, and sometimes the Bundy ranch house. But her testimony dovetailed neatly with defense suspicions about the government's failure to produce Love's notes and computer records. This further frustrated Myhre, who saw the judge granting the defense more latitude every day.

Hinson's revelation wasn't in itself shocking. FBI agents had been part of the investigation and indeed were sitting directly behind the government's table as Hinson gave her testimony in the courtroom. But their failure to disclose information and the mocking tone of some of the prosecutors clearly appeared to grate on the judge.

As jurors prepared to enter the courtroom on November 7, 2017, Navarro called for yet another delay. The FBI's hillside surveillance camera and its monitor feed in the trailer had not been previously disclosed to the defense. In fact, prosecutors had scoffed at the contention that the Bundys had been under video surveillance and within the sights of federal snipers. The "fantastical fishing expedition," as the prosecution called it, had caught a whopper of a Brady evidence-violation. A Brady violation occurs when the prosecution suppresses admissible evidence favorable to the accused.

As she granted a delay in the proceedings, Navarro ordered prosecutors to turn over records regarding the surveillance camera and any evidence detailing the presence of armed agents positioned around the family's home. "Certainly, something is available that could be provided to the jury," she said in frustration as the defense alleged prosecutorial misconduct. She declined to dismiss the case— at least for the time being.

Hinson's revelation threatened to make a lie of the indictment, thereby invalidating it. Weksler complained that "Nobody has ever testified about surveilling the Bundy Ranch," or about the FBI's role in the roundup.

Myhre countered, "We have turned over all video surveillance that the government is aware of or in possession of." He offered an FBI agent's memo stating that an ATV had damaged the camera, which was later moved to a hillside overlooking the Bundy supporters' Camp Liberty meeting place near the ranch. The camera was in service only from April 5 to April 8, he said. A Bundy family nephew, Arthur Scott Sessions, testified that he saw three objects that appeared to be cameras. That was enough for Navarro to order Myhre to scour all files for any material related to government camera recordings or notes produced during their use.

The government's costly criminal roundup was going the way of the cattle impoundment and taking the reputations of the prosecutors with it. For her part, Navarro was for the first time noticeably amenable to releasing at least some of the defendants from detention during trial, suggesting that a halfway house or home-confinement scenario might be possible. Most of these defendants were eventually released with conditions. Only Cliven Bundy, reminding the court that he had two other sons and other defendants still in detention, refused the offer.

When the trial resumed, the testimony of Mary Jo Rugwell, a long-time BLM supervisor, provided a dry but credible reminder of the issues at the heart of the Bundy mess. Soon to be eclipsed by more dramatic turns in the trial, Rugwell's testimony under Schiess's examination was yet another reminder that Bundy had been a well-documented scofflaw for a long time. Excoriated at every turn by the defense, the BLM had been more than patient with the rancher and his cockeyed constitutional views about its jurisdiction over federal land.

Rugwell also explained to the jury that the ephemeral grazing lease at the time Bundy stopped paying his fees was approximately $1.30 per Animal Unit Month (AUM), meaning his herd could legally graze for about $15 per animal per year. This nominal cost was approximately one-tenth the amount Bundy would have had to pay to graze his cattle on private land. He had simply refused to pay the federal government and started down a road that more than two decades later had led to the brink of a bloodbath and Navarro's courtroom.

Because the available forage was especially impacted by the area's near-constant drought conditions, the Bundy Ranch had never been approved for more than 106 animals, Rugwell recalled. At the time the standoff ended, nearly four hundred cows had been impounded and more than nine hundred more had been identified. Bundy had simply let his herd grow out of control, along with his opinion that he held ancestral grazing rights in the area.

But the case was no longer really about a BLM grazing violation or wandering cows, and there was little that credible testimony from federal-service veterans Terry Petrie, Rand Stover, and others could do about it. In his December 18, 2017, motion attempting to preclude defenses that the prosecution deemed legally invalid, Myhre's frustration with the direction of the trial was palpable.

As the Bundy case eroded by the day, Myhre scrambled to exclude what the judge had previously ruled were invalid defenses and inadmissible evidence. But something had changed on the bench. Navarro, the no-nonsense jurist who had substantially limited the defense team in the retrial of the accused gunmen, grew steadily less impressed with the prosecution and the ethical quagmire Love had created, and she increasingly appeared to be giving her attention to the steady drumbeat of requests by Whipple, Weksler, and Norwood about the fear the Bundy family had felt and by which Payne said he was moved to act.

Myhre appeared to be on solid legal ground when he sought a pretrial ruling from Navarro that established clear and conservative bounds of admissible evidence. From the prosecutor's perspective, defenses that pointed to instigation, provocation, self-defense or the defense of others, and entrapment should have been forbidden. And it was also inappropriate to attack the validity of the 1998 and 2013 federal court orders associated with the impoundment as part of the defense. The cattle roundup had been legally approved, and the federal officers present to provide security had proper jurisdiction, he wrote, calling the defense effort a "thinly veiled attempt" at jury nullification. Jurors are duty-bound to follow the law as instructed, and nullifying the law because jurors don't agree with it is illegal. Payne, for instance, may have sincerely believed that the Bundys faced "a threat of unlawful violence" and that he was provoked by "the government's own unreasonable conduct," but this wasn't an affirmative defense.

Although Bundy's attorney argued that his client was entrapped through the instigation and provocation of the government, Myhre continued to define the prosecution's position:

> Whatever the term "sniper" means to the defendants—it reduces to this: cops have guns and have special training, each of which is allowed. The government has no evidence, none, that snipers, or any other federal office, used force of any kind—let alone excessive force—against the defendants or anyone else. Neither do the defendants. And no matter how the defendants perceived the officers' conduct, the officers' use of a camera or "snipers," or their proximity to and purpose for being near the Bundy home on April 5–7, do not constitute immediacy of harm days later on April 12.

Myhre reminded the court once again that armed federal officers were in the wash carrying out court orders signed in the very courtroom in which they were trying the case:

> No matter how many ways the defendants try to argue it, instigation or provocation as a basis for self-defense is simply not available. To the extent defendants seek to offer evidence of surveillance cameras, uniforms, number of officers, weapons carried, and training the officers receive, none of that is relevant to show excessive force or a reason to assault officers. This type of evidence amounts to nullification arguments…
>
> Imagine a defendant assembling a group of armed followers to assault Metro officers conducting crowd control on the Strip on New Year's Eve, and then claiming, as a defense, that

the assembled armed followers were there only to protect the crowd against the Metro officers using force against the crowd.

But a paragraph contained in the indictment made the prosecution's argument far more difficult. It alleged that the defendants were "stating falsely, among other things, that the Bundy Ranch was surrounded by BLM snipers."

Fresh from detention, Ammon Bundy was once again in front of television news cameras with his mother, Carol, at his side, confidently opining, "I don't think there is a jury in this country that will convict us. The truth is on our side." By then, he knew that the deck was finally stacked in favor of the defense.

On the last morning, the sidewalk in front of the federal courthouse was more crowded than usual with banners and signs and the blowing of the shofar, a ram's horn referred to in the Old Testament whose sound signified, among other things, the Almighty's power.

The religious symbolism continued inside the building when Ryan Bundy led a group prayer in the crowded hallway outside Navarro's courtroom. Ranchers removed their hats and caps out of respect as the rancher's son, as ever, blended prayer with liberty and faith in the Constitution and the Founding Fathers. At long last, he even had a kind word for Judge Navarro: "She chose the side of thee and liberty.... Father in heaven, we need thy protection. We need our men home.... We need freedom back on this day."

An estimated one hundred supporters of the family squeezed into every space in the courtroom not occupied by federal personnel or the press. Many were rural people who knew and respected the Bundys' stance and had driven in from Bunkerville and southern Utah to attend a historic moment they believed was inspired by God.

In an eleventh-hour motion to bring the judge back from the brink of dismissal, Myhre reminded the court that the government had provided 1.5 terabytes of information, evidence, video, and still photography in the largest disclosure in the history of the Las Vegas office. The prosecution had practiced good faith, and its failures had been unintentional or, at worst, negligent. He also argued that the violent potential of the case made concealing witnesses' identities necessary to prevent threats "with witness protection in mind." He added, almost desperately, that despite the sheer size of the document dump and concerns about the witnesses, "the government never let these obstacles stand in the way of diligently working to fulfill its discovery obligations."

Navarro did not agree. In a measured, almost professorial voice, she calmly dispatched with one motion to dismiss on double-jeopardy grounds and moved on to whether the prosecution's failure to disclose more than a thousand pages of mostly FBI documents, as well as any evidence from its surveillance cameras, constituted a due-process violation. It was a high bar, for mere negligence wouldn't have been enough to move from mistrial to a dismissal with prejudice, meaning that the defendants couldn't be retried under the same indictment. Navarro quoted from the Ninth Circuit's *Restrepo* decision, which held that the government's conduct must be "so grossly shocking and so outrageous as to violate the universal sense of justice" under the conscious direction of the prosecution.

"Now, dismissal under this 'extremely high' standard is appropriate only in 'extreme cases in which the government's conduct violates fundamental fairness,'" the judge said, quoting from the Ninth Circuit's *Pedrin* case.

"Here in this case, both the prosecution and the investigative agencies are equally responsible for the failure to produce Brady materials to the defense," she said. In the gallery, Bundy supporters wept. Behind the prosecution's table, the FBI agents were silent and still. She continued:

> In the prior mistrial hearing, the court explained, in detail, that numerous documents, and the information contained in such documents, should have been provided to the defense and the court finds this conduct especially egregious because the government chose not to provide this evidence, even after the defense specifically requested it.

The court finds the prosecution's representations that it was unaware of the materiality of the Brady evidence is [sic] grossly shocking.... the prosecution denied the defense its opportunity to provide favorable evidence to support their theories as a result of the government's withholding of evidence and this amounts to a Brady violation.

Navarro took pains to include the FBI's investigative role in her dressing down. "Clearly, the FBI was involved in the prosecution of this case," she said. "Based on the prosecution's failure to look for evidence outside of that provided by the FBI and the FBI's failure to provide evidence that is potentially exculpatory to the prosecution for discovery purposes, the court finds that a universal sense of justice has been violated." She also predicted that more evidence potentially beneficial to the defendants existed in the FBI's possession.

Navarro then explained the legal underpinnings of the court's supervisory powers, which grant a judge the ability to remedy unconstitutional or statutory violations, protect the judicial integrity of the process, and act to deter future illegal conduct due to flagrant misbehavior and substantial prejudice. She found that multiple evidence violations had occurred "because the government failed to produce evidence that bolstered the defense and was useful to rebut the government's theory" and "willfully failed to disclose potentially exculpatory" evidence. The judge went out of her way to point out that most of that evidence was generated by and in the possession of the FBI.

In a trial that included so much video evidence in discovery, it was the lack of available evidence from an FBI surveillance camera that in the end helped save the defense. By taking the FBI agents' word that no recordings existed, or were misplaced, Navarro concluded,

The court finds that the FBI's failure to timely produce information to the prosecution amounts to reckless disregard or flagrant misbehavior, especially in light of the fact that the FBI was directly involved in the operation, prior to the operation, during, and after the alleged conspiracy timeline.

She called the prosecution's representations about whether armed officers positioned on the hillside were technically "snipers" disingenuous and found ample evidence of "flagrant prosecutorial misconduct in this case."

Finding no alternative sanctions sufficient to protect due process, and determined to hold prosecutors and investigators "to the ethical standards which regulate the legal profession as a whole," Navarro made her final decision: "The court finds that the government's conduct in this case was indeed outrageous, amounting to a due process violation, and that a new trial is not an adequate sanction for this due process violation."

The dismissal with prejudice sent cheers and cries of joy through the stunned courtroom. As order was restored, Navarro vacated the detention orders of the defendants and set aside a time to do the same for the remaining defendants who had been scheduled for the next judicial go-round.

As word of the stunning rebuke spread and the defendants began to appear outside the courthouse to face the waiting press, the government was battered from all sides. The self-righteous cackles of the Bundy backers were to be expected, but trackers of far-right extremists and defenders of the environment also pummeled prosecutors.

"The result can only embolden anti-government extremists, especially in western states, and make future confrontations and standoffs with the government more likely," the Anti-Defamation League's Jonathan Greenblatt offered in a statement. Jennifer Rokala of the Center for Western Priorities warned, "The Bundy family took up arms against the US government, endangering the lives of the men and women who work tirelessly to protect America's public lands. Letting the Bundys walk free on a technicality should send a chill down the spines of anyone who values our parks, wildlife refuges, and all public lands."

"Federal prosecutors clearly bungled the case and let the Bundys get away with breaking the law," Kieran Suckling of the Center for Biological Diversity jabbed in his statement to the press, labeling the dismissal of the case as "just a horrific outcome." A relentless critic of the rancher's actions, the Center successfully sought to intervene in a little-noticed and legally nonsensical lawsuit filed by Bundy that called for the transfer of Nevada's federal public lands into state control by declaratory judgment.

Given the opportunity to humbly admit that he was wrong when he asserted that the federal government lacked jurisdiction over the land in question, Cliven Bundy returned to a familiar theme—victimhood: "I'm not used to being free. I've been a political prisoner for right at 700 days today. I come into this courtroom an innocent man and I'm going to leave as an innocent man."

But the judge hadn't ruled on his guilt or innocence. She had found that the prosecution had egregiously violated the rules of evidence and marred the defendants' constitutional right to a fair trial. Unlike Bundy, Navarro knew her Constitution. In her judicial capacity and jurisdiction, she followed the law and ruled in his favor out of an abundance of fairness in a court that Bundy failed to respect or recognize. Instead, he questioned why land-management bureaucracies, such as the BLM, Forest Service, and Park Service, would have need for "armies," neglecting to acknowledge his role in inviting militia backers to his self-styled "range war emergency."

But those hoping for a scintilla of contrition would have to wait until well after Cliven's cows came home. He had his victory and a platform of reporters and willing listeners. "My defense is a fifteen-second defense," he bragged from under his cowboy hat. "I graze my cattle on Clark County, Nevada, land and I have no contract with the federal government. This court has no jurisdiction or authority over this matter. And I've put up with this court in America as a political prisoner for two years."

He called out the "aiders and abettors out there" who'd participated in "taking freedom away from Americans," answered more reporters' questions, and posed for selfies with admirers.

The Bunkerville rancher's story beamed around the world faster than a cowhand can pull on his boots.

Lonesome Bull

While still standing in the shadow of the Lloyd D. George U.S. Courthouse following the dismissal, Cliven Bundy told reporters that he looked forward to returning to the ranch, being with his family, enjoying a steak, and getting back on his land. But a funny thing happened on the way to riding off into the Nevada sunset. Neither he nor his sons were finished sharing their views, and they appeared confident that the public was waiting for more than melons and beef from the men from Bunkerville.

Bundy went free, but some of America's wealthiest citizens benefited from his courtroom victory. That noble-rancher imagery was gold to the behemoth range operators. Although some outfits could claim more than a century on the land, cattlemen had long been selling out to corporate titans who knew far more about tax shelters and banking than roping and branding. In Nevada, Cliven's 160 deeded acres amounted to a postage stamp next to the Winecup Gamble Ranch in northeastern Elko County. Once owned by Silver State ranching king John Sparks in the late 1800s, in 2016 it was put on the market for $77 million, which included 247,000 deeded acres with another 558,080 acres under grazing lease and still another 142,800 acres available for lease from adjacent ranches. The Winecup Gamble Ranch wasn't owned by a calloused Nevada stockman but by Paul Fireman, one of the nation's largest landowners and founder of the investment firm Fireman Capital Partners. The TS Ranch at Dunphy and Battle Mountain had historic roots going back to the 1870s, but these days the 400,000-acre spread was owned by a subsidiary of Newmont Goldcorp.

However disingenuous Bundy's "not guilty" claim, the imagery that his story generated was useful to the Trump administration as it worked methodically to gut Obama administration policies designed to protect the environment and define new wild lands for status as national monuments. Under Secretary Ryan Zinke and his replacement, former oil and gas lobbyist David Bernhardt, conservation programs were rebranded as the work of radical environmentalists, and public lands were thrown open to oil and gas exploration and to hydraulic fracturing—a method of petroleum extraction potentially far more devastating to precious water tables than any bureaucrat's regulation. Interior's inspector general's office had already opened an ethics investigation of Bernhardt for possible "conflict of interest and other violations" committed during his brief tenure as deputy secretary. Bernhardt was suspected of continuing his lobbying work as he transitioned into government service, derailing the release of an Interior study of the impact of pesticide toxicity on endangered species, concealing private meetings with corporate interests, and shilling for former clients while in office.

Budget cuts at Interior were coupled with looser restrictions on mining and budget-funding cuts that threatened to devastate the national parks system. Much-vilified environmental organizations, which had spent decades in a successful ground game against the destruction of habitat and wildlife in courts across the country, decried Trump's clear disdain for the Endangered Species Act, which had been signed into law in 1973 by Richard Nixon. Bundy differed from Trump on multiple issues, including immigration policy, but when it came to rebranding environmental protections as "socialism," he was along for the ride.

In a decision that horrified environmentalists but was cheered by western ranchers, Trump announced in July 2019 a plan to dismantle the BLM in Washington, streamlining the agency and moving its headquarters to Grand Junction, Colorado. With nearly all the 388,000 square miles under BLM purview located in a dozen western states, the decision made political sense. Previous candidates and public officials had suggested a similar move, and a large majority of the BLM's ten thousand employees were already in the West. Nevada was in line to absorb fifty new employees, with Grand

Junction slated to receive just thirty. It was a move seen as mostly symbolic and was criticized as a sign that the BLM's future was in peril, but it was heralded by ranchers and extractive-industry leaders as a sign that their concerns were being heard.

Bundy and his allies understood the power of symbolism. His continued outspokenness was welcome news to organizations such as the American Legislative Exchange Council (ALEC), which had benefited from the rancher's legal entanglement as it argued about supposed overreach on public lands. Backed by billionaire brothers Charles and David Koch, ALEC resolved to press state legislatures for the transfer of public lands to state control. With its stated purpose of working with "state legislators dedicated to the principles of limited government, free markets and federalism," and with help from a $10-million annual budget, by 2019 ALEC boasted of its members representing more than sixty million Americans as it made progress toward transferring federal public lands "in the best interests of the nation."

Bundy found another ally in the American Lands Council (ALC), which since its inception in 2012 continued to work at the county level in the West to wrest control of federal lands and enthused that its members included more than a thousand elected officials. If its unstated goal was to facilitate the transfer of public lands into corporate hands, the curious might not suspect this from reading its mission statement, which called for the "lawful, peaceful path to better, more accountable management of our public lands and natural resources."

Surely no one individual would have been more pleased with Bundy's courtroom success than his ally Bert Smith, the so-called godfather of the Sagebrush Rebellion and one-time Ruby Valley, Nevada, rancher who had started ALC with a $35,000 check and had papered the land with hundreds of thousands of his friend Cleon Skousen's pocket Constitutions. Smith died in April 2016 at age ninety-five. His far-right, federalist interpretation of the Constitution and his own reactionary LDS beliefs reflected Bundy's own views on public lands and the supposed socialist perils of environmentalism. Smith, who had co-founded the Freeman Institute (later called the National Center for Constitutional Studies) with Skousen in 1971, also provided funding for the less well-known National Federal Lands Conference and was suspected of backing other alphabet organizations that proposed changes in federal land and water policies. Late in his life, Smith called Bundy "a hero of the range livestock operator on the public land."

However much Bundy had missed his home range, it hadn't prevented him from selling off approximately four hundred of his cattle during his time in detention. However little regard he had for the federal government, it was an undeniable fact that he'd let his herd expand far beyond the land's capacity to provide forage. Bundy Ranch had gotten a lot lighter, even as the BLM had indefinitely postponed its impoundment, which remained legally binding and just as disregarded. The cattle wandered far and were considered "essentially feral" by traditional ranching standards. At trial, Whipple attempted to rebrand the herd in more scientific terms, asserting they'd been bred to survive in harsh desert conditions and weren't as aggressive as they were resilient. Their form of resilience had led to the cancellation of dove-hunting season in the area, due to the cattle's menacing of the hunters.

Cliven didn't stay on the ranch long. After only three weeks, he was back standing before a herd whose company he seemed to enjoy most—not the ones with horns and hooves but those who favored hats and boots. It was enough to make some folks wonder who was minding the cattle, and whether those cows were getting lonesome. Bundy and family members took their show on the road, heading north to Paradise, Montana, where the rancher addressed two hundred like-minded members of the Coalition of Western Property Owners (COWPO) on his favorite topic—the unconstitutional overreach of the federal government's control of public lands in the West. As the *Missoulian* reported, Bundy received a standing ovation when he implored the crowd to "Go and read your Constitution and start acting like you're a sovereign state." Like a confidence man from a Sinclair Lewis satire come to life, the rancher Bundy was back preaching the gospel of Gadsden, states' rights, glory, and freedom.

Bundy took time during one public appearance to chastise the presidentially pardoned Oregon ranchers Dwight and Steven Hammond for once again following BLM grazing rules. At a meeting in Nephi, Utah, before a local gathering of the super-conservative Independent American Party, the rancher called their decision "the worst thing, the terriblest thing, that would happen for the Hammonds." Notable was the crowd size—just a dozen or so.

The rancher's road show was not without controversy. His challenged interpretation of the Constitution aside, he occasionally encountered detractors. Members of Montana's Backcountry Hunters & Anglers (BHA) outdoor organization staged their own protest against Bundy's dream of turning all federal land over to the states. To outdoors enthusiasts and those who enjoy federal public lands for recreation, Bundy is not a noble cowboy. The BHA National Board Chair Ryan Busse later wrote:

> When someone stole things or grazed cattle on a place they did not have permission, we called them thieves. I was raised as an American, and I was taught that our founding fathers wanted to shift power from British royalty and give it to the people. When people want to return this power to the corporate royalty of today, I call that treasonous.

The Bundy brothers had been fortunate in the Malheur occupation and were found not guilty at trial. Ranchers Dwight and Steven Hammond were pardoned by President Trump in July 2018, after Forrest Lucas, an Indiana oil tycoon and friend of Vice President Mike Pence, brought their case to the president's attention. Trump called the Hammonds prosecution "overzealous," and Lucas sent a private jet to pick them up at federal prison in California and transport them back to their home in eastern Oregon.

Others among the twenty-seven defendants charged under federal law in the standoff weren't as lucky. By then, the public-lands issue was being played politically for all it was worth.

Ammon and Ryan Bundy weren't finished on the stump. On the final day of filing for Nevada's 2018 election cycle, Ryan decided to run for governor of Nevada. He struck themes familiar to anyone who had followed his family's story. He told Las Vegas public radio station KNPR that he saw "atrocities taking place by the government both on the state and the federal level" and reminded listeners, "The United States—I don't see as one country, I see the United States as 50 separate sovereign individual countries—so to speak—that we are united for common cause and purposes." The interview gave him time to once again speak of federal overreach: "Nevada is only 10 percent of the state that it believes it is. The rest of it is being controlled as a territory and there is nothing constitutional about that."

Ryan Bundy was back, but not exactly by popular demand. On Election Day, he received just 1.4 percent, or 13,891 out of nearly 950,000 votes cast.

Of all the Bundy brothers, it was Ammon who appeared most comfortable in the spotlight. Fond of casting his family's plight and his personal journey in religious terms, he settled back into life in Emmett, Idaho, as an auto fleet manager, but soon he admitted that life was not the same. How could it be—after nearly two years of detention, the fight of a lifetime in federal court, and all that media attention? In an interview with the *Idaho Statesman*, he mused, "Life has never, ever been the same—in a good and a hard way. I think it'll take years and years to kind of dissolve."

But he didn't want to pass up the spotlight either, taking to the road often to speak at conferences on everything from the dangers of environmentalism to the sanctity of the Second Amendment. Federal land ownership, his recurring theme, echoed his father's message and that of Skousen, Bert Smith, and all those Nevada sagebrush rebels who had stepped up before. Like the others, Ammon created his own problems when he strayed from a specific narrative and began to riff. In a rally in Modesto, California, he said all talk of water shortages was "a lie" promulgated by socialist environmentalists when they knew the truth: that the earth's water supply was replenished by ice from asteroids.

In time, the Bundys would be quoted on many topics unrelated to cattle ranching or federal land issues. In one interview, Cliven balked at Trump's controversial plans to build a wall at the US-Mexico border, saying it "never did sit very good with me." His sons concurred.

Ammon told *BuzzFeed News* that he believed the president was a nationalist who made decisions that benefit the nation and not the individual. He said, "That is not freedom, and that is not what America was built upon." But when Ammon renounced the militia movement as filled with "hate, and fear, and almost warmongering," he was betraying the very people who had armed themselves as citizen warriors, traveled across state lines, and stood up for his family.

Like his father, Ammon softened his right-wing rhetoric by name-dropping African American civil rights icons such as Rosa Parks and Dr. Martin Luther King Jr. Some in his almost exclusively white audiences talked of feeling "disenfranchised" by the federal government. The Bundys' story had come to illustrate and reinforce a familiar western theme of alienation from and victimization by distant Washington bureaucrats.

Then Ammon Bundy went further in a meeting at a Smithfield, Utah, high school recreation center, associating the family's grazing dispute and federal fight with nothing less than a sacred "battle of high priests," pitting his father and attorney Whipple against the U.S. attorney who prosecuted his family, the chief judge in the Malheur case, and former Senate Majority Leader Harry Reid. He invoked his family's ties to Bunkerville, saying his ancestors had been sent to the desert more than 140 years earlier by the LDS faith's second president, Brigham Young himself. He'd been directed by the Almighty to travel to Oregon with armed militia backers to take over the Malheur Refuge, an act that had compelled the LDS Church to issue a statement denying that the act that led to the loss of one life was "justified on a scriptural basis."

Those in attendance then heard Ammon Bundy say that socialists, globalists, and environmentalists had infiltrated the LDS Church and called environmentalism an un-Christian form of religion. He read from the Book of Mormon Third Nephi and the Old Testament's Book of Judges and draped his family's struggle in a spiritual light and in terms of good and evil. After extolling the virtues of the

LDS Church and endorsing the veracity of the Book of Mormon, he added that his family was "being prosecuted by a high priest of The Church of Jesus Christ of Latter-day Saints." He said such things because "the truth matters."

Given his extremist views, it was probably inevitable that Ammon Bundy would become associated with Washington State legislator Matt Shea, a right-wing politician and militia associate who had once introduced a bill designed to divide Washington into two states. Shea's relationship with Bundy was exposed in a 108-page investigative report released by the legislature in 2019 that labeled the lawmaker a "domestic terrorist" who envisioned a "Christian insurrection." Although Shea's party and caucus sprinted to distance themselves from him, he refused to resign for reportedly helping Ammon Bundy plot the Malheur action.

Other Bundy allies fared little better. Roger Stone, a Trump confidant, was found guilty in November 2019 of lying and obstructing a congressional investigation of Russia's interference in the 2016 election. Trump commuted Stone's forty-month-prison term in July 2020, then pardoned him in December. Lawyer Larry Klayman in 2019 found himself fighting the suspension of his law license in the District of Columbia. In a twist of legal irony reminiscent of a dog chasing and chewing on its own tail, Klayman sued Stone for defamation and dragged the provocateur through a deposition during which he responded with a fusillade of epithets.

Perhaps it had to do with Bundy's religion's long obsession with bloodlines and familial ancestry, but biographers and investigative journalists searching in the twenty-first century for keys to Cliven's personality and motivation inevitably found information that linked him to everyone from the plotters of the 1857 massacre at Mountain Meadows, the largest mass murder of nonindigenous people in American history up to that date, to polygamists chased from the Utah Territory's Dixie to the Arizona Strip and all the way into Mexico. It was true that the region's historical influencers were eclectic, ranging from the hearty pioneer stock dispatched by Brigham Young to the horse and cattle thieves who pastured stolen livestock around the Pahranagat Valley. Although less chronicled by outsiders, it was also true that the region had a long history of tax protest. Skeptics would be forgiven for suspecting there was something in the water, or perhaps in the LDS faith's history of persecution and paranoia, that influenced Bundy's politics.

On the Bundy range, politics, religion, and ranching were inseparable. Their story produced a spate of compelling literature; the blend of cowboy and Mormon mystiques proved irresistible. Other observers focused on the eerie rise of the American militia and its relationship to land disputes. Some saw the Bundy action as mere political theater in the greater but less-publicized environmental tragedy in the West. As with most things related to Bundy, authors brought their own personal and political views to the page and created a fascinating mosaic of the man and his mission. The rancher's critics generally agreed with historian and conservationist Betsy Gaines Quammen's conclusion that "Bundy has convinced himself and others that God wants him to go to war over our public lands." It wasn't hard to hear the voice of Bundy's fiery forefathers in the rancher's pronouncements.

More than a century earlier, Theodore Roosevelt had spoken his own truth as the father of America's conservation movement, which he considered a "new nationalism": "We have become great because of the lavish use of our resources. But the time has come to inquire seriously what will happen when our forests are gone, when the coal, the iron, the oil and the gas are exhausted, when the soils have still further impoverished and washed into the streams, polluting the rivers, denuding the fields." This was a truth no longer in fashion in the Trump White House, which through rapid deregulation brought its own brand of economic nationalism to the Great American Commons: the politics of plunder.

To that end, former Interior solicitor John Leshy calls the public lands' destiny a matter that Americans must decide for themselves as part of a national identity: "There is nothing in the Constitution that says we have to keep these places, so it's up to every generation of Americans to decide whether they want to keep them or not, and how they want them to be managed."

For Ammon, the priestly sounding Bundy son, the truth also had a long memory. At the Malheur takeover, he'd sounded like a prophet, not from a holy book but from the website of ALEC or the American Lands Council: "While we're here," he'd said, "what we're going to be doing is freeing these lands up, getting the ranchers back to ranching, getting the miners back to mining, getting the loggers back to logging, where they can do it under the protection of the people—and not be afraid of this tyranny that has been upon them."

It was the tyranny of following BLM grazing regulations. And in the case of Cliven Bundy, those regulations had been flouted for a quarter century. Although sent reeling by Judge Navarro's withering decision, federal prosecutors regrouped and petitioned the Ninth Circuit Court of Appeals to reinstate criminal charges against Bundy and other defendants. They were immediately vilified for beating a dead horse. Myhre had accepted a demotion with the naming of Dayle Elieson as Nevada's U.S. attorney, and the DOJ's investigation of the FBI's and the prosecutors' conduct remained incomplete.

The dismissal provided a field day for Larry Klayman, who had been kept at a distance from the trial proceedings by the judge, but who let anyone within earshot know his legal views of the case. Chest-thumping on right-wing websites, Klayman's rhetoric reflected a popular view among Bundy followers, that Navarro had followed the law only after realizing the defendants would likely be acquitted. He invoked "Dirty Harry" Reid into his counterconspiracy, along with former President Obama and the "Deep State holdovers in the U.S. Attorney's Office" on the prosecution team. He gloated, "They're hoping for a Hail Mary at the 9th Circuit, because otherwise Myhre and company, their careers are over."

Klayman's enthusiasm faded after Bundy's civil suit calling for federal public land in Nevada to be returned to state control was laughed out of court by presiding District Judge James Crockett. In an eight-page dismissal, Crockett restated what other judges had been saying for nearly a quarter century and American historians had recognized since 1848. No matter how the rancher felt about it, Crockett wrote, "It is simply delusional to maintain that all public land within the boundaries of Nevada belongs to the State of Nevada.... It is painfully obvious that the claims asserted by Bundy in the instant matter rest upon the fundamentally flawed notion

advanced by Bundy since 1998 regarding ownership of federal public lands in Nevada." Klayman, so quick to find conspiracy, promised
to appeal, accused the judge of being in the "hip pocket" of the federal government, and criticized him for being discourteous.

Like a rooster who takes credit for every sunrise, from his Idaho
home Ammon Bundy drew small crowds wherever he went and
found almost-lurking socialism and threatened freedoms associated
with almost every public controversy. When the novel coronavirus
swept across the country, killing many thousands and buckling the
economy, Bundy violated stay-at-home rules in a "Liberty" quar-
antine rebellion, and at one point he informed his audience of
medical-science skeptics that "I actually want the virus" in order to
gain immunity to it. As with other far-right protests of pandemic-
containment measures, he attracted plenty of armed militia volunteers to provide security.

Intoxicated by their place in the new American conservative Zeitgeist, the Bundys appeared unfazed by the damage they'd helped
unleash. In addition to the violent death of LaVoy Finicum, several
of their most faithful supporters remained behind bars. Gregory
Burleson wasn't scheduled to be released from prison until 2075.
Todd Engel's family and friends continued their efforts to raise funds
to support his appeal from a sentence that would keep him behind
bars until 2028. Jerry DeLemus's attempt to have his seven-year sentence set aside was unsuccessful.

Bundy's image as a noble cowboy didn't square with the facts,
and when his family used social media to call out their "Range War
Emergency" and included associates of the American militia movement in their email blasts, they set the stage for what had all the
makings of a bloodbath in Toquop Wash. The question was whether
there would ever be a higher price to pay.

Delayed in part by the devastating coronavirus pandemic that
killed more than 300,000 Americans before the end of 2020, the
prosecution's appeal of the dismissal with prejudice finally reached
oral arguments before the U.S. Ninth Circuit Court of Appeals
on May 29, 2020. In keeping with the times, the hearing before
the three-judge panel was conducted by teleconference and live-

streamed on the appeals court's website. Given all the video, audio, and social media that was entered into evidence in the criminal investigation, it seemed only fitting.

In order to have the case remanded for a new trial, U.S. Attorney Elizabeth White had to persuade the appeals court that Judge Navarro had erred when she ruled that the prosecution's failure to provide evidence caused a due-process violation "so grossly shocking and so outrageous as to violate the universal sense of justice." White kept the argument simple, reminding the court that the dismissal was based on a failure to disclose just eight documents in a case with an eighty-seven-page discovery log listing hundreds of thousands of pages of documents, audio and video tapes, and more than four hundred FBI agent memos.

"The record shows here that the government worked tirelessly and tried diligently to comply with all of its obligations," White said. But, she allowed, "In undertaking this enormous task, we missed a few things. We overlooked a document here, or we didn't appreciate the potential relevance of a document there. And in light of the District Court's finding of materiality, what is clear is that we fell short. We fell short with respect to these eight items. But falling short simply does not warrant the extreme sanction of dismissing a criminal indictment, and particularly dismissing it with prejudice."

Although he was kept away from the defense table during the trial, attorney Larry Klayman represented Cliven Bundy before the appeals court. He was at his barbwire best. "There was flagrant abuse here, gross abuse," Klayman said. "And Judge Navarro made the exact correct decision."

Klayman noted to the court that his client had already spent nearly two years in detention, some of that time in solitary confinement. Sensing the increasing possibility of a remand, he then pursued the assistance of the appeals court in ensuring that a damning 2017 BLM whistleblower memo received judicial notice. The memo of BLM veteran Larry Wooten alleged that federal officials kept "kill lists," disparaged the Bundys' Mormon faith, and celebrated when family members were roughed up prior to the standoff. This motion was taken into consideration by the court.

Assistant federal public defender Amy Cleary represented the remaining defendants, and she detailed areas where the court determined that the prosecution had been not just incomplete in its discovery but also deceptive with the judge and defense. She reminded the appeals court, "That is why this is such an egregious case. And it's a troubling case, and it's a rare case."

Although the appeals court was known as the "slowest of the circuits" when it came to publishing its decisions, it moved relatively swiftly in August, with affirming Judge Navarro's decision and denying the prosecution's attempt to revive the Bundy prosecution.

The celebration was tempered by the knowledge that the BLM still considered Bundy in violation of the rules so many other ranchers followed. "They still say I'm trespassing," Bundy told the Associated Press, and reminding the outside world, "I have no contract with the federal government." Cliven Bundy remained emboldened by his courtroom victory, however long it lasted, and was entirely comfortable with his actions. "I have a lot of faith in the Heavenly Father and I feel like he's protecting me and blessed me in many, many ways," the rancher told a friendly reporter. "So with that faith, I don't have a lot of fear."

Bundy's faith was unshaken, but the result of the 2020 presidential election left his allies in corporate ranching and the extractive industries less sanguine. The public-lands pendulum was about to swing again with the victory of former Vice President Joe Biden. Environmentalists predicted that the new administration would work quickly to undo President Trump's sweeping deregulation. "They'll be starting right out of the gate," Harvard Law School Environmental and Energy Law Program Director Jody Freeman said. Although some of the regulatory cleanup could be accomplished with a stroke of a pen, rebuilding hollowed-out departments and making real progress might take much longer. Biden was expected to restore the boundaries of Utah's Bears Ears and Grand Staircase–Escalante national monuments, which was certain to rekindle regional debate and cries of federal overreach from ranchers and drillers alike.

The Environmental Protection Agency and Department of the Interior, some speculated, would once again function with the interests of the planet and public lands in mind. Biden's announced creation of a cabinet-level position to address the climate change crisis, and his nomination of former Secretary of State John Kerry to head it as a member of the National Security Council, placed the president-elect in good stead with those who had longed for bold leadership on the global-warming issue. Climate science would be a "top-tier issue," and no longer the butt of a joke, inside the White House.

Yet even optimists acknowledged that it might take years to recover from the Trump administration's broad deregulation and its fire sale of oil and gas leases. From the sagebrush to cyberspace, the endless fight for control of West's vast but fragile public lands continued.

Acknowledgments

My first of many thanks goes to my wife, Sally Denton, a great writer, editor, coach, and friend. Thanks as well to my inspiring daughter, Amelia, for always being in my corner. Thanks also to Sara Denton, intrepid matriarch of a great Nevada family. And a special thanks to my family and friends who support me through every endeavor.

One day, I suspect, energetic law-school students will take it upon themselves to chronicle how the technology-associated evidence-gathering done in *U.S. v. Bundy et al.* created a blessing and a complication for all concerned. That the serve-and-volley of the Las Vegas trials went so smoothly was a testament to the professionalism of U.S. District Court Judge Gloria Navarro and her staff, as well as the worthy combatants.

At the valiant University of Nevada Press, I am grateful for Acting Director JoAnne Banducci, Marketing and Sales Manager Sara Hendrickson, Marketing Assistant Iris Saltus, acquiring editor Margaret F. Dalrymple, copyeditor Daniel Montero, project editor Sara Vélez Mallea, indexer Cynthia J. Coan, proofreader Luke Torn, UNLV History Professor Michael Green, former directors Clark Whitehorn and Justin Race, and former editorial-production manager Alrica Goldstein.

In recent years, I have covered parts of this story for several publications, including the *Daily Beast*, the *Las Vegas Review-Journal*, *The Nevada Independent*, and Reuters, as well as Public Radio Station KNPR in Las Vegas. I'd like to thank past and current editors who encouraged me to follow this story either as a reporter or columnist and to lend my own perspective to it: John Avlon, Michael Hengel, Ben Klayman, Frank McGurdy, Justin Miller, Thomas Mitchell, Jon Ralston, Bill Tarrant, and Elizabeth Thompson.

Some remarkable reporters took on the daunting task of attempting to corral this big, underreported, and easily misunderstood story. They are some of the best journalists I've ever watched work. At the risk of leaving some out: Erin Alberty, Robert Anglen, Maxine Bernstein, Nicole Blanchard, Henry Brean, Jim Brunner, Sandra Chereb, Rachel Christiansen, Sean Dolan, David Ferrara, Josh Gerstein, John M. Glionna, David Gutman, Mike Heuer, Jeremy Jacobs, Ryan Lenz, Doug McMillan, Katharine Miezkowski, Dave Montero, Thomas Moriarty, Vanessa Murphy, Tim Pearce, Gary Andrew Poole, Ken Ritter, Joe Schoenmann, Leah Sottile, Rex Stenninger, Phil Taylor, Rob Taylor, Debra Cassens Weiss, Tay Wiles, Lance Williams, Jenny Wilson, and Jennifer Yachnin. Deadline journalism is much maligned in the Trump era and has never been more important to keeping the public accurately informed, no matter how contentious the issue. While working on this story, I saw reporters yelled at and called "fake news," and worse. Just outside the Las Vegas courtroom, I saw one rancher crudely attempt to menace a reporter. She didn't back down. The good ones never do.

The Bundy standoff and Malheur takeover not only attracted worldwide press attention to remote areas of the West, casting an intense light on the controversial subject of federal public lands, but they also have inspired talented long-form writers to tell their versions of events from their own interesting perspectives. A lot of good work has been done, with more to come. The topic reverberates far beyond the West and strikes at the heart of the American psyche as we decide whether to accept the fact that our country's natural resources and environmentally sensitive spaces, however vast, are limited and threatened. For writers, the range is open. I'll see you on the trail.

Sources of Quotations

Key phrases in boldface italics refer to quotations.

Prologue—Back Road to Gold Butte

x ***One could write a post-war history:*** Ketcham, "The Great Republican Land Heist," *Harpers* (February 2015). https://harpers.org/archive /2015/02/the-great-republican-land-heist/.

xi ***"The nation wasn't formed":*** Leshy, quoted in Powell, "Public Lands," *Harvard Law Today*, March 15, 2018.

xii ***"Conservation is a great moral issue":*** Theodore Roosevelt in his "New Nationalism Speech," September 1, 1910.

xiv ***"chloroform in print":*** Twain, *Roughing It*, chap. 16.

xv ***"And for this purpose I have established the Constitution of this land":*** Doctrine and Covenants, 101: 79–80.

xviii ***"When I see the forces":*** Author interview with Cliven Bundy, April 5, 2014.

xviii ***"the public lands in Nevada":*** Judge Lloyd D. George, decision, July 2013.

xix ***"You know, our fathers come":*** Author interview with Bundy, April 5, 2014.

xxi ***"You can go around":*** BLM Officer directing author, April 5, 2014.

Chapter 1: We Join the Revolution Already in Progress

3 ***"Notice is hereby given":*** Official BLM notice posted March 24, 2014.

3 ***"ready to do battle":*** Cliven Bundy, written statement, March 24, 2014.

4 ***"range war emergency":*** Cliven Bundy missive, March 24, 2014.

4 ***"appropriate legal remedies":*** Cliven Bundy's notifications to contractors, Match 24, 2014.

5 ***"force, violence and economic harm":*** *US v. Bundy et al.*, March 2, 2016.

5 ***"his soul to the devil":*** "BLM's Conundrum: What to Do with Bundy's Cows," enews.net, February 26, 2016.

6 ***a family historian:*** Hafen, *Far from Cactus Flats*.

7 ***"I have always thought of the Bundys":*** Hafen, *Far from Cactus Flats*, 10.

7 ***"learned quickly the trickster temperament":*** Bennion, *Desert Patriarchy*, ix.

7 ***"Hope, in spite of heartache":*** Hafen, *Far from Cactus Flats*, 208.

8 *"With dad gone"*: Cliven Bundy, quoted in *Washington County News* (St. George, Utah), May 14, 1964.

9 *"I didn't hardly see"*: Bundy author interview, April 18, 2014.

9 *"ephemeral…for livestock grazing"*: US District Judge Johnnie B. Rawlinson's ruling re: Bundy's federal grazing permit, November 4, 1998.

10 *"Bundy appears to be the last"*: Kenric Ward, *Saints in Babylon*, 101–2; *"a noble cause"*: Vin Suprynowicz, *Las Vegas Review-Journal*; *"the arrogant practitioners"*: Tim Findley, *Range Magazine*.

10 *"Do we want to be run"*: Cliven Bundy, quoted in *Daily Spectrum* (St. George, Utah), June 1989.

10 *Administrative Notices of Intent*: Bundy missive, February 28, 1993.

11 *"if fully implemented.... The decision from the BLM"*: U.S. District Judge Johnnie Rawlinson, litigation decision, *U.S. v. Cliven Bundy*, November 3, 1998.

12 *"has no right to occupy"*: Bureau of Land Management memorandum, 2002, Re: Bundy Grazing Allotment.

12 *"whatever it takes"*: "Constructive Notice," Cliven Bundy statement, April 2014.

14 *"First, I'm fighting this thing"*: *Daily Spectrum* (St. George, Utah), April 2014.

14 *"They got themselves into trouble"*: Unnamed Utah livestock auction owner, ibid.

15 *"All those cowboys"*: Cliven Bundy in a video titled *Range War, 2014*. See https://www.youtube.com/watch? v=y75A1hwRLzc.

16 *"I've done quite a bit"*: Bundy statement, April 5, 2014.

16 *"false, deceitful and deceptive"*: *U.S. v. Bundy*, superseding indictment.

16 *"snipers against Bundy"*: Ibid.

16 *"They have my cattle"*: Facebook post, Cliven Bundy, April 2014.

17 *"Heaven forbid, we don't want"*: Author interview with Las Vegan Eric Farnsworth, April 5, 2014.

17 *"You'd better have funeral plans…inbred bastard…I'm trying to do everything"*: Author interview with Clark County commissioner Tom Collins, April 7, 2014.

18 *"No cow justifies"*: Governor Brian Sandoval statement, April 8, 2014.

19 *"huge advocate against government"*: Blaine Cooper, on social media, produced in *U.S. v. Bundy*, March 2, 2016.

19 *"I say we go their [sic] armed together"*: Ibid.

20 *"some Jews"*: *Missoula Independent*, June 2014.

20 *"a national organization…defense of public…At such a point"*: Website, West Mountain Rangers, Facebook page.

21 *"When I first arrived"*: Ryan Payne, YouTube interview, April 7, 2014.

21 *"I have raised cattle"*: Cliven Bundy public statement, *The Blaze*, April 9, 2014.

22 *"Time we stopped all this":* Pete Santilli, statement, internet radio broadcast, *U.S. v. Bundy* indictment.

22 *deceitful: U.S. v. Bundy* superseding indictment, March 2, 2016.

22 *"armed with assault rifles":* Cliven Bundy social media statement, ibid.

22 *"If this is not the issue…all Americans anywhere":* Pete Santilli, from ibid.

22 *"take our land back":* Cliven Bundy, public statement, April 12, 2014.

23 *"I don't believe in firing":* Santilli, internet broadcast, April 8, 2014.

23 *"BLM is in violation":* Ibid.

23 *"the BLM knows":* Ibid.

23 *"We want BLM to always retreat":* Ibid.

24 *"my country back…I'm off to war":* Social-media statement, Ricky Lovelien, Montana State Defense Force, reported in the *Nevada Independent*, March 19, 2017.

24 *"killing cops…I see all those":* Gregory Burleson, Facebook post, 2014, quoted in *U.S. v. Bundy* superseding indictment, March 2, 2016.

24 *"I prayed upon it":* Brandon Rapolla, "The Battle Over Bunkerville: The Bundys, the Federal Government, and the New Militia Movement," *Frontline*, May 16, 2017.

25 *"face-to-face confrontation…thousands of people":* Santilli, internet radio statement, April 2014.

27 *"She's yellin":* Todd Engel, testimony, *U.S. v. Bundy*, July 18, 2018.

27 *"These folks":* Ibid.

29 *"a tense game of chicken":* "War in the West," *Southern Poverty Law Center Intelligence Report*, August 20, 2015.

29 *"Good morning, citizens":* Cliven Bundy, public statement, April 12, 2014.

29 *"The BLM is going to cease…What I would hope":* Gillespie public statement, April 12, 2014.

29 *"trying to get some legs":* Cliven Bundy, quoted in "War in the West," *Southern Poverty Law Center Intelligence Report*, August 20, 2015.

29 *"My intention is to keep":* Gillespie told the crowd at Bunkerville, April 12, 2014.

30 *"We want those arms":* Bundy, public statement, April 12, 2014.

30 *"God is going to be with us":* Ibid.

31 *"Can't breach this":* *U.S. v. Bundy*, superseding indictment, March 2, 2016.

33 *"It is impossible to overstate":* Michael Vanderboegh, social-media interview, April 2014, produced during *U.S. v. Bundy*.

33 *"Well, for a minute there":* McGuire on social media, April 2014, produced during *U.S. v. Bundy*.

34 *"I faced off":* Burleson on Facebook post, April 12–13, 2014, quoted in *U.S. v. Bundy*.

34 *"We locked them down"*: Payne, quoted in *U.S. v. Bundy*.

34 *"a safe and peaceful operation"*: Kornze public statement. April 12, 2014.

35 *"Given the circumstances"*: Governor Brian Sandoval statement. April 11, 2014.

35 *"Those people who hold themselves"*: Reid, quoted in *Las Vegas Review-Journal*, April 2014.

35 *"Hopefully we will look back"*: Larry Pratt, Gun Owners of America, at National Rifle Association annual meeting, April 2014.

35 *"I'm worried about the lies"*: Hannity, April 24, 2014.

36 *"surprise midnight raid"*: Richard Mack, quoted by Hannity, *Fox News*, April 16, 2014.

36 *"We believe these armed extremists"*: Heidi Beirich, SPLC website, January 4, 2016.

36 *"Deadbeat on the Range"*: Timothy Egan, "Deadbeat on the Range," *New York Times*, April 17, 2014.

37 *"does not condone"*: Nevada Cattlemen's Association.

37 **Please do not judge:** Cattlemen's Association, quoted in *Las Vegas Review-Journal*, "Nevada Rancher Questions Bundy's Legal Strategy," April 17, 2014.

37 *"Negros are enslaved"*: Cliven Bundy public statement, April 23, 2014.

37 *"downright racist"*: Hannity on *Fox News*. April 24, 2014.

38 *"The district is a microcosm"*: Horsford public statement, April 2014.

38 *"Here's the thing, I'm a wondering"*: Cliven Bundy public statement, interview, April 24, 2014.

38 *"I said all along"*: "Sheriff Breaks Silence, Says BLM, Bundy Share Blame for Near Catastrophe," *Las Vegas Sun*, July 2, 2014.

39 *"hateful racist"*: Reid in interview with *Las Vegas Review-Journal*, April 24, 2014.

39 *"We were actually strategizing"*: Mack, "The Real Story," *Fox News*, April 15, 2014.

Chapter 2: You Don't Need a Reason to Start a Revolution

41 *"from out of nowhere"*: Anonymous witness, CNN.COM, June 9, 2014.

41 *"This is the start"*: Associated Press, June 9, 2014.

41 *"a man who was willing"*: Ibid.

42 *"Stand down!"*: Jerad Miller statement, June 8, 2014.

42 *"wingnut Bonnie and Clyde duo"*: John P. Avalon and John L. Smith, "Patriot Politics Created the Las Vegas Killers," *The Daily Beast*, June 9, 2014.

42 *"I feel sorry for any federal"*: Jerad Miller to KRNV-TV, April 13, 2014.

42 *"Not very many people"*: Ammon Bundy, Associated Press, June 10, 2014.

43 *"with fascism"*: Las Vegas Metro undersheriff Kevin McMahill, Associated Press, June 10, 2014.

43 *"I will be supporting"*: Jerad Miller Facebook posts.

43 *"is no greater cause"*: Ibid.

43 *"Either you stand with freedom"*: Ibid.

44 *"All politics in this country"*: Ibid.

44 *"The dawn of a new day"*: Jerad Miller statement, Miller Facebook post, quoted in Avlon and Smith, "Patriot Politics Created the Las Vegas Killers," *The Daily Beast*, June 9, 2014.

46 *"leaderless resistance"*: Letter, Texas KKK Grand Dragon Louis Beam, 1983.

47 *"Since the entire purpose"*: Ibid.

47 *"a personality that is already violent"*: Glen Wallace, quoted in Joel Dyer, *Harvest of Rage*, 40.

47 *"a child of necessity"*: Letter, Texas KKK Grand Dragon Louis Beam, 1983.

48 *"Soon there will be millions"*: Ibid.

50 *"This is the next Waco!"*: Jerad Miller, Facebook post.

52 *"Sovereign citizens do not represent"*: FBI's Counterterrorism Analysis Section, "Sovereign Citizens: A Growing Domestic Threat to Law Enforcement," September 1, 2011. Available at: https://leb.fbi.gov /articles/featured-articles/sovereign-citizens-a-growing-domestic -threat-to-law-enforcement.

54 *"He found people"*: Shari Kaufman, Mahan Courtroom statement, March 2011, author column.

54 *"ahead of the posse"*: U.S. Senator Harry Reid announcing his retirement, 2015.

55 *"I, Cliven D. Bundy, have been"*: Bundy Ranch blog, bundyranch.blog spot.com, January 1, 2015.

55 *"For more than twenty years"*: *U.S. v. Hammond* indictment.

56 *"endangered the lives of numerous"*: BLM memo.

56 *"light up the whole country"*: Grandson testimony, *U.S. v. Hammond*, U.S. Court of Appeals, Ninth Circuit, February 7, 2014.

56 *"really, really good folks"*: Bill Hoyt, Oregon Cattlemen's Association, Associated Press, Jeff Barnard, June 20, 2010.

57 *"I understand that there are"*: U.S. Attorney Billy Williams, *Burns Times Herald*, December 7, 2015.

58 *"first responders"*: *Pacific Patriots Network* website, 2018.

59 *"We realize that they are abusing"*: Ryan Bundy, Public Radio Station KNPR, *State of Nevada*, interview with Joe Schoenmann, July 6, 2018.

59 *"Neither Ammon Bundy nor anyone"*: Allen Schroeder to Sheriff Ward, January 4, 2016.

59 *"The Hammond family have refused":* Ammon Bundy statement, January 4, 2016.

60 *"Our purpose as we have shown":* Ammon Bundy public statement, January 4, 2016.

61 *"That was my main source of income":* Oregon Public Broadcasting. January 2016.

62 *"had to do a lot of soul-searching":* Finicum YouTube video, August 14, 2015.

62 *"I sent a letter to the BLM":* Ibid.

62 *"I'm telling them right now":* Finicum interview with MSNBC, January 6, 2018.

63 *"Just shoot me":* Shawna Cox cell phone video of his February killing. March 14, 2016.

64 *"life was cut short":* Finicum, *Only by Blood and Suffering*, 283.

64 *"in fact, necessary":* Deschutes County district attorney Dan Norris statement, March 8, 2016.

Chapter 3: Ghost Dancing Through Deseret

65 *"You will not take one single cow":* Ryan Bundy, recorded statement with FBI, March 2014.

65 *"We are coming":* Ibid.

66 *"If the standoff with the Bundys":* Cliven Bundy statement, KUEU radio interview, 2014.

67 *"born-again constitutionalism":* W. Cleon Skousen statement, United Press International, June 20, 1982.

67 *"Nearly every problem":* Ibid.

67 *"the conservative answer to the Brookings Institute":* Ibid.

67 *"American slave children":* Ibid.

68 *"clearly understood that the Lord":* Ammon Bundy public comment, January 4, 2016.

68 *"Come to Harney County":* Ibid.

68 *"battle of high priests":* Ammon Bundy, quoted in *Idaho State Journal*, July 22, 2018.

68 *"While the disagreement occurring":* Official LDS Church response to Bundy action in Malheur occupation, January 4, 2016.

69 *"We can talk about the Bundys":* Matthew Bowman, quoted in thinkprogress.org, January 4, 2016.

69 *"that God had a work for me":* Joseph Smith, founder of the Church of Jesus Christ of Latter-day Saints, in the Book of Mormon.

70 *"It would be the first of hundreds":* Denton, *American Massacre*, 4.

70 *"an insipid mess":* Twain, *Roughing It*, ch. 16.

72 *"must be exterminated":* Missouri Governor Lilburn Boggs. Research source, James B. Allen, assistant church historian, LDS.org.

72 *"to run her dead husband's":* Stegner, *Mormon Country*, 60.

73 *"like a new flight out of Egypt":* Ibid.

73 *"The secretary had taken over":* Ibid., 60.

74 *"Mormonism had been conceived":* Ibid., 63.

74 *"Come immediately and prepare":* Billington and Ridge, *Westward Expansion*, 184.

75 *"No man can buy land here":* Ibid.

75 *"Rigid controls":* Stegner, *Mormon Country*.

75 *"Young organized the mass movement":* Denton, *American Massacre*, 10.

75 *"an immense bookkeeping":* DeVoto, *The Year of Decision 1846*, 99.

76 *"The kindness of these Mormons":* Nevins, *Frémont*, 418.

76 *"He has been called a hypocrite":* Burton, *The City of Saints*, via Pat Bagley, *Salt Lake Tribune*, January 5, 2013.

77 *"for the creation of Salt Lake City":* Porte, *Emerson in His Journals*, 379.

77 *"The Mormons could have made Nevada":* Lillard, *The Desert Challenge*, 15.

78 *put "the skids":* "Utah's Dixie steeped in slave culture, historian says," Will Bagley. *Salt Lake Tribune*, December 10, 2012.

78 *"I have witnessed their devotion":* Herbert Hoover, quoted in the *Mormon Times*, September 26, 2015.

79 *"Tonight I speak for all Americans":* John F. Kennedy speech in the Mormon Tabernacle, September 23, 1960.

80 *"there is no place for them":* Stegner, *Mormon Country*, 346.

80 *"The new westerners sought":* Dant, *Losing Eden*, 189.

82 *"some Indian children for sale":* Daniel W. Jones, Oral History, "Forty Years Among the Indians," Full text at Gutenburg.com; *Utah Historical Quarterly* 12, nos. 1–4 (Salt Lake City, Utah, 1944).

82 *"They offered them to the Mormons":* Jones, quoted in Van Hoak, "And Who Shall Save the Children."

83 *"clad in sackcloth":* John Ragsdale Jr., *The Urban Lawyer* 48, no. 3 (Summer 2016).

85 *"all former disputes":* Treaty of Ruby Valley, October 1, 1863.

87 *"My brothers, you would make war":* Numaga, quoted in Ferol Egan, *Sand in a Whirlwind*, 102.

88 *"that hostilities and all depredations":* Treaty of Peace and Friendship made at Ruby Valley, signed on August 1, 1863.

89 *"This land is yours":* Reno *Gazette-Journal*, September 19, 1975.

90 *"of what these white man laws":* Ibid.

90 *"in order to establish a tribal organization":* Reno *Gazette-Journal*, October 25, 1937.

91 *"One of the surest consequences":* Statement of the Rev. R.J. Rushdoony, Western Shoshone Mission, quoted by Howard Buffett in *Congressional Record*, April 7, 1952, appendix 2, 631.

93 *"payment of any claim":* Indian Claims Commission Act 1962.

93 *"by gradual encroachment":* Ibid.

94 *"If the government wins":* Jack Anderson syndicated column, April 28, 1984.

94 *"The Justice Department is trying":* Quoted in ibid.

95 *"The Danns shouldn't need a permit":* Assistant Attorney General Robert McConnell, *U.S. v. Dann*, oral argument, November 5, 1984.

95 *"If you sell your property":* Reno Gazette-Journal, November 6, 1984.

95 *"To construe the word 'payment'":* Ibid.

96 *"You can't just snap your fingers":* Public statement, Western Shoshone Tribal Attorney Michael Lieder, November 5, 2014.

96 *"hidebound ranchers":* Leduff, "Range War in Nevada Pits U.S. Against Two Shoshone Sisters," *New York Times*, October 30, 2002.

97 *"years and likely millions of dollars":* Elko BLM Office Manager Helen Hagen, *Elko Daily Free Press*, September 23, 2002.

97 *"They pay their fees and they're good stewards":* BLM State Director Bob Abbey, *Elko Daily Free Press*, September 23, 2002.

98 *"At some point you have to let":* Janine Hansen, Leader of the Nevada Committee for Full Statehood, ibid.

98 *"have a meeting":* Los Angeles Times, September 24, 1991.

98 *"Depending on who is asked":* Leduff, "Range War in Nevada Pits U.S. against Two Shoshone Sisters," *New York Times*, October 30, 2002.

98 *"intransigent old-timers":* Ibid.

99 *"a money-waving campaign":* Ian Zabarte, quoted in *Reno Gazette-Journal*, July 18, 2001.

99 *"We need it":* Larry Piffero, quoted in *Elko Daily Free Press*, August 24, 1999.

99 *"The majority of the Western Shoshone":* Ibid.

99 *"To come back now and say it's not fair":* Harry Reid, quoted by Associated Press, July 20, 2000.

100 *"The tribe twice has voted":* Associated Press, March 10, 2006.

101 *"Indians love horses":* Carrie Dann interview, *London Sunday Times*, April 23, 2006.

101 *"I believe government officials lied":* Felix Ike quoted in ibid.

101 *"Our tribe has decided":* Judith Graham, "Indians: $140 Million Isn't Justice," *Chicago Tribune*, January 1, 2004.

101 *"with her boots on:":* Patricia Paul, quoted in Associated Press, April 24, 2005.

102 *"This was Mary's life's work":* Carrie Dann, quoted in ibid.

102 *"Our land is not for sale":* Western Shoshone leader Allen Moss, ibid.

102 *"mind terrorism":* Quoted in ibid.

Chapter 4: Saddle Born

104 *"I happen to be one"*: Public statement, Ronald Reagan, 1980, Salt Lake City.

104 *"In one way or another"*: Department of Interior website, doi.gov: https://www.doi.gov/whoweare/history.

105 *"You seem to be the idol"*: 1869 letter from Mark Twain to Cornelius Vanderbilt. "Open Letter to Cornelius Vanderbilt," Archive, Marktwainstudies.com.

107 *"to use what nature's given"*: John F. Kennedy speech, Las Vegas, September 28, 1963. Available at JFK-Archives.blogspot.com.

108 *"A wilderness, in contrast…The idea of wilderness"*: Wilderness Society executive Howard Zahniser, "The Need for Wilderness Areas," *The Living Wilderness*, 1956–1957, Winter–Spring, No. 59.

112 *"should be of only those lands"*: Public Lands Law Review Commission, 1970.

112 *"the public lands be retained"*: Federal Land Policy and Management Act of 1976.

113 *"management of the public lands"*: Ibid.

114 *"the last of the big federal"*: Nies, *Unreal City*, 177.

114 *"canceled the blank check"*: United Press International, March 27, 1977.

114 *"We intend to exercise"*: Ibid.

114 *"a deep personal commitment"*: Wiley and Gottlieb, *Empires in the Sun*, 60.

115 *"The old interests"*: Undersecretary of Interior James Joseph, speech, 1979.

116 *"As long as there's room for negotiation"*: Nevada Governor Mike O'Callaghan, quoted in the *Reno Gazette-Journal*, April 29, 1977.

116 *"Western types who are used"*: Andrus speech, October 31, 1977.

116 *"We have begun to make"*: *Washington Post*, April 3, 1977.

117 *"doing a lot of praying"*: unnamed oil and gas executive, quoted in the *Washington Post*, May 7, 1977.

117 *"In two centuries"*: *Reno Gazette-Journal*, April 9, 1977.

117 *"the little fiefdoms"*: *Philadelphia Inquirer*, August 7, 1977.

117 *"alienated virtually every powerful"*: *Washington Post*, October 31, 1977.

118 *"constitutional liberties"*: The Environmental Complex, published by the Heritage Foundation, November 1977.

118 *"provide an effective voice"*: Ibid.

119 *"The environmental movement"*: Ibid.

119 *"primarily for livestock"*: *Washington Post*, March 27, 1977.

120 *"I do not know how many"*: Watt statement before Congress, January 7, 1981.

120 *"He cannot speak without"*: "How James Watt Survives," *Rolling Stone*, June 9, 1983.

120 *"Watt only has two constituents"*: Gaylord Nelson, Wilderness Society Chairman, *Rolling Stone*, June 9, 1983.

121 *"a black, a woman"*: Watt remark, quoted at a U.S. Chamber of Commerce breakfast, September 21, 1983.

121 *Top 10 Worst Cabinet Members:* No author, *Time*. See http://content .time.com/time/specials/packages/article/0,28804,1858691_18586 90_1858648,00. html (page 6 of 10).

121 *"Things were going well"*: Coates, "Sagebrush Rebellion on Hold," *Chicago Tribune*, March 16, 1986.

121 *"ruggedly handsome"*: Ibid.

122 *"Most of us who spearheaded"*: Ibid.

122 *"It is the land grab"*: Coates, "Sagebrush Rebellion."

122 *"If I said the land"*: Ibid.

123 *"I am trusting God"*: Buursma, "Scandal Damaging Ministry," May 3, 1987.

123 *"Never, never trust your government"*: James Watt, quoted in *Los Angeles Times*, February 23, 1995.

124 *"I don't think the federal government"*: Mike Anderson, interview by Robert D. McCracken, in "Destiny Denied: Esmeralda County Citizens Speak out on Public Lands Issues," *Esmeralda County Press* (Goldfield, Nevada), 2014, p. 145.

125 *"All the Colvins"*: Ben Colvin, quoted in oral history, Esmeralda County History Project, 2013.

125 *"They were running horses"*: Ibid.

126 *"I don't really even care"*: BLM Nevada director Bob Abbey, quoted in Associated Press, August 10, 2001.

126 *"Grazing on public land"*: Associated Press, November 15, 2001.

126 *"I'd still be paying"*: Associated Press, December 20, 2001.

127 *"The way the bureaucrats"*: Colvin oral history, Esmeralda County History Project, 2013.

127 *"My family, in one way"*: Wayne Hage, quoted from his Vimeo video interview. February 27, 2010.

128 *President Harry S. Truman declared Elko:* United Press International, March 22, 1952.

128 *"The big cattle outfits"*: Hage, quoted in *The New American*, May 20, 2002.

129 *"before they passed the Wild and Free"*: Hage video interview, February 27, 2010.

129 *"The main value right today"*: Ibid.

130 *The MX raised concerns:* Wilson, "The Missile Gap the MX Can't Close," *Washington Post*, December 14, 1980.

130 *"In this instance, a small number":* Wiley and Gottlieb, *Empires in the Sun,* 210.

131 *"This isn't Kansas":* Hage, quoted in *Reno Gazette-Journal,* January 31, 1980.

131 *"I have $1 million worth":* Ibid.

132 *"I've grown to love and admire":* U.S. Air Force Brig. General Gary Hecker, *Tonopah Times,* October 24, 1979.

132 *"For many years, because their land":* Hulse, *The Silver State,* 14.

133 *"Our fathers came to this western":* Speech, LDS Church President Spencer W. Kimball, May 5, 1981. See www.LDS.org, or Jacob W. Olmstead's "The Mormon Heirarchy and the MX," *Journal of Mormon History* 33, Issue 3 (2007). See https://digitalcommons.usu.edu/cgi /viewcontent.cgi? article=1051&context=mormonhistory.

133 *"save a lot of duplication":* Hage, quoted in *Reno Gazette-Journal,* February 1, 1985.

134 *"The linkage is clear":* *Elko Daily Free Press,* June 10, 1992.

134 *"bad rancher":* Ibid.

135 *"If you don't have the water rights":* Hage statement, 2004 federal hearing.

135 *idiosyncratic view…court invites them to try:* U.S. District Judge Clive Jones statement in *U.S. v. Hage.*

136 *"with the standard arrogant":* Ibid.

136 *"Defendants openly trespassed":* U.S. Ninth Circuit Court of Appeals Judge Susan Graber, quoted in *Albuquerque Journal,* January 19, 2016.

137 *"A dispassionate observer":* Ibid.

137 *"It looks to me like":* Wayne Hage Jr. in *Las Vegas Review-Journal,* January 18, 2016.

137 *"become a retirement community":* Dick Carver, quoted in Associated Press, October 9, 1993.

137 *"There is no such thing":* *Los Angeles Times,* December 3, 1995.

138 *"My friends would have drilled":* Ibid.

139 *"rose to a position":* Carver, Southern Poverty Law Center website. www.splccenter.org.

139 *"religious ideology popular":* Antidefamation League website. www.adl.org.

140 *"The weapon I have in my pocket":* *Reno Gazette-Journal,* May 3, 1995.

140 *"We've worked very hard":* *Reno Gazette-Journal,* March 9, 1995.

141 *"We're in a Civil War":* *Seattle Post-Intelligencer,* April 2, 1995.

141 *"There is going to be no bloodshed":* Carver statement as a guest of Win Back the Midwest, September 20, 1995.

141 *"cowards…the incendiary rhetoric":* *Reno Gazette-Journal,* August 8, 1995.

142 *"My work is to take care":* Ibid.

142 *"owns and has the power":* U.S. District Judge Lloyd George, March 15, 1996.

143 *"Now it's time to come together":* U.S. Attorney General Janet Reno, statement reported in the *New York Times*, March 6, 1996.

143 *"It is time to find common ground":* Ibid.

143 *"We made our point":* Ibid.

144 *They bristled at the decision:* Kim Raff, "Drought Pushed Nevada Ranchers to Take on Washington," *New York Times*, July 2, 2015.

145 *"This is not an easy job":* Ibid.

145 *A closer look revealed:* Lance Williams and Katharine Mieszkowski, "Ranchers Denied the Drought While Collecting Drought Subsidies," revealnews.org, December 3, 2015.

145 *"The ranchers generate public sympathy":* Statement to Reuters, June 3, 2015.

145 *In 2019, Furtado:* Daniel Patterson whistleblower complaint, October 4, 2019.

146 *"Grazing on upland areas":* BLM public statement, at blm.gov, p. 506.

146 *"Sometimes you just have to":* Thomas Mitchell, *Elko Daily Free Press*, June 21, 2015.

146 *Blue Eagle Ranch:* Author interview with Jeanne Sharp Howerton, 2020.

147 *United Cattle & Packing:* Robert D. McCracken, *United Cattle & Packing: The Rise and Fall of Nevada's Largest Ranch*, 2012.

147 *"The restrictions sometimes":* Author interview with Jeanne Sharp Howerton, 2020.

148 *During a break between shows:* Author interview with David Stanley, 2014.

149 *"Ranchers face the same pressures":* Author interview with Jeanne Sharpe Howerton.

149 *Increasingly in modern Nevada:* Author interview with Michael Stankovic, 2020.

Chapter 5: The Senator from Searchlight

154 *"And to add insult":* Shepperson, "The Maverick and the Cowboy," *Nevada Historical Society Quarterly* (Spring 1983): 13–22.

155 *"The ordinary working cowhand":* Ibid.

155 *"outside the home environment":* Martin, "Nevada," quoted in Shepperson, "The Maverick," 17.

155 *"In a sad and negative way":* Ibid.

156 *"The lack of constructive national land":* Donahue, *The Western Range Revisited*, 49.

156 *"failed to precipitate":* Ibid.

156 *"So, at the very moment":* Quoted in ibid.

157 *"There is gold here":* Reid, *The Good Fight*, 49.

158 *"At the beginning of the century":* Ibid., 27.

158 *"When I was a boy":* Ibid., 27.

160 *"My friends begged me not to":* Reid, *The Good Fight*, 238.

160 *"Mr. Cleanface":* FBI surveillance tape in *U.S. v. Joseph V. Agosto*, 1979.

162 *"peculiar condition":* King and Elliot, *Hang Tough*, 216.

163 *"After becoming governor I got exercised":* Quoted in ibid.

164 *"I was allergic to horses":* Interview with Tom Mullen for togovern.com, also found in List interview at ag.nv.gov.

164 *Bing Crosby, Joel McCrea, Dean Witter:* Denton et al., *A Liberal Conscience: Ralph Denton, Nevadan*, 124.

165 *"His goals were simple and parochial":* Elliott, *Senator Alan Bible and the Politics of the New West*, 203–4.

165 *"He labored long on behalf":* Ibid.

166 *"As Reid and others":* Emily Green, "Quenching Las Vegas's Thirst," *Las Vegas Sun*, June 2008.

166 *"I didn't know the intensity":* Author interview with Reid, 2019.

168 *"good for the park":* Associated Press, December 16, 1999.

168 *"It became obvious":* Quoted in ibid.

168 *"With the formation of the Great Basin":* Jon Ralston, *Reno Gazette-Journal*, July 12, 2015.

168 *"Now instead of having to share":* Reno Gazette-Journal, December 17, 1999.

170 *"In the early 1980s":* Quoted in ibid.

170 *"The day I voted for that bill":* Author interview with Reid, 2019.

170 *"important to Southern Nevada":* Congressional Record, Vol. 148, No. 137, October 17, 2002, pp. 10769–771.

171 *"The sheer number of public lands":* Ibid.

171 *"The name alone made the eyes glaze":* Chuck Neubauer, *Los Angeles Times*, June 23, 2003.

171 *"What Reid did not explain":* Ibid.

172 *"more suitable for development":* www.summerlin.com

173 *"Lots of people have children":* Chuck Neubauer and Richard T. Cooper, "In Nevada, the Name to Know Is Reid," *Los Angeles Times*, June 23, 2003.

173 *"Putting aside the jokes":* Ibid.

174 *"at the time the law was enacted":* Ibid.

174 *"Those of us who wrote":* Ibid.

175 *"in desperate need of protection":* Ibid.

176 *"good friend of the environment":* Reno Gazette-Journal.

178 *"a license to steal":* Quoted in Harkinson, "Harry Reid, Gold Member," *Mother Jones*, March–April, 2009.

178 *"They [the mining companies] own":* Ibid.

178 *"Thinking that people here are voting":* Quoted in ibid.

179 *"one of the mining industry's":* Ibid.

179 *"the last great boondoggle":* Quoted in ibid.

180 *"a law that has been out of step":* "Campaign for Responsible Mining," Pew Charitable Trusts, 2009. See www.pewtrusts.org.

180 *"This is a pirate story":* Quoted in ibid.

181 *"The law allows claimholders":* Ibid.

181 *"complete reclamation":* Nevada Mining Association statement. www .nevadamining.org, and "Overview of Mining—Nevada Legislature, Presession Issue Briefing," December 7, 2010, https://www.leg.state .nv.us/Division/Research/LegInfo/Orientation/2010–11/Handouts /Dec7/13-MiningHandouts.pdf."

182 *"All roads to reform":* "Campaign for Responsible Mining," Pew Charitable Trusts, 2009. See www.pewtrusts.org.

182 *"I don't see it this year":* Reid interview, Gannett News Service, August 10, 2008.

183 *"You have to look at what's best":* Author interview with Reid, 2019.

183 *"One of the real difficult things":* Ibid.

183 *"the vast majority of ranching":* Ibid.

184 *"When she realized":* Ibid.

184 *"One of the good qualities":* Ibid.

184 *"Part of their problem was":* Ibid.

184 *"Now, this is really landmark":* Ibid.

187 *"The relationship between the two":* James E. Faust, speeches.byu.edu, "What's in It for Me?"

187 *"I learned from him the meaning":* Obituary, James E. Faust, August, 1995, www.churchofjesuschrist.org.

187 *"an oddly Sidney Greenstreet–like figure":* "Please Explain This Water Lobbyist," June 20, 2009. See www. Chanceofrain.com.

188 *"You mean to tell me":* Quoted in Schoenmann, "What's the Deal with Consultant Contracts?" *Las Vegas Sun,* June 20, 2009.

188 *"You can't find a qualified":* Quoted in ibid.

188 *"The native Westerner specializes":* Emily Green, "Quenching Las Vegas's Thirst," *Las Vegas Sun,* June 2008.

189 *"If you want water":* Ibid.

190 *"The severe drought has Las Vegas":* Mike O'Callaghan, *Las Vegas Sun,* February 2004.

191 *"Maya wasn't a real politician":* *Los Angeles Times,* June 5, 2006.

192 *"It's a complicated legacy":* Author interview with Fulkerson, 2019.

192 *"Yucca Mountain was stopped":* Ibid.

193 *"snowshoed, hiked":* Ibid.

194 *"I'd rather flush toilets":* Author interview with Reid, 2019.

194   *"The serious ramifications":* Letter, July 12, 2004, Nevada Ad Hoc Water Network.

194   *"Former Governor Mike O'Callaghan":* Ibid.

196   *"an incredibly criminal, intentional act":* Judge Larry Hicks in *U.S. v. Whittemore*, 2013; *USA Today*, September 30, 2013.

197   *"after an impressive and successful":* www.abbeystubbsfordllc.com.

197   *"expected to receive":* Denton, *The Profiteers*, 162.

198   *"would be on the basis":* U.S. Senate Committee on Appropriations, Subcommittee on Military Construction, 1981.

198   *"the General Motors":* *Time*, March 10, 1958.

199   *"Perhaps the most important":* www.coyotesprings.com.

199   *"In Nevada the Name to Know is Reid":* *Los Angeles Times*.

200   *"surrounded by important lands":* www.basinandrangewatch.org.

200   *"Senator Reid is a dear friend":* Huntsman presentation, June 2017.

201   *"When I was elected to Congress":* Author interview with Reid, 2019.

Chapter 6: When the Cows Come Home...to Roost

202   *"stimulate insurrection":* file://localhost/. (Rightwingwatch.org http//: www.rightwingwatch.org: post: michael-savage-obama -wants-to-mow-down-white-crackers-fight-a-war-against-white -people:); Brian Tashman, rightwingwatch.org, Sept. 3, 2014.

204   *"taken on a life":* Thomas Moriarty, "Mine Owner Pleads for Calm Over Oath Keepers' Presence After Threats to BLM." *Mail Tribune (Medford, Ore.)*, April 15, 2015.

205   *"We will continue to pursue":* Quoted in *Las Vegas Review-Journal*, June 24, 2015.

205   *"I want to know if this is an interview":* "American Patriot: Inside the Armed Uprising Against the Federal Government." *Frontline*, May 16, 2017.

206   *"to put some BLM agent":* Blogpost, www.americanredoubt.com, 2016.

207   *"may now find themselves":* Blogpost, David Codrea, www.oath keepers.org, February 18, 2016.

207   *"The rule of law has now been":* *U.S. v. Bundy*, 2016.

208   *"They have my house surrounded":* Prosecution statement, *U.S. v. Bundy*, 2016.

208   *"a resounding message":* Ibid.

208   *"massive armed assault":* *U.S. v. Bundy*, superseding indictment, 2016.

208   *"The 200 Followers in the wash":* FBI legal brief of Agent Joel Willis, April 12, 2014.

209   *"Outnumbered by more than 4:1":* Ibid.

209   *"On or about April 7, 2014":* Indictment, *U.S. v. Bundy*, 2016.

210 *"We're going to shoot to kill"*: *Chicago Tribune* News Service, March 30, 2016.

210 *"violent extremism"*: "Congress should confront the rise of violent extremism on America's Public Lands." Matt Lee-Ashley. See http://www.americanprogress.org, March 24, 2016.

211 *"you don't have a government"*: Quoted in Reuters, January 16, 2016.

211 *"I like him"*: Trump to Sean Hannity, *Fox News*, 2014.

211 *"pitchforks and torches time"*: Sheriff David Clark on Twitter, October 15, 2016.

211 *"grabbing my musket"*: Joe Walsh tweet, @WalshFreedom, *Washington Post*, Oct. 26, 2016.

212 *"unfortunate and tragic"*: Cruz on Glenn Beck, *Fox News*.

212 *"It always starts like this"*: See www.rightwingwatch.org, C-SPAN, https://www.c-span.org/video/? 318743–5/freedom-summit-mike -huckabee.

212 *"I'm not here to jump"*: Statement during April 2014 Freedom Summit.

213 *"leaders and organizers"*: *U.S. v. Bundy*, 2016.

214 *"foreign entity"*: David Bundy statement, 2014.

214 *"He's a danger"*: U.S. Magistrate Judge Cam Ferenbach, *U.S. v. Bundy*, 2016.

214 *"They [federal authorities] have to sleep"*: *Courthouse News*, May 17, 2016.

215 *"the entire picture"*: Associated Press, June 26, 2016.

216 *"These homegrown militias"*: Grijalva and Thompson, "Homegrown Anti-Government Militias Threaten Public Safety," June 30, 2016.

216 *"could be intimidating"*: Associated Press, July 10, 2016.

217 *"credible risk"*: *U.S. v. Bundy*, 2016.

217 *"because I want to keep"*: "Trump Could Tamp Down the Bundys," www.eenews.net, November 10, 2016.

218 *"gun it, gun it"*: Shawna Cox cell phone video, 2016.

219 *"from the works of the devil"*: *Shauna Cox v. U.S. Government*, February 18, 2016.

219 *"Welcome to another day"*: *Los Angeles Times*, October 27, 2016.

219 *"And I'd like to be tall"*: Court proceedings, *U.S. v. Bundy*, 2016.

220 *"extreme disappointment"*: U.S. Attorney Billy Williams, public statement, October 2016.

221 *"stating him saying slur language"*: Bundy Ranch blog, 2017.

221 *"Republicans hate public lands"*: *Washington Post*, June 13, 2017.

224 *"My time has been very much"*: Ryan Bundy statement before U.S. Magistrate Judge George Foley Jr., *U.S. v. Bundy*, February 2017.

225 *"There comes a time when personalities"*: Quoted in *USA Today Network*, February 6, 2017.

226 *"This isn't an undercard":* Associated Press, February 4, 2017.

226 *"They're not the Bundys":* Ibid.

228 *"They kept the pressure on":* Myhre opening statement, *U.S. v. Parker et al.,* February 4, 2017.

229 *"This case, folks":* Tanasi opening statement, *U.S. v. Bundy,* February 9, 2017.

230 *"History tells us about protesters":* Ibid.

230 *"one of history's most popular martyrs":* Ibid.

231 *"I had nothing to gain":* Engel opening statement, *U.S. v. Bundy,* February 9, 2017.

231 *"You see her legs":* Leventhal opening statement, *U.S. v. Bundy,* February 9, 2017.

232 *"they show that a few days":* Jackson opening statement, *U.S. v. Bundy,* February 9, 2017.

232 *"One thing—after this happened":* Ibid.

234 *"Nothing would have happened":* Perez opening statement, *U.S. v. Bundy,* February 9, 2017.

234 *"potential to not only taint":* Chaffetz letter to DefBLM inspector general, February 14, 2017.

241 *"bad judgment, lack of discipline": High Country News,* July 6, 2017.

242 *"The horror of this recent shooting":* Brenda Weksler and Ryan Norwood defense motion, *U.S. v. Bundy,* October 3, 2017.

243 *"Bundy continues to demand":* Bret Whipple statement, *U.S. v. Bundy,* October 5, 2017.

244 *"professional gadfly notorious":* Klayman profile, Southern Poverty Law Center website: https://www.splcenter.org/fighting-hate /extremist-files/individual/larry-klayman.

244 *"Bret [Whipple] can't handle this":* Author interview with Klayman, 2017.

244 *"The assertions made by Bundy":* Decision, Ninth Circuit Court of Appeals, March 30, 2017.

245 *"I think this is the most important":* "Barred from the defense table, birther lawyer Klayman remains in Cliven Bundy's corner as trial begins." John L. Smith, *The Nevada Independent,* November 5, 2017.

246 *"After the meeting we made":* Testimony of Mary Hinson, *U.S. v. Bundy,* November 3, 2017.

247 *"fantastical fishing expedition":* Prosecution statement, *U.S. v. Bundy,* November 3, 2017.

250 *"Whatever the term 'sniper'":* Ibid.

251 *"I don't think there is":* Ammon Bundy comments to press, December 2017.

251 *"She chose the side of thee":* Ryan Bundy statement, *U.S. v. Bundy,* December 2017.

252 *"with witness protection in mind":* U.S. v. Bundy, December 2017.

252 *"so grossly shocking":* Ibid.

254 *"The result can only embolden":* Jonathan Greenblatt, Anti-Defamation League.

254 *"The Bundy family took up arms":* Jennifer Rokala, Center for Western Priorities.

254 *"Federal prosecutors clearly":* Kieran Suckling, Center for Biological Diversity.

255 *"I'm not used to being free":* Cilven Bundy statement to the press.

255 *"My defense is a fifteen-second defense":* Ibid.

Epilogue: Lonesome Bull

257 *"conflict of interest and other violations":* Department of the Interior inspector general report, "Interior chief Bernhardt under inspector general probe," Timothy Gardner, Reuters, April 15, 2019.

258 *"state legislators dedicated":* "About ALEC–American Legislative Exchange Council," www.alec.org.

258 *"lawful, peaceful path":* Mission Statement, www.americanlands council.org.

259 *"a hero of the range":* "'Mr. Sagebrush Rebellion' Bankrolls Push to Seize Federal Land," www.eenews.net, March 18, 2016.

259 *"essentially feral":* "Bundy Keeps Selling Cattle as BLM Contemplates New Roundup," www.eenews.net, November 20, 2017.

259 *"Go and read your Constitution":* Quoted in *Missoulian*, January 20, 2018.

260 *"the worst thing, the terriblest thing":* Quoted in *Salt Lake Tribune*, June 9, 2019.

260 *"When someone stole things":* Ibid.

261 *"atrocities taking place":* State of Nevada, KNPR, July 6, 2018.

261 *"Life has never, ever":* Quoted in *Idaho Statesman*, November 10, 2018.

262 *"never did sit very good":* Quoted in *The Guardian*, November 29, 2018.

262 *"That is not freedom":* Buzzfeed News, December 6, 2018.

262 *"battle of high priests":* Ammon Bundy, quoted in *Idaho State Journal*, July 22, 2018.

263 *fusillade of epithets:* Ed Brayton, "Klayman vs. Stone: Battle of the Crackpots," Patheos.com, February 29, 2020.

264 *"Bundy has convinced himself":* Betsy Gaines Quammen, *American Zion.*

264 *"We have become great":* Theodore Roosevelt, "New Nationalism" speech, Delivered May 13, 1908, at the Conference of the Conservation of Natural Resources.

264 *"There is nothing in the Constitution":* Leshy interview in "Public

Lands a Priceless Legacy for Future." Harvard University Center for the Environment, Environment.harvard.edu, March 9, 2018.

265 *"While we're here":* YouTube video, January 2018.

265 *"Dirty Harry" Reid:* www.eenews.net, April 10, 2019.

265 *"It is simply delusional":* District Judge James Crockett statement.

266 *"I actually want the virus":* Ammon Bundy interview, CNN, April 10, 2020.

267 *"so grossly shocking and so outrageous":* U.S. Ninth Circuit Court of Appeals live video broadcast, *U.S. v. Cliven Bundy*, No. 18–10287, May 29, 2020. See https://www.ca9. uscourts.gov/media/view_video .php? pk_vid=0000017470.

267 *"There was flagrant abuse":* Ibid.

268 *"That is why this is such an egregious":* Ibid.

268 *"slowest of the circuits":* Paul J. Killion, "How Long Will My Ninth Circuit Civil Appeal Take?" Duane Morris LLP. See https://www .lexology.com/library/detail.aspx?g=3cc1dc3c-67c1–4273–97e2 –645b5eb6c1ba.

268 *"They still say I'm trespassing":* www.dailycaller.com, January 27, 2019.

268 *"They'll be starting":* "Biden to Move Fast to Strike Down Trump's Environmental Agenda," by Stephen McGee and Bobby Magill, November 7, 2020, news.bloomberglaw.com

269 *"top-tier issue":* Randy Bell, Director of the Global Energy Center, November 24, 2020, published in atlanticcouncil.org.

Selected Bibliography

Books

Abbey, Edward. *One Life at a Time, Please*. New York: Henry Holt and Company, 1989.

———. *The Serpents of Paradise: A Reader*. New York: Henry Holt and Company, 1995.

Bagley, Will. *Blood of the Prophets: Brigham Young and the Massacre at Mountain Meadows*. Norman: University of Oklahoma Press, 2002.

Bennion, Janet. *Desert Patriarchy: Mormon and Mennonite Communities in the Chihuahua Valley*. Tucson: University of Arizona Press, 2004.

Billington, Ray Allen, and Martin Ridge. *Westward Expansion: A History of the American Frontier*. Albuquerque: University of New Mexico Press, 2002.

Bowman, Matthew. *The Mormon People: The Making of an American Faith*. New York: Random House, 2012.

Burton, Sir Richard. *The City of the Saints: Among the Mormons and Across the Rocky Mountains to California*. Torrington, Wyo.: Narrative Press, 2003.

Clemens, Samuel. *Roughing It*. Hartford, Conn.: American Publishing Company, 1872.

Cox, Shawna. *Last Rancher Standing: The Cliven Bundy Story a Close-up View*. Rochester, N.Y.: Legends Library, 2014.

Dant, Sara. *Losing Eden: An Environmental History of the American West*. New York: Wiley Blackwell, 2016.

Denton, Ralph, with Michael S. Green and R. T. King. *A Liberal Conscience: Ralph Denton, Nevadan*. Reno: University of Nevada Oral History Program, 2001.

Denton, Sally. *American Massacre: The Tragedy at Mountain Meadows*. New York: Alfred A. Knopf, 2003.

———. *The Plots Against the President: FDR, a Nation in Crisis, and the Rise of the American Right*. New York: Bloomsbury Press, 2012.

———. *The Profiteers: Bechtel and the Men Who Built the World*. New York: Simon & Schuster, 2016.

DeVoto, Bernard. *The Year of Decision 1846*. New York: St. Martin's Griffin, 2000.

———. *The Western Paradox: A Conservation Reader*. New Haven, Conn.: Yale University Press, 2001.

Donahue, Debra L. *The Western Range Revisited*. Oklahoma City: University of Oklahoma Press, 1999.

Dyer, Joel. *Harvest of Rage: Why Oklahoma City Is Only the Beginning*. Boulder, Col.: Westview Press, 1998.

Egan, Ferol. *Sand in a Whirlwind: The Paiute Indian War of 1860*. New York: Doubleday, 1972.

Elliott, Gary E. *Senator Alan Bible and the Politics of the New West*. Reno: University of Nevada Press, 1994.

Finicum, LaVoy. *Only by Blood and Suffering: Regaining Lost Freedom*. N.p.: Self-published, copyright Jeanette Finicum, 2017.

Flores, Dan. *American Serengeti: The Las Big Animals of the Great Plains*. Lawrence: University Press of Kansas, 2016.

Fradkin, Philip L. *Sagebrush Country: Land and the American West*. Tucson: University of Arizona Press, 1989.

——. *Wanderings of an Environmental Journalist: In Alaska and the American West*. Albuquerque: University of New Mexico Press, 1993.

Green, Michael S. *Nevada: A History of the Silver State*. Reno: University of Nevada Press, 2015.

Hafen, Lyman. *Far from Cactus Flats: The 20th Century Story of a Harsh Land, a Proud Family, and a Lost Son*. St. George, Utah: Arizona Strip Interpretive Association, 2006.

Hage, Wayne. *Storm over Rangelands: Private Rights in Federal Lands*. Bellevue, Wash.: Free Enterprise Press, 1989.

Hulse, James W. *The Silver State: Nevada's Heritage Reinterpreted*. Reno: University of Nevada Press, 1991.

Ketcham, Christopher. *This Land: How Cowboys, Capitalism, and Corruption Are Ruining the American West*. New York: Viking, 2019.

King, R. T., and Gary Elliott. *Hang Tough: Grant Sawyer, An Activist in the Governor's Mansion*. Reno: University of Nevada Oral History Program, 1993.

Krakauer, Jon. *Under the Banner of Heaven: A Story of Violent Faith*. New York: Anchor Books, 2004.

Leshy, John. *Debunking Creation Myths about America's Public Lands*. Salt Lake City: University of Utah Press, 2018.

Lillard, Richard G. *The Desert Challenge: An Interpretation of Nevada*. New York: Alfred A. Knopf, 1942.

Limerick, Patricia Nelson. *Something in the Soil*. New York: W. W. Norton, 2000.

Madsen, Brigham D. *The Northern Shoshoni*. Caldwell, Ida.: Caxton Press, 2007.

McCann, Anthony. *Shadowlands: Fear and Freedom at the Oregon Standoff*. New York: Bloomsbury Publishing, 2019.

McCracken, Robert D. *The United Cattle & Packing Company: The Rise and Fall of Nevada's Largest Ranch*. Pahrump, Nev.: Nye County Press, 2012.

———. *Destiny Denied: Esmeralda County Citizens Speak Out on Public Lands Issues*. Goldfield, Nev.: Esmeralda County Press, 2014.

Nevins, Allan. *Frémont: Pathmarker of the West*. Lincoln: University of Nebraska, 1992.

Nies, Judith. *Unreal City: Las Vegas, Black Mesa, and the Fate of the West*. New York: Nation Books, 2014.

Pogue, James. *Chosen Country: A Rebellion in the West*. New York: Henry Holt and Company, 2018.

Porte, Joel, ed. *Emerson in His Journals*. Cambridge: Harvard University Press, 1982.

Quammen, Betsy Gaines. *American Zion: Cliven Bundy, God, and Public Lands in the West*. Salt Lake City: Torrey Publishing, 2020.

Reid, Harry. *Searchlight: The Camp that Didn't Fail*. Reno: University of Nevada Press, 1998.

Reid, Harry, with Mark Warren. *The Good Fight: Hard Lessons from Searchlight to Washington*. New York: G. P. Putnam's Sons, 2008.

Reisner, Marc. *Cadillac Desert: The American West and Its Disappearing Water*. New York: Penguin Books, 1986.

Skillen, James R. *The Nation's Largest Landlord: The Bureau of Land Management in the American West*. Lawrence: University of Kansas Press, 2009.

Stegner, Wallace. *Mormon Country*. Lincoln: University of Nebraska Press, 1981.

Stickler, Michael L. *Cliven Bundy: American Patriot*. N.p.: The Vision Group, 2017.

Temple, John. *Up in Arms: How the Bundy Family Hijacked Public Lands, Outfoxed the Federal Government, and Ignited the Patriot Militia Movement*. New York: Ben Bella Books, 2019.

Turner, Wallace. *The Mormon Establishment: How Does This Uniquely American Religion Rule the Lives of Two and a Half Million Americans Today?* Boston: Houghton Mifflin, 1966.

Udall, Stewart L. *The Forgotten Founders: Rethinking the History of the Old West*. Washington, D.C.: Island Press, 2002.

Ward, Kenric F. *Saints in Babylon: Mormons and Las Vegas*. Bloomington, Ind.: First Books Library, 2002.

Watts, Lyle. *The Western Range: Letter from the Secretary of Agriculture, 1936*. U.S. Government Document.

Wiley, Peter, and Robert Gottlieb. *Empires in the Sun: The Rise of the New American West*. Tucson: University of Arizona Press, 1982.

Young, James A., and B. Abbott Sparks. *Cattle in the Cold Desert*. Reno: University of Nevada Press, 2002.

Selected Periodicals

Avlon, John P., and John L. Smith. "I Created the Las Vegas Killers." *Daily Beast*, June 9, 2014.

Buursma, Bruce. "Scandal Damaging Ministry." *Chicago Tribune*, May 3, 1987.

Coates, James. "Sagebrush Rebellion on Hold, Group Lights Other Legal Fires." *Chicago Tribune*, March 16, 1986.

Egan, Timothy. "Deadbeat on the Range." *New York Times*, April 17, 2014.

FBI Counterterrorism Analysis Section. "Sovereign Citizens: A Growing Domestic Threat to Law Enforcement, September 1, 2011." Available at: https://leb.fbi.gov/articles/featured-articles/sovereign-citizens-a-grow ing-domestic-threat-to-law-enforcement.

Graham, Judith. "Indians: $140 Million Isn't Justice." *Chicago Tribune*, January 1, 2004.

Green, Emily. "Quenching Las Vegas's Thirst." *Las Vegas Sun*, June 2008.

Grijalva, Raúl, and Bennie Thompson. "Homegrown Anti-Government Militias Threaten Public Safety." *High Country News*, June 30, 2016.

Harkinson, Josh. "Harry Reid, Gold Member." *Mother Jones*, March–April, 2009.

Ketcham, Christopher. "The Great Republican Land Heist." *Harper's*, February 2015.

LeDuff, Charles. "Range War in Nevada Pits U.S. Against Two Shoshone Sisters." *New York Times*, October 30, 2002.

Martin, Anne. "Nevada: Beautiful Desert of Buried Hopes." *Nation*, July 26, 1922.

Neubauer, Chuck, and Richard T. Cooper. "In Nevada, the Name to Know Is Reid." *Los Angeles Times*, June 23, 2003.

Powell, Alvin. "Public Lands 'A Priceless Legacy for Future.'" *Harvard Law Today*, March 15, 2018.

Shepperson, Wilbur. "The Maverick and the Cowboy." *Nevada State Historical Society Quarterly* (Spring 1983): 13–22.

Van Hoak, Stephen P. "And Who Shall Have the Children?: The Indian Slave Trade in the Southern Great Basin, 1800–1865." *Nevada Historical Quarterly* 41, no. 1 (Spring 1998): 3–25.

Author's note: The remarkable Bundy saga was covered by many news outlets and in multiple mediums. Here is what amounts to a sample of the hundreds of articles and commentaries from which this book benefited:

> *Albuquerque Journal, Arizona Daily Star, Arizona Republic,* Associated Press, *Burns Times-Herald, Carson Appeal, Chicago Tribune, Daily Beast, Daily Spectrum, Denver Post, Deseret News, Elko Daily Free*

Press, Esquire, Harper's, Harvard Law Today, High Country News, Idaho Statesman, Las Vegas Review-Journal, Las Vegas Sun, Los Angeles Times, Malheur Enterprise, Mason Valley News, Medford Mail Tribune, Mesquite Local News, Missoula Independent, Missoulian, Nevada State Journal, Newsweek, New Yorker, New York Times, Oregonian, Range, Reno Gazette-Journal, Reuters, *Salt Lake Tribune, San Francisco Chronicle, Santa Fe New Mexican, Seattle Times, The Guardian, Wall Street Journal, Washington County News, Washington Post, Time.*

Television and websites sourced: blm.gov, biologicaldiversity.org, *CNN*, eenews.net, epa.gov, *Fox News*, *KLAS*-*TV*-Las Vegas, *KTNV*-Las Vegas, *MSNBC*, Oregon Public Broadcasting, Oregonwild.org, *PBS Frontline*, Pacific Patriots Network, Reboubt.com, Revealnews.org, West Mountain Rangers.

Index

Abbey, Bob, 97, 126

Adams, John, 44

Aerojet-General Corporation, 197–98

African American civil rights activists, 262

agrarian communalism, 74, 75

agri-business, 148, 155

airports: development of, 175

alienation from federal government: as theme in western politics, 262

All-American Society (*later* Freeman Institute), 67, 258–59

America: Freedom to Fascism (film), 53

American Gaming Hall of Fame, 201

American Indian Movement, 92, 98

American Lands Council (ALC), xiii, 212, 258, 265

American Legislative Exchange Council (ALEC), xiii, 258, 265

America Reloaded (fictional documentary), 205

America's Promise Ministries, 48

Anderson, Jack, 94

Andrus, Cecil, 114, 115, 116–17, 118, 139

Anti-Defamation League, 139, 254

antigovernment extremists: activity, increase in, 203; Bundy Ranch–Waco scenarios compared by, 50; emboldening of, 254; as folk heroes, 64; leaderless resistance espoused by, 46; victory for, 33; worldview of, 21

antigovernment organizations, 46, 51, 203, 210

anti-Islam activity, 204

Antiquities Act (1906), 222

Arapine (Western Ute), 82

Arizona Strip, 6–7, 263

armed occupation: Mormon views on, 68–69

arms race, 130, 131

arms/weapons, 17, 18, 19, 22–23, 24, 32, 52, 242

Arnold, Ron, 134

arson *versus* prescribed burns: cases involving, 55–60

Atlas Shrugged (Rand), 69

atomic weapons tests, 130, 131

Babbitt, Bruce, 123, 138–39

Backcountry Hunters & Anglers (BHA), 260

Bagley, Will, 78

Bannock tribe, 85, 87

Bannock War (1878), 86

Barclay, Rick, 203, 204

Baring, Walter, 163, 165

Barrick Gold, 179

Battle Mountain–ranching families, 144

Beam, Louis, 46, 47–48

Bears Ears monument, 222, 268

Bechtel, 197

Beck, Alyn, 40–41

About the Author

Native Nevadan John L. Smith is a longtime Silver State journalist and the author of more than a dozen books, including *The Westside Slugger: Joe Neal's Lifelong Fight for Social Justice*. An award-winning columnist, in 2016 he was inducted into the Nevada Press Association Hall of Fame. That same year, Smith and his colleagues were honored with the James Foley Medill Medal for Courage in Journalism, the Ancil Payne Award from the University of Oregon, and the Society of Professional Journalists Award for Ethics. Smith writes a weekly column for *The Nevada Independent* and is a contributor to Nevada Public Radio's *State of Nevada* and a wide range of publications. The father of an adult daughter, Amelia, he is married to the writer Sally Denton.